Force Platform Cookbook

Code Samples and Best Practices

By Second Edition Authors: Stefanie Anderson, Steven Anderson, Mysti Berry, Phil Choi, Leah Cutter, Mark Leonard, Chris McGuire, and Garen Torikian
Editor: Mysti Berry

With contributions by additional members of the salesforce.com Technology and Services organizations

Force Platform Cookbook

ISBN: 978-0-9789639-4-1 0-9789739-4-6

The authors would like to thank additional contributors Dave Carroll, Simon Fell, Steve Fisher, Chris Fry, Richard Greenwald, Larry Jovanovic, Andrea Leszek, Markus Spohn, Nick Tran, and Craig Weissman. Additional thanks to Andrew Albert, Grant Anderson, Gavin Austin, Eric Bezar, Manoj Cheenath, Bulent Cinarkaya, Bill Eidson, Matthew Friend, Adam Gross, Michelle Jowitt, Paul Kopacki, Sarah Marovich, Reena Mathew, Taggart Matthiesen, Yudi Nagata, Kavindra Patel, Igor Pesenson, Vahn Phan, Varadarajan Rajaram, Bhavana Rehani, EJ Rice, Jim Rivera, Emad Salman, Mary Scotton, Jerry Sherman, Sagar Wanaselja, Jill Wetzler, and Sarah Whitlock for their advice and support. Special thanks to the editor and lead writer of the First Edition, Caroline Roth.

Table of Contents

Welcome

Congratulations! You are part of a growing movement of innovative application developers who are curious about the future of computing, and who no longer want to accept the status quo. Maybe your organization has just purchased Salesforce licenses, or maybe you've been using Salesforce for a while and want to extend its capabilities. Maybe you've got a brilliant business idea and are looking for the best and fastest way to start making money, or maybe you're just curious about this thing called Apex and want to keep your skill set up to date with the latest technology.

No matter what angle you're coming from, this book will help application developers leverage the power of salesforce.com's cloud computing platform to build fully-functional, integrated Web applications that free you and your organization from the drudgery of maintaining your own software and hardware stacks. Instead, you can spend your time and money on the ideas and innovations that make your business applications special, whether you're a lone developer looking for your first round of venture funding or part of a multi-billion-dollar company with hundreds of thousands of employees.

About This Book

This book provides over 80 recipes for using the Force Platform API, developing Apex scripts, and creating Visualforce pages. Written by developers for developers, the *Force Platform Cookbook: Code Samples and Best Practices* helps developers become familiar with common Force Platform programming techniques and best practices.

To get the most out of the recipes in this book, make sure you understand the experience you should have, and the tools to supplement these recipes:

- *Intended Audience* on page 2
- *Conventions* on page 2
- *The Sample Recruiting App* on page 3

1

- *Code Samples* on page 4
- *Additional Resources* on page 5
- *Sending Feedback* on page 7

 Note: This book indicates the recipes for which salesforce.com Training & Certification has provided example code or other information. To enroll in courses that provide even more information and practical experience, see `www.salesforce.com/training`.

Intended Audience

Developers who are already familiar with the native capabilities of the Force Platform can most easily implement the recipes in this book. Before working with the recipes you find here, you should be familiar with the concepts, techniques, and best practices described in the following books:

- *Force Platform Fundamentals: An Introduction to Custom Application Development in the Cloud*, available on the Developer Force website at
  `http://wiki.apexdevnet.com/index.php/Force_Platform_Fundamentals`
- *Force Platform Developer Guide: Advanced Programming Techniques for Cloud Computing*, available on the Developer Force website at
  `wiki.apexdevnet.com/index.php/Force_Platform_Developer_Guide`

To get the most out of this book, you should also have experience with at least one of the following:

- HTML and JavaScript
- Java
- C#.NET
- VB.NET
- PHP
- Python
- Ruby
- Perl
- Any other Web-services-enabled programming language

Conventions

This book uses typographical conventions:

Convention	Description
SELECT Name FROM Account	In an example, Courier font indicates items that you should type as shown. In a syntax statement, Courier font also indicates items that you should type as shown, except for question marks and square brackets.
SELECT *fieldname* FROM *objectname*	In an example or syntax statement, italics represent variables. You supply the actual value.
?	In a syntax statement, the question mark indicates the element preceding it is optional. You may omit the element or include one.
WHERE [*conditionexpression*]	In a syntax statement, square brackets surround an element that may be repeated up to the limits for that element. You may omit the element, or include one or more of them.

The Sample Recruiting App

Some of the recipes in this book require a custom app for illustration. In these cases, this book uses the custom Recruiting app that was developed as part of *Force Platform Fundamentals: An Introduction to Custom Application Development in the Cloud*. The schema for this Recruiting app is pictured in the following entity-relationship diagram and can be downloaded from wiki.apexdevnet.com/index.php/Force_Platform_Cookbook.

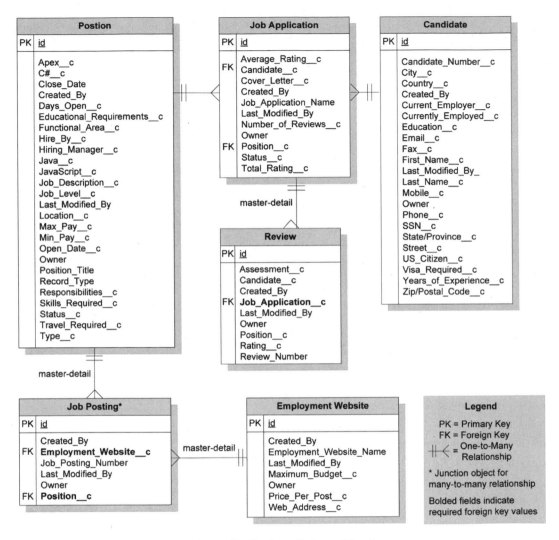

Figure 1: Schema for the Sample Recruiting App

Code Samples

An online version of this book is available on the Developer Force website at wiki.apexdevnet.com/index.php/Force_Platform_Cookbook. This website also includes links to the code samples found in this book, as well as any errata that are discovered after publication.

Additional Resources

A variety of resources are available to supplement this book.

Documentation

Before working with the recipes in this book, you should work through the first two books in the series: *Force Platform Fundamentals: An Introduction to Custom Application Development in the Cloud*, available on the Developer Force website at `http://wiki.apexdevnet.com/index.php/Force_Platform_Fundamentals`, and *Force Platform Developer Guide: Advanced Programming Techniques for Cloud Computing*, available on the Developer Force website at `wiki.apexdevnet.com/index.php/Force_Platform_Developer_Guide`

Native Force Platform Point-and-Click Functionality:

- Access the Help & Training window by clicking **Help** or **Help & Training** in the upper-right corner of any Salesforce page. Alternatively, access a context-sensitive view of the Help & Training window by clicking **Help for this Page** on the right side of any page title bar, or the help link on the right side of any related list.
- Review white papers, multimedia presentations, and other documentation in the Native Framework section of the Developer Force website at `wiki.apexdevnet.com/index.php/Native_Framework`.
- Review tips and best practices at `www.salesforce.com/community`.

Visualforce:

- Read the *Visualforce Developer's Guide*, available at `http://www.salesforce.com/us/developer/docs/pages/index.htm`.
- Review white papers, multimedia presentations, and other documentation in the Visualforce section of the Developer Force website at `http://wiki.apexdevnet.com/index.php/Visualforce`.

Apex:

- Read the *Apex Developer's Guide*, available at `www.salesforce.com/us/developer/docs/apexcode/index.htm`.
- Review white papers, multimedia presentations, and other documentation in the Apex section of the Developer Force website at `http://wiki.apexdevnet.com/index.php/Apex_and_Visualforce`.

Force Platform Web Services API:

- Read the *Force Platform Web Services API Developer's Guide*, available at `www.salesforce.com/apidoc`.

- Review whitepapers, multimedia presentations, and other documentation in the API section of the Developer Force website at `wiki.apexdevnet.com/index.php/Web_Services_API`.

- Review white papers, multimedia presentations, and other documentation in the API section of the Developer Force website at `wiki.apexdevnet.com/index.php/Web_Services_API`.

- Read the *Force Platform Metadata API Developer's Guide*, available at http://www.salesforce.com/us/developer/docs/api_meta/index.htm.

Training Courses

Training classes are also available from salesforce.com Training & Certification. You can find a complete list of courses at `www.salesforce.com/training`.

Free Developer Edition Account

If you have not already done so, visit the Developer Force website at developer.force.com and click **Getting Started** to sign up for a free, two-user Developer Edition organization.

Integrated Development Tools

The Force Platform provides developer's tools that are tightly integrated with the platform. You may wish to select a tool and become familiar with it before working with the recipes in this book.

- The Force Platform Migration Tool is generally available. To access it, log in to your Salesforce organization and select **Setup ➤ Develop ➤ Tools** and click **Force Platform Migration Tool**.
- The Force Platform IDE is the world's first integrated development environment for cloud computing. Based on Eclipse technology, the Force Platform IDE provides professional developers and development teams the tools to code, test, deploy, and version Force Platform components, including Apex, Visualforce, custom objects, layouts, and more. For information about this tool, see `http://wiki.apexdevnet.com/index.php/Force.com_IDE`.
- The latest version of AJAX Tools, a Force Platform AppExchange package alternative to the Force Platform IDE, includes syntax-highlighting, a lightweight version of Force Platform Explorer, and code samples. To download the latest version, go to `http://www.salesforce.com/appexchange/detail_overview.jsp?NavCode__c=&id=a0330000002foeKAAQ`
- Force Platform Explorer is a lightweight, .NET-based tool that lets you browse the schema within your organization, edit data values, and build and test SOQL and SOSL queries While the Force Platform IDE and AJAX Tools include a lightweight version of this handy application, the stand-alone .NET version of Force Platform Explorer includes more functionality, including the ability to test SOSL statements, view documents, and update

database values. To download it, go to
`wiki.apexdevnet.com/index.php/Apex_Explorer`.

- For Mac users, SoqlXplorer is a great counterpart to the Force Platform Explorer for Windows. SoqlXplorer provides metadata exploration, a SOQL query tester, and a graphical schema view for examining object relationships (a piece of functionality that's only available on the Mac OS X platform!). Download SoqlXplorer from Simon Fell's PocketSOAP website at `www.pocketsoap.com/osx/soqlx`. After the download automatically extracts itself, drag the SoqlXplorer icon to your Applications folder to complete the installation.

For other great Salesforce tools and utilities built exclusively for Mac OS X, see `www.pocketsoap.com/osx`.

 Tip: Visit Salesforce.com Ideas at ideas.salesforce.com and see what users are asking for. Salesforce.com Ideas is a forum where salesforce.com customers can suggest new product concepts, promote favorite enhancements, interact with product managers and other customers, and preview what salesforce.com is planning to deliver in future releases. You can use Salesforce.com Ideas both to find ideas for new applications, and to post your pet peeves about how the platform works for you.

Sending Feedback

The authors made every effort to ensure the accuracy of the information contained within this book, but neither they nor salesforce.com assumes any responsibility or liability for any errors or inaccuracies that may appear. If you do find any errors, please send feedback to `docfeedback@salesforce.com`, or visit the Developer Force discussion boards at `www.salesforce.com/developer/community/index.jsp`.

Understanding the Force Platform

The Force Platform makes it easy to build applications for cloud computing. It is the world's first platform for building, sharing, and running business applications in the cloud. Force Platform is unique among development platforms for the following reasons:

Delivery

The Force Platform runs in a hosted, multitenant environment. That means you can access any app you build on the platform from anywhere in the world with just an Internet connection and a Web browser. No servers or databases need to be maintained, and no software needs to be installed or upgraded. Instead, salesforce.com provides a hosted environment in which the latest features and functionality are seamlessly available to all users with every new release. And you'll have the peace of mind of knowing that any app you were using or building before the new release will work just as well after the release too, regardless of whether it was a standard CRM app from salesforce.com or a custom app you developed on your own.

As a developer, the platform's multitenant architecture also means that you never have to worry about scaling your apps from one to one thousand or even to one million users—all of the infrastructure to handle such growth is provided free of charge, automatically behind the scenes. That leaves you more time to focus on your business problems and solutions, rather than spending time trying to anticipate the pressures that increased usage might exert on your apps.

Distribution

Any app written on the platform has access to a built-in community of potential customers on the Force Platform AppExchange at `www.salesforce.com/appexchange/`. Unlike traditional software, where you have to create an install wizard and send your code to a manufacturer to cut hundreds of CDs, you can easily share and distribute your app on the AppExchange with only a few clicks of the mouse. You can quickly share your apps privately with just the people you want, or you can publish your apps for anyone to download.

If you do publish an app publicly, the community of users on the AppExchange can take your app for a test drive and review comments from other users about how well it worked. Additionally, information about the users who end up downloading your app is sent directly to you in the form of a new lead in any Salesforce organization that you specify. When you're ready to release new versions of your app, the AppExchange also helps you communicate and manage the upgrade process for all of your users. You can track which of your customers is on which version of your app, and you never have to worry that your users have broken or deleted any component your app relies on.

Development

The Force Platform comes with a wide variety of built-in, point-and-click functionality that can help you build your apps faster. Need a way to store data in your app? Define new database objects, fields, and relationships declaratively with the mouse, rather than by composing SQL CREATE statements. Need to control which users have access to different kinds of data? Again, no coding necessary—just use the security and sharing framework to define permissions at different levels of granularity, from individual fields to entire objects and applications. The Force Platform includes point-and-click tools for everything from string localization to workflow rules and approval processes, from custom reports and dashboards to page layouts and data import wizards—which means you can spend less time recreating the "plumbing" that makes your applications run and more time on the unique functionality that sets your apps apart from your competitor's.

And what happens when you want to go beyond the capabilities of the point-and-click tools the platform provides? The Force Platform Web Services API, Apex, and Visualforce give you the flexibility you need to build the applications you want. Integrate third-party Web services with embedded mashups, change the logic behind every function with Apex classes and triggers, and redesign the user interface the way you want with Visualforce. You're limited only by your imagination!

The Force Platform includes a number of tools that can help you develop apps. These tools allow you to define the data, business logic, and user interface for an application. The recipes in this book focus on these tools.

Using Force Platform Tools and Technologies

The Force Platform includes a number of tools that can help you build apps. These tools allow you to define the data, business logic, and user interface for an application.

Force Platform Point-and-Click Setup Tools

The Force Platform includes declarative, point-and-click setup tools that allow administrators and developers to quickly build common application components without writing any code. Also known as *native* platform functionality, these setup tools allow you to effortlessly build:

Data Components

Data components are equivalent to the "model" in the Model-View-Controller (MVC) application development paradigm. They include:

- **Custom objects**

  Similar to a database table, a Salesforce object is a structure for storing data about a certain type of entity, such as a person, account, or job application. Salesforce includes over a dozen standard objects that support default apps like Sales and Service & Support, but it also allows you to build custom objects for your own application needs. In Salesforce, each object automatically includes built-in features like a user interface, a security and sharing model, workflow processes, search, and much more.

- **Custom fields**

  Similar to a column in a database table, a Salesforce field is a property of an object, such as the first name of a contact or the status of an opportunity. Salesforce fields support over a dozen different field types, such as auto-number, checkbox, date/time, and multi-select picklists.

- **Custom relationships**

  Similar to the way primary and foreign keys work in a relational database, a Salesforce relationship defines a connection between two objects in which matching values in a specified field in both objects are used to link related data.

- **Field history**

  Salesforce field history allows you to track changes to fields on a particular object just by selecting a checkbox on a custom object and field definition. Users can then review audit logs for changes to sensitive records without any additional development work.

Business Logic Components

Business logic components are equivalent to the "controller" in the Model-View-Controller (MVC) application development paradigm. They include:

- **Security and permission settings**

  Salesforce security and permissions tools, such as user profiles, organization-wide defaults, the role hierarchy, sharing rules, and manual sharing, allow you to control the data that users can view and edit, either with broad generalizations or with a fine level of detail.

- **Formula fields and validation rules**

  Formula fields, default field values, and validation rules allow you to use Excel-like syntax to calculate certain data automatically, maintain data quality, and add custom error messages to your apps.

- **Workflow rules**

Workflow rules are processes triggered by user activity or according to a schedule. These processes can automatically assign tasks to users, send email alerts to multiple recipients, update field values in records, and even generate SOAP messages to external Web services.

- **Approval processes**

  Approvals allow you to set up a chain of users who can approve the creation of sensitive types of records, such as new contracts or vacation requests.

- **Email**

  Email functionality in Salesforce allows you to email contacts, leads, person accounts, and users in your organization directly from account, contact, lead, opportunity, case, campaign, or custom object pages.

User Interface Components

User interface components are equivalent to the "view" in the Model-View-Controller (MVC) application development paradigm. They include:

- **Tabs**

  Tabs give users a starting point for viewing, editing, and entering information for a particular object. When a user clicks a tab at the top of the page, the corresponding tab home page for that object appears.

- **Page layouts**

  Regardless of whether a particular object has a tab, all objects can be viewed or edited. Page layouts allow you to organize the fields, custom links, related lists, and other components that appear on those pages.

- **Custom views**

  Custom views allow users to filter the records they see for a particular object, based on criteria they specify.

- **Reports and Dashboards**

  Salesforce includes a full-featured report building tool, including custom report types that allow you to view data for any combination of objects, and dynamic dashboards that give users a bird's eye view of their application data.

- **Console**

  Salesforce Console allows you to set up a page that displays multiple objects at a time, streamlining the user experience. It includes a list view of several different objects at the top of the page, a detail view in the main window, customizable sidebar components, and mini-detail views of related information in a dynamic AJAX-based interface.

With this native functionality, app developers can build extensive, full-featured applications that handle many business needs. For a more thorough introduction to the native functionality provided by the platform, read *Force Platform Fundamentals: An Introduction to Custom Application Development in the Cloud*, available on the Developer Force website at `wiki.apexdevnet.com/index.php/Force_Platform_Fundamentals`.

Visualforce

Visualforce is a tag-based markup language that allows developers to develop their own custom interfaces using standard Salesforce components. Visualforce pages deliver the ability to create custom pages for your Force Platform applications. Visualforce pages includes a set of tags to describe a variety of rich components into your page design. These components bring the full power of the metadata-drivenForce Platform to your pages, while giving you complete freedom to design pages to suit your specific user interface requirements. The components can either be controlled by the same logic that's used in standard Salesforce pages, or developers can associate their own logic with a controller written in Apex. With this architecture, designers and developers can easily split up the work that goes with building a new application—designers can focus on the user interface, while developers can work on the business logic that drives the app.

Apex

Apex is a strongly-typed, object-oriented programming language for executing flow and transaction control statements on the Force Platform server in conjunction with database queries, inserts, updates, and deletes. Using syntax that looks like Java and acts like database stored procedures, Apex allows you to add business logic to your applications in a more efficient, integrated way than is possible with the Force Platform API.

You can manage and invoke Apex scripts using the following constructs:

- **Classes**

A *class* is a template or blueprint from which Apex objects are created. Classes consist of other classes, user-defined methods, variables, exception types, and static initialization code.

Once successfully saved, class methods or variables can be invoked by other Apex scripts, or through the Force Platform Web Services API (or AJAX Toolkit) for methods that have been designated with the `webService` keyword.

In most cases, Apex classes are modeled on their counterparts in Java and can be quickly understood by those who are familiar with them.

- **Triggers**

  A *trigger* is an Apex script that executes before or after specific data manipulation language (DML) events occur, such as before object records are inserted into the database, or after records have been deleted. Other than Apex Web service methods, triggers provide the primary means for instantiating Apex.

- **Anonymous blocks**

  An *anonymous block* is an Apex script that does not get stored in the metadata, but that can be compiled and executed through the use of the `executeanonymous()` API call or the equivalent in the AJAX toolkit.

Force Platform Mobile

Force Platform Mobile is a Salesforce feature that enables users to access their Salesforce data from mobile devices running the mobile client application. The Force Platform Mobile client application exchanges data with Salesforce over wireless carrier networks, and stores a local copy of the user's data in its own database on the mobile device. Users can edit local copies of their Salesforce records when a wireless connection is unavailable, and transmit those changes when a wireless connection becomes available.

Force Platform Mobile works with Apex and Visualforce to extend functionality.

The Force Platform Web Services API

The API defines a Web service that enables full, reliable access to all of the data in an organization. With more than 20 different calls, the API allows you to request metadata related to standard and custom objects, maintain passwords, perform searches, create custom objects and fields, and much more. Use the API in any language that supports Web services, or within an s-control by using the AJAX Toolkit.

The Force Platform Migration Tool

The Force Platform Migration Tool is a Java/Ant-based command-line utility for moving metadata between a local directory and a Salesforce organization. You can use the Force Platform Migration Tool to retrieve components, create scripted deployment, and repeat deployment patterns.

Force Platform IDE

The Force Platform IDE is a plug-in for the Eclipse IDE that provides special help for developing and deploying Apex classes, Apex triggers, Visualforce pages, and metadata components.

The Metadata API

The metadata API allows you to manage setup and customization information (metadata) for your organizations:

- Work with setup configuration as XML metadata files
- Migrate configuration changes between organizations
- Create your own tools for managing organization and application metadata

You can modify metadata in *test* organizations on Developer Edition or Sandbox, and then deploy tested changes to *production* organizations on Enterprise Edition or Unlimited Editions. You can also create scripts to populate a new organization with your custom objects, custom fields, and other components.

Chapter 1

Modifying and Extending the Salesforce Application

This chapter contains recipes that help you make basic modifications to the Salesforce application.

Point-and-Click Setup Tools

With the Salesforce user interface, nearly all of the data and functionality you need is just a click away. Still, you might find that a few modifications here and there could make you even more efficient. For example, you might have a need to add a custom button to a list view to give users the ability to update all of the records in the list at one time. Or perhaps you would like to see data from different types of objects calculated and displayed in one spot. And of course, after you've customized these aspects of your app, you want to give users some custom documentation that describes how to use it. All of this is possible, and easy to do, on the Force Platform!

In this chapter, you'll learn how to create custom buttons, such as a **Mass Delete** and a **Mass Update** button, override the action of a standard Salesforce button, pass parameters into your custom button or link code, redirect users to a different URL when they go to a standard Salesforce page, and provide custom help documentation with your app. You'll also learn how to model many-to-many relationships between objects, how to retrieve and display data from related records, and how to block record creation according to data on related records. We'll use a combination of native

- Overriding a Standard Page
- Dynamically Updating a Page
- Overriding a Page for Some, but not All, Users
- Creating Tabbed Accounts
- Adding CSS to Visualforce Pages
- Editing Multiple Records Using a Visualforce List Controller
- Registering a Custom Domain for Your Force Platform Site
- Using Force Platform Site-Specific Merge Fields
- Customizing the Look and Feel of Your Force Platform Site
- Integrating Your Force Platform Site with Google Analytics
- Adding a Feed to Your Force Platform Site
- Using Dynamic Apex

and composite platform features to easily and quickly customize your Salesforce organization.

Visualforce

Similar to the way Apex dramatically increases the power of developers to customize business logic, Visualforce dramatically increases the power of developers to customize the user interface. With this markup language, each tag corresponds to a coarse or fine-grained component, such as a section of a page, a related list, or a field. The components can either be controlled by the same logic that's used in standard pages, or developers can associate their own logic with a controller written in . With this architecture, designers and developers can easily split up the work that goes with building a new application—designers can focus on the user interface, while developers can work on the business logic that drives the app.

Sites

Salesforce organizations contain valuable information about partners, solutions, products, users, ideas, and other business data. Some of this information would be useful to people outside your organization, but only users with the right access and permissions can view and use it. In the past, to make this data available to the general public, you had to set up a Web server, create custom Web pages (JSP, PHP, or other), and perform API integration between your site and your organization. Additionally, if you wanted to collect information using a Web form, you had to program your pages to perform data validation.

Apex

Apex enables a new class of applications and features to be developed and deployed on the platform by providing the ability to capture business logic and rules. The language uses a combination of Java-like syntax with API functions and SOQL to let you define triggers, classes, and other representations of business logic that can interact with the platform at a low level. Conceptually similar to a stored procedure system, Apex allows almost any kind of transactional, complex logic to be developed and run entirely in the cloud.

Creating a Mass Delete Button

Problem

You want to add a button to the top of the Contacts related list in an account detail page that allows users to select multiple contacts in the list and delete all of them at once.

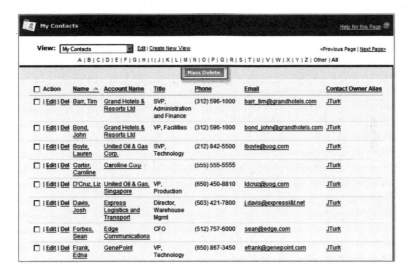

Figure 2: A Mass Delete Button on a Contacts List View

Solution

Create a new button on Contact, and then add the button to the related list on the Account page layout.

To create this mass delete button:

1. Click **Setup ➤ Customize ➤ Contacts ➤ Buttons and Links**.

    Tip: For a new button on a custom object, navigate to **Setup ➤ Create ➤ Objects**, and click the name of the object.

2. In the Custom Buttons and Links related list, click **New**. Assign it the following attributes:

   - `Label`: Mass Delete
   - `Name`: Mass_Delete_Contacts
   - `Description`: Contacts related list button on an account detail page to allow users to select multiple contacts in the list and delete all of them at once.

- Display Type: List Button
- Display Checkboxes: Selected
- Behavior: Execute JavaScript
- Content Source: OnClick JavaScript

3. In the code for the button, use the GETRECORDIDS() function to acquire the IDs of the contacts that the user selects. The code then performs the appropriate logic, updates the database using the AJAX Toolkit, and refreshes the page as confirmation to the user.

For example:

```
// Include and initialize the AJAX Toolkit javascript library
//
{!REQUIRESCRIPT("/soap/ajax/10.0/connection.js")}


// Get the list of accounts that should be deleted.
// Use the $ObjectType merge field to indicate the type of
// record Ids that are expected.
//
var idsToDelete = {!GETRECORDIDS( $ObjectType.Contact )};
var deleteWarning = 'Are you sure you wish to delete ' +
                    idsToDelete.length + ' contacts?';

if (idsToDelete.length && (window.confirm(deleteWarning))) {

    // Delete the records, and pass a function into the call
    // so that the toolkit refreshes the current page
    // asynchronously when the call succeeds.
    //
    sforce.connection.deleteIds(idsToDelete,
            function() {navigateToUrl(window.location.href);});

} else if (idsToDelete.length == 0) {
    alert("Please select the contacts you wish to delete.");
}
```

4. Click **Check Syntax**.
5. Click **Save**.
6. Add the button to the Contacts related list on the Account page layout:

    a. Click **Setup ➤ Customize ➤ Accounts ➤ Page Layouts**.

    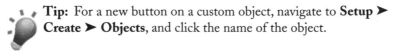 **Tip:** For a new button on a custom object, navigate to **Setup ➤ Create ➤ Objects**, and click the name of the object.

    b. Click **Edit** next to the page layout you want to customize.

   c. From the Related Lists Section, double-click the Contacts related list to edit it.

   d. In the Custom Buttons section, select the Mass Delete button in the Available buttons list and click **Add**.

   e. Click **OK** to close the popup.

   f. Click **Save** on the page layout. Your changes are not saved until you do so.

7. Optionally, enhance the usability of your app even more by adding the Mass Delete button to the Contacts Search Results and List View layouts as well:

   a. Click **Setup ➤ Customize ➤ Contacts ➤ Search Layouts**.

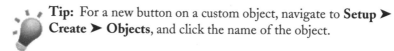

       Tip: For a new button on a custom object, navigate to **Setup ➤ Create ➤ Objects**, and click the name of the object.

   b. Click **Edit** next to the search layout you want to customize. You can add buttons to the Search Results and List View search layouts.

   c. In the Custom Buttons section, use the arrows to move the Mass Delete button to the `Selected Buttons` list.

   d. Click **Save** on the page layout.

8. Open an account record and scroll to the Contacts related list to view the button.

Discussion

The GETRECORDIDS() function is the crucial call in any mass action list button. It returns an array of string record IDs for the selected records in the list view or related list. It always takes a single $ObjectType merge field with the specified type of the records that are included in the list (for example, $ObjectType.Case or $ObjectType.Position__c).

If you're creating a mass delete button for a list of activities, you must specify whether the activities are tasks or events. If tasks, use $ObjectType.Task in your call to GETRECORDIDS(). If events, use $ObjectType.Event instead.

       Note: The GETRECORDIDS() function is only available in custom buttons and links. The $ObjectType merge field is only available in Visualforce pages, custom buttons and links, and validation rules.

       Tip: If you'd rather not go to the trouble of creating this button yourself, install it and others like it for free by going to Force Platform AppExchange and searching for the Mass Delete app. Installing this package includes a mass delete custom button for each standard object. The custom list button for activity lists also deletes all selected tasks or events at once.

See Also

- *Creating a Mass Update Button* on page 20
- "Getting Started with Custom Buttons and Links," a Breeze presentation available at salesforce.breezecentral.com/buttonsandlinks
- "Embedded Mash-Up Samples," a PDF available at blogs.salesforce.com/features/files/salesforce_useful_scontrols.pdf
- "Operators and Functions" in the Salesforce online help
- "Understanding Global Variables" in the Salesforce online help
- *AJAX Toolkit Developer's Guide*

Creating a Mass Update Button

Problem

You want to add a button to the top of a list of records that allows users to select multiple items in the list and perform the same updates on all of them.

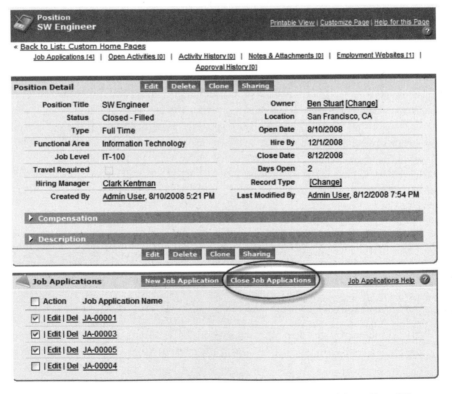

Figure 3: A Mass Close Button for Job Applications on a Positions Detail Page

Solution

Create a custom mass action list button on the object that's associated with the records that appear in the list.

To illustrate this solution, we'll enhance the sample Recruiting application by giving users a quick way to close multiple job applications after a position has closed. Instead of forcing users to open each job application and change its Stage and Status fields, we'll set up a list button called **Reject Applications** to do this for us.

To implement this solution on your own, use the same general procedure for creating a list button as was described in the recipe for *Creating a Mass Delete Button* on page 17. Instead of using the JavaScript code for the mass delete button, though, swap in the following code:

```
// Include and initialize the AJAX Toolkit javascript library
//
{!REQUIRESCRIPT("/soap/ajax/10.0/connection.js")}

// Get the list of job applications that should be closed by using the
// $ObjectType merge field to indicate the type of record Ids that
// are expected.
//
var jobAppIdArr = {!GETRECORDIDS( $ObjectType.Job_Application__c )};

if (jobAppIdArr == null || jobAppIdArr.length == 0) {
    alert("Please select the job applications you wish to reject.");

} else {

    // Retrieving the job applications that should be deleted from
    // the database is inefficient and unnecessary. Instead, create
    // new job application records for each job application that
    // should be updated, store them in an array, and then use the
    // update API call.
    //
    var jobApps = new Array();

    for (var i = 0; i < jobAppIdArr.length; i++) {
        var jobApp = new sforce.SObject("Job_Application__c");

        // Since we'll be using the update call, we must set the id
        // on the new job application record.
        //
        jobApp.Id = jobAppIdArr[i];

        // Next set the appropriate fields to reject the
        //application.
        //
        jobApp.Status__c = "Closed";
        jobApp.Stage__c = "Closed - Rejected";

        // Finally add the record to our array.
        //
        jobApps.push(jobApp);
```

```
    }

    // Now make the update API call in a try statement so we can
    // catch any errors. Save the resulting array so we can also
    // check for problems with individual records.
    //
    var callCompleted = false;
    try {
        var result = sforce.connection.update(jobApps);
        callCompleted = true;

    } catch(error) {
        alert("Failed to update Job Applications with error: " + error);

    }

    // Now check for problems with individual records.
    //
    if (callCompleted) {
        for (var i = 0; i < result.length; i++) {
            if (!result[i].getBoolean("success")) {
                alert("Job Application (id='" + jobAppIdArr[i] +
                    "') could not be updated with error: " +
                    result[i].errors);
            }
        }

        // Finally, refresh the browser to provide confirmation
        // to the user that the job applications were rejected.
        //
        window.location.reload(true);
    }
}
```

See Also

- *The Sample Recruiting App* on page 3
- *Creating a Mass Delete Button* on page 17
- "Getting Started with Custom Buttons and Links," a Breeze presentation available at salesforce.breezecentral.com/buttonsandlinks
- "Embedded Mash-Up Samples," a PDF available at blogs.salesforce.com/features/files/salesforce_useful_scontrols.pdf
- "Operators and Functions" in the Salesforce online help
- "Understanding Global Variables" in the Salesforce online help

Creating a Custom Detail Page Button

Problem

You want to add a custom button to the account detail page.

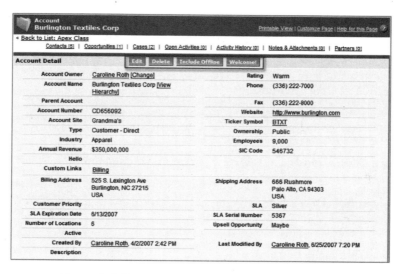

Figure 4: A Custom Button on an Account Detail Page

Solution

First define the button, then add it to the appropriate page layout. For example, the following procedure creates a simple button that, when clicked, displays a popup dialog with a welcome message.

1. Define the button:

    a. Click **Setup ➤ Customize ➤ Accounts ➤ Buttons and Links**.

    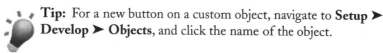 **Tip:** For a new button on a custom object, navigate to **Setup ➤ Develop ➤ Objects**, and click the name of the object.

    b. In the Custom Buttons and Links related list, click **New**.

    c. Name the button and set its attributes as follows:

    - `Label`: Welcome!
    - `Name`: Welcome
    - `Description`: Welcome message to user.
    - `Display Type`: Detail Page Button

- `Behavior`: Execute JavaScript
- `Content Source`: OnClick JavaScript

 Tip: Since there's a limited amount of space in the button bar, keep the button label as short as possible.

    d. In the body of the button, enter the following JavaScript code:

```
alert ("Hello {!User.FirstName}");
```

    e. Click **Check Syntax**.
    f. Click **Save**.

2. Add the button to the Account page layout:

    a. Click **Setup ➤ Customize ➤ Accounts ➤ Page Layouts**.

 Tip: For a new button on a custom object, navigate to **Setup ➤ Develop ➤ Objects**, and click the name of the object.

    b. Click **Edit** next to page layout you want to customize.
    c. From the Button Section, double-click the Detail Page Buttons item to edit it.
    d. Select the Welcome! button in the Available buttons list and click **Add**.
    e. Click **OK** to close the popup.
    f. Click **Save** on the page layout. Your changes are not saved until you do so.

Discussion

Custom buttons allow you to build custom actions directly into Salesforce. A button can navigate to a URL, or execute JavaScript when a user clicks it. It can open a new window, display in the existing window, or perform an action behind the scenes.

 Tip: If you define a button that displays in a new window, you can control the properties of that window by clicking **Window Open Properties** in the button's detail page.

Because buttons are more recognizable and easy to find on a page than custom links, use them for your most important value-add functionality.

See Also

- *Creating a Mass Delete Button* on page 17
- *Creating a Mass Update Button* on page 20

- *Creating a Button with Apex* on page 25
- "Getting Started with Custom Buttons and Links," a Breeze presentation available at salesforce.breezecentral.com/buttonsandlinks
- "Embedded Mash-Up Samples," a PDF available at blogs.salesforce.com/features/files/salesforce_useful_scontrols.pdf
- "Operators and Functions" in the Salesforce online help
- "Understanding Global Variables" in the Salesforce online help

Using Special Characters in Custom Links

Problem

You have customers who are using non-English versions of Internet Explorer 6 or another browser, and URLs in and custom links aren't passing special characters properly. The characters either don't show up, or the entire line of code is copied.

Solution

Encode the URLs with the `encodeURI()` JavaScript function. For example:

```
<script language="JavaScript">
function redirect()
   {parent.frames.location.replace(encodeURI("/003/e?retURL=" +
      "%2F{!Contact.Id}&con4_lkid={!Account.Id}&" +
      "con4{!Account.Name}&00N30000001KqeH=" +
      "{!Account.Account_Name_Localized__c}" +
      "&cancelURL=%2F{!Account.Id}"))}
   redirect();
</script>
```

Creating a Button with Apex

Problem

You want to create a new button that executes logic written in Apex.

Solution

Define a `webService` method in Apex and then call it using the AJAX Toolkit in a button.

For example, suppose you want to create a **Mass Add Notes** button on accounts:

1. Define the Web service method in Apex by clicking **Setup ➤ Develop ➤ Apex Classes,** clicking **New,** and adding the following code into the body of your new class:

```
global class MassNoteInsert{

  WebService static Integer insertNotes(String iTitle,
                                        String iBody,
                                        Id[] iParentIds) {
    Note[] notes = new Note[0];
    for (Id iParentId : iParentIds) {
        notes.add(new Note(parentId = iParentId,
                           title = iTitle, body = iBody));
    }
    insert notes; //Bulk Insert
    return notes.size();
  }

}
```

2. Then, click **Setup ➤ Customize ➤ Accounts ➤ Buttons and Links**, and click **New** in the Custom Buttons and Links related list.

3. Name the button and assign it the following attributes:

   - `Display Type`: List Button
   - `Behavior`: Execute JavaScript
   - `Content Source`: OnClick JavaScript

4. In the code for the button, enter:

```
{!REQUIRESCRIPT("/soap/ajax/14.0/connection.js")}
{!REQUIRESCRIPT("/soap/ajax/14.0/apex.js")}


var idsToInsert= {!GETRECORDIDS( $ObjectType.Account )};
var noteTitle = prompt("Please enter the title of the note");
var noteBody = prompt("Please enter the body of the note");

if (idsToInsert.length) {

    // Now make a synchronous call to the Apex Web service
    // method
    var result = sforce.apex.execute(
      "MassNoteInsert",        // class
      "insertNotes",           // method
      {iTitle : noteTitle,     // method arguments
       iBody: noteBody,
       iParentIds: idsToInsert });

    alert(result[0] + " notes inserted!"); //response
} else if (idsToInsert.length == 0) {
    alert("Please select the accounts to which" +
          " you would like to add notes.");
}
```

5. Click **Save**.
6. Click **Setup ➤ Customize ➤ Accounts ➤ Search Layouts** and add the button to the Accounts List View layout.

To test this new button, visit the Accounts tab and click **Go!** to view a list of accounts. Select one or more accounts and click **Mass Add Notes**.

See Also

- *Creating a Mass Delete Button* on page 17
- *Creating a Mass Update Button* on page 20

Overriding a Standard Button

Problem

You want to override what happens when a user clicks a standard button, such as **New** or **Edit**.

Solution

To override a button on a standard object:

1. Click **Setup ➤ Customize**, select the name of the object, and then click **Buttons and Links**.
2. In the Standard Buttons and Links related list, click **Override** next to the name of the button you want to change.
3. Select **Visualforce Page** as the content type.
4. Select a Visualforce page from the content name drop-down list.

   Only Visualforce pages that use the standard controller for the object on which the button appears can be selected. For example, if you want to use a page to override the **Edit** button on accounts, the page markup must include the `standardController="Account"` attribute on the `<apex:page>` tag:

   ```
   <apex:page standardController="Account">

       ... page content here ...

   </apex:page>
   ```

5. Click **Save**.

To override a button on a custom object:

1. Click **Setup ➤ Create ➤ Objects** and select the name of the object.

2. Scroll down to the Standard Buttons and Links related list and click **Override** next to the name of the button you want to override.

3. Select **Visualforce Page** as the content type.

4. Select a Visualforce page from the content name drop-down list.

   Only Visualforce pages that use the standard controller for the object on which the button appears can be selected. For example, if you want to use a page to override the **Edit** button on accounts, the page markup must include the `standardController="Account"` attribute on the `<apex:page>` tag:

   ```
   <apex:page standardController="Account">

        ... page content here ...

   </apex:page>
   ```

5. Click **Save**.

Discussion

For standard and custom objects in the application, you can override the following standard buttons:

- New
- View
- Edit
- Delete
- Clone
- Accept

Additionally, some standard objects also have special actions. For example, Leads have Convert, Change Status, Add to Campaign, and others. These actions can also be overridden.

However, because Visualforce pages are only available through the Salesforce user interface, overriding the **New** button for contacts has no effect on new contacts that are created via Apex or the API.

You can only override standard buttons that appear on an object's detail page or list views. Buttons that only appear on an edit page or in reports can't be overridden.

As a final note, button overrides shouldn't be confused with Apex triggers, which execute in tandem with the typical behavior. Button overrides replace the standard behavior entirely. For example, if you override the **Delete** button on Accounts and a user attempts to delete an account, it won't necessarily be deleted. Instead, the user is forwarded on to the URL of your choosing, which may or may not include code to delete the account. If you define an Apex delete trigger on Accounts, however, the normal delete behavior still occurs, as long as the trigger doesn't prevent deletion by adding an error to the record.

See Also

- *Overriding a Standard Page* on page 46
- *Overriding a Page for Some, but not All, Users* on page 53

Creating a Consistent Look and Feel with Static Resources

Problem

You want all of your Visualforce pages to have a consistent look and feel that can easily be updated.

Solution

Create a *static resource* from a Cascading Style Sheet and include it in your Visualforce pages. A static resource; is a file or archive that you upload and then reference in a Visualforce page.

To create a static resource from a stylesheet:

1. Click **Setup ➤ Develop ➤ Static Resources**.
2. Click **New Static Resource**.
3. In the `Name` text box, enter `myStyleSheet`. This name is used to identify the resource in Visualforce markup.
4. In the `Description` text area, enter `My site-wide stylesheet`.
5. Next to the `File` text box, click **Browse** to navigate to a local copy of your stylesheet.
6. Click **Save**.

To reference the stylesheet in a page, create the following Visualforce page:

```
<apex:page showHeader="false">
  <apex:styleSheet value="{!$Resource.myStyleSheet}"/>
  <!-- Your content goes here -->
  <h1>My Style</h1>
  <p>This page uses styles from my stylesheet.
     The stylesheet is a static resource.</p>
</apex:page>
```

To change the look of your pages, all you need to do is update the static resource with your new styles, and every page that uses that static resource displays with your new style.

Discussion

Static resources can be used for many other purposes, not just stylesheets. A static resource can be an archive (such as .zip and .jar files), image, stylesheet, JavaScript, or any other type of file you want to use in your Visualforce pages.

A static resource name can only contain alphanumeric characters, must begin with a letter, and must be unique in your organization. If you reference a static resource in Visualforce markup and then change the name of the resource, the Visualforce markup is updated to reflect that change.

A single static resource can be up to 5 MB in size, and an organization can have up to 250 MB of static resources, total.

See Also

- Managing Static Resources in the Salesforce online help
- *Visualforce Developer's Guide*

Formatting a Currency

Problem

You want to display a currency value, but the API doesn't return currencies in a formatted state.

Solution

Use Visualforce to display currencies in a manner that is correctly formatted for your users. The following Visualforce page will show Opportunity date and amount values in the format for their locale.

```
<apex:page standardController="Opportunity">
    <apex:pageBlock title="Opportunity Fields">
        <apex:pageBlockSection >
            <apex:outputField value="{!opportunity.closedate}"/>
            <apex:outputField value="{!opportunity.amount}"/>
        </apex:pageBlockSection>
    </apex:pageBlock>
</apex:page>
```

Discussion

The Visualforce `<apex:outputfield>` component does the formatting automatically for users in all locales.

Building a Table of Data in a Visualforce Page

Problem

You want to display a set of records in a table in a Visualforce page.

Solution

Define a custom controller that returns the set of records you want to display, and then use the `<dataTable>` tag to display the results. For example, assume that you want to display the contacts associated with a record in a table.

1. Create a controller so that it returns a list of associated contacts with an account record:

```
public class mySecondController {

  public Account getAccount() {
    return [select id, name,
             (select id, firstname, lastname
              from Contacts limit 5)
             from Account where id =
              :System.currentPageReference()
              .getParameters().get('id')];
  }

 public String getName() {
   return 'My Second Custom Controller';
 }
}
```

2. Iterate over the resulting contacts with the `<dataTable>` tag. This tag allows us to define an iteration variable that we can use to access the fields on each contact:

```
<apex:page controller="mySecondController" tabStyle="Account">

  <apex:pageBlock title="Hello {!$User.FirstName}!">
    You belong to the {!account.name} account.
  </apex:pageBlock>
  <apex:pageBlock title="Contacts">
    <apex:dataTable value="{!account.Contacts}"
                    var="contact"
                    cellPadding="4" border="1">
      <apex:column >
        {!contact.FirstName}
      </apex:column>
      <apex:column >
        {!contact.LastName}
      </apex:column>
    </apex:dataTable>
  </apex:pageBlock>
</apex:page>
```

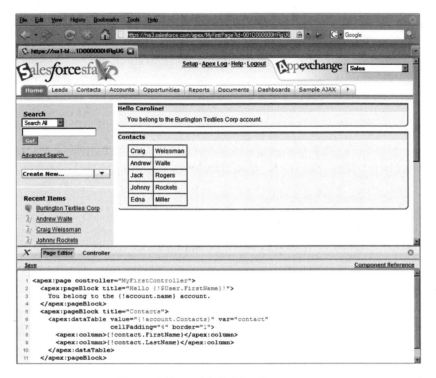

Figure 5: The <dataTable> Component

Discussion

Notice that the `<apex:dataTable>` tag supports styling attributes like `cellPadding` and `border`. You can also style individual data elements with HTML tags. For example, the following `<apex:dataTable>` component makes the last name of each contact bold:

```
<apex:dataTable value="{!account.Contacts}" var="contact"
              cellPadding="4" border="1">
  <apex:column>{!contact.FirstName}</apex:column>
  <apex:column><b>{!contact.LastName}</b></apex:column>
</apex:dataTable>
```

See Also

- *Using Query String Parameters in a Visualforce Page* on page 139
- *Building a Form in a Visualforce Page* on page 33
- *Using AJAX in a Visualforce Page* on page 141
- *Creating a Wizard with Visualforce Pages* on page 35

Building a Form in a Visualforce Page

Problem

You want to create a Visualforce page that captures input from users.

Solution

Use the `<apex:form>` tag with one or more input components and a `<apex:commandLink>` or `<apex:commandButton>` tag to submit the form.

Discussion

To gather data for fields that are defined on a custom or standard object, use the `<apex:inputField>` tag. This tag renders the appropriate input widget based on the field's type. For example, if you use an `<apex:inputField>` tag to display a date field, a calendar widget displays on the form. If you use an `<apex:inputField>` tag to display a picklist field, a drop-down list displays instead.

For example, the following page allows users to edit and save the name of an account.

```
<apex:page standardController="Account">
  <apex:form>
    <apex:pageBlock title="Hello {!$User.FirstName}!">
      You belong to the {!account.name} account.<p/>
      Account Name:
      <apex:inputField value="{!account.name}"/>
      <p/>
      <apex:commandButton action="{!save}"
                          value="Save New Account Name"/>
    </apex:pageBlock>
  </apex:form>
</apex:page>
```

 Note: Remember, for this page to display account data, the ID of a valid account record must be specified as a query parameter in the URL for the page.

Notice that the `<apex:commandButton>` tag is associated with the save action of the standard controller, which performs the same action as the **Save** button on the standard edit page. The `<apex:inputField>` tag is bound to the account name field by setting the value attribute with an expression containing dot notation.

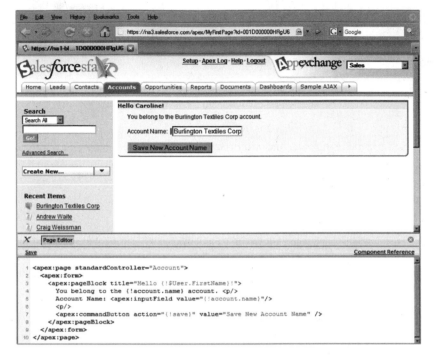

Figure 6: The <apex:form> Component with a Single Input Field

The <apex:inputField> tag can be used with either standard or custom controllers and enforces all security restrictions and other flags on the field, such as whether a value for the field is required, or whether it must be unique from the value on all other records of that type. Its only drawback is that if it's used to display variables in a custom controller that aren't bound to an object field, the variables might not display the way you want them to.

To gather data for these variables, use the apex:inputCheckbox, apex:inputHidden, apex:inputSecret, apex:inputText, or apex:inputTextarea tags instead. To learn more about these tags, browse the component library by clicking **Component Reference** in the Page Editor or accessing it through the Salesforce online help.

See Also

- *Using Query String Parameters in a Visualforce Page* on page 139
- *Building a Table of Data in a Visualforce Page* on page 31
- *Using AJAX in a Visualforce Page* on page 141
- *Creating a Wizard with Visualforce Pages* on page 35

Creating a Wizard with Visualforce Pages

Problem

You want to create a three-step opportunity wizard that allows users to create an opportunity at the same time as a related contact, account, and contact role:

- The first step captures information related to the account and contact
- The second step captures information related to the opportunity
- The final step shows which records will be created and allows the user to save or cancel

Solution

Define three Visualforce pages for each of the three steps in the wizard, plus a single custom controller that sets up navigation between each of the pages and tracks the data that the user enters.

The code for the three pages and the controller is included here; however, it's important to understand the best procedure for creating them because each of the three pages references the controller, and the controller references each of the three pages. In what appears to be a Catch-22, you can't create the controller without the pages, but the pages have to exist in order for you to refer to them in the controller.

Luckily, we can work our way out of this conundrum because we can define a page that's completely empty. To create the wizard pages and controller:

1. Navigate to the URL for the first page:
   `https://<host>.salesforce.com/apex/opptyStep1`
2. Click **Create Page newOpptyStep1**.
3. Repeat the two steps above for the other pages in the wizard: `opptyStep2` and `opptyStep3`.

    Note: Although you can create an empty page, the reverse is not true. In order for a page to refer to a controller, the controller has to exist with all of its methods and properties.

   Now all three of the pages exist. Even though they are empty, they need to exist before we can create a controller that refers to them.

4. Create the `newOpportunityController` controller by adding it as an attribute to the `<apex:page>` tag on one of your pages (for example, `<apex:page controller="newOpportunityController">`, and clicking **Create Apex controller newOpportunityController**. Paste in all of the following controller code:

```
/*
 * This class is the controller behind the New Customer Opportunity
```

```
 * wizard. The new wizard is comprised of three pages, each of
 * which utilizes the same instance of this controller.
 */
public class newOpportunityController {

    // These four class variables maintain the state of the wizard.
    // When users enter data into the wizard, their input is stored
    // in these variables.
    Account account;
    Contact contact;
    Opportunity opportunity;
    OpportunityContactRole role;


    // The next four methods return one of each of the four class
    // variables. If this is the first time the method is called,
    // it creates an empty record for the variable.
    public Account getAccount() {
        if(account == null) account = new Account();
        return account;
    }

    public Contact getContact() {
        if(contact == null) contact = new Contact();
        return contact;
    }

    public Opportunity getOpportunity() {
        if(opportunity == null) opportunity = new Opportunity();
        return opportunity;
    }

    public OpportunityContactRole getRole() {
        if(role == null) role = new OpportunityContactRole();
        return role;
    }


    // The next three methods are used to control navigation through
    // the wizard. Each returns a reference to one of the three pages
    // in the wizard.
    public PageReference step1() {
        return Page.newOpptyStep1;
    }

    public PageReference step2() {
        return Page.newOpptyStep2;
    }

    public PageReference step3() {
        return Page.newOpptyStep3;
    }

    // This method performs the final save for all four objects, and
    // then navigates the user to the detail page for the new
    // opportunity.
```

```
    public PageReference save() {

        // Create the account. Before inserting, copy the contact's
        // phone number into the account phone number field.
        account.phone = contact.phone;
        insert account;

        // Create the contact. Before inserting, use the id field
        // that's created once the account is inserted to create
        // the relationship between the contact and the account.
        contact.accountId = account.id;
        insert contact;

        // Create the opportunity. Before inserting, create
        // another relationship with the account.
        opportunity.accountId = account.id;
        insert opportunity;

        // Create the junction contact role between the opportunity
        // and the contact.
        role.opportunityId = opportunity.id;
        role.contactId = contact.id;
        insert role;

        // Finally, send the user to the detail page for
        // the new opportunity.
        // Note that using '/' in the new PageReference object keeps
        // the user in the current instance of salesforce, rather than
        // redirecting him or her elsewhere.
        PageReference opptyPage = new PageReference('/' +
                                                    opportunity.id);
        opptyPage.setRedirect(true);

        return opptyPage;
    }
}
```

5. Save the controller.

6. Navigate to the URL for the first page:
   `https://<host>.salesforce.com/apex/opptyStep1` and copy in the following:

```
<apex:page controller="newOpportunityController"
           tabStyle="Opportunity">
  <apex:sectionHeader title="New Customer Opportunity"
                      subtitle="Step 1 of 3"/>
  <apex:form>
    <apex:pageBlock title="Customer Information">

      <!-- This facet tag defines the "Next" button that appears
           in the footer of the pageBlock. It calls the step2()
           controller method, which returns a pageReference to
           the next step of the wizard. -->
```

```
    <apex:facet name="footer">
      <apex:commandButton action="{!step2}" value="Next"
                          styleClass="btn"/>
    </apex:facet>
    <apex:pageBlockSection title="Account Information">

    <!-- <apex:panelGrid> tags organize data in the same way as
          a table. It places all child elements in successive cells,

          in left-to-right, top-to-bottom order -->
    <!-- <apex:outputLabel> and <apex:inputField> tags can be
          bound together with the for and id attribute values,
          respectively. -->
    <apex:panelGrid columns="2">
      <apex:outputLabel value="Account Name" for="accountName"/>
      <apex:inputField id="accountName" value="{!account.name}"/>
      <apex:outputLabel value="Account Site" for="accountSite"/>
      <apex:inputField id="accountSite" value="{!account.site}"/>
    </apex:panelGrid>
    </apex:pageBlockSection>
    <apex:pageBlockSection title="Contact Information">
      <apex:panelGrid columns="2">
        <apex:outputLabel value="First Name"
                          for="contactFirstName"/>
        <apex:inputField id="contactFirstName"
                          value="{!contact.firstName}"/>
        <apex:outputLabel value="Last Name" for="contactLastName"/>
        <apex:inputField id="contactLastName"
                          value="{!contact.lastName}"/>
        <apex:outputLabel value="Phone" for="contactPhone"/>
        <apex:inputField id="contactPhone"
                          value="{!contact.phone}"/>
      </apex:panelGrid>
    </apex:pageBlockSection>
  </apex:pageBlock>
  </apex:form>
</apex:page>
```

7. Save the page.
8. Navigate to the URL for the first page:
   `https://<host>.salesforce.com/apex/opptyStep2` and copy in the following:

```
<apex:page controller="newOpportunityController"
          tabStyle="Opportunity">
  <apex:sectionHeader title="New Customer Opportunity"
                      subtitle="Step 2 of 3"/>
  <apex:form>
    <apex:pageBlock title="Opportunity Information">
      <apex:facet name="footer">
        <apex:outputPanel>
          <apex:commandButton action="{!step1}" value="Previous"
                              styleClass="btn"/>
          <apex:commandButton action="{!step3}" value="Next"
```

```
                                      styleClass="btn"/>
            </apex:outputPanel>
         </apex:facet>
         <apex:pageBlockSection title="Opportunity Information">
            <apex:panelGrid columns="2">
               <apex:outputLabel value="Opportunity Name"
                              for="opportunityName"/>
               <apex:inputField id="opportunityName"
                              value="{!opportunity.name}"/>
               <apex:outputLabel value="Amount"
                              for="opportunityAmount"/>
               <apex:inputField id="opportunityAmount"
                              value="{!opportunity.amount}"/>
               <apex:outputLabel value="Close Date"
                              for="opportunityCloseDate"/>
               <apex:inputField id="opportunityCloseDate"
                              value="{!opportunity.closeDate}"/>
               <apex:outputLabel value="Stage"
                              for="opportunityStageName"/>
               <apex:inputField id="opportunityStageName"
                              value="{!opportunity.stageName}"/>
               <apex:outputLabel value="Role for Contact:
                                    {!contact.firstName}
                                    {!contact.lastName}"
                              for="contactRole"/>
               <apex:inputField id="contactRole"
                              value="{!role.role}"/>
            </apex:panelGrid>
         </apex:pageBlockSection>
      </apex:pageBlock>
   </apex:form>
</apex:page>
```

9. Save the page.
10. Navigate to the URL for the first page:
    `https://<host>.salesforce.com/apex/opptyStep3` and copy in the following:

```
<apex:page controller="newOpportunityController"
           tabStyle="Opportunity">
   <apex:sectionHeader title="New Customer Opportunity"
                     subtitle="Step 3 of 3"/>
   <apex:form>
      <apex:pageBlock title="Confirmation">
         <apex:facet name="footer">
            <apex:outputPanel>
               <apex:commandButton action="{!step2}" value="Previous"
                              styleClass="btn"/>
               <apex:commandButton action="{!save}" value="Save"
                              styleClass="btn"/>
            </apex:outputPanel>
         </apex:facet>
         <apex:pageBlockSection title="Account Information">
            <apex:panelGrid columns="2">
```

```
        <apex:outputText value="Account Name"/>
        <apex:outputText value="{!account.name}"/>
        <apex:outputText value="Account Site"/>
        <apex:outputText value="{!account.site}"/>
    </apex:panelGrid>
  </apex:pageBlockSection>
  <apex:pageBlockSection title="Contact Information">
    <apex:panelGrid columns="2">
        <apex:outputText value="First Name"/>
        <apex:outputText value="{!contact.firstName}"/>
        <apex:outputText value="Last Name"/>
        <apex:outputText value="{!contact.lastName}"/>
        <apex:outputText value="Phone"/>
        <apex:outputText value="{!contact.phone}"/>
        <apex:outputText value="Role"/>
        <apex:outputText value="{!role.role}"/>
    </apex:panelGrid>
  </apex:pageBlockSection>
  <apex:pageBlockSection title="Opportunity Information">
    <apex:panelGrid columns="2">
        <apex:outputText value="Opportunity Name"/>
        <apex:outputText value="{!opportunity.name}"/>
        <apex:outputText value="Amount"/>
        <apex:outputText value="{!opportunity.amount}"/>
        <apex:outputText value="Close Date"/>
        <apex:outputText value="{!opportunity.closeDate}"/>
    </apex:panelGrid>
  </apex:pageBlockSection>
  </apex:pageBlock>
 </apex:form>
</apex:page>
```

11. Save the page.

You'll now have a wizard that is composed of the following three pages:

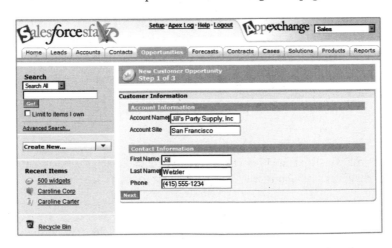

Figure 7: Step 1 of the New Customer Opportunity Wizard

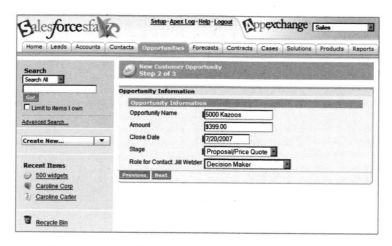

Figure 8: Step 2 of the New Customer Opportunity Wizard

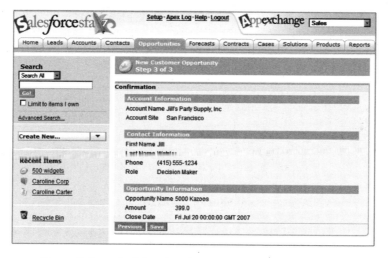

Figure 9: Step 3 of the New Customer Opportunity Wizard

You can start the wizard by navigating to the first page:
`https://<host>.salesforce.com/apex/opptyStep1`.

Discussion

On page 1 of the wizard, data about the associated contact and account is gathered from the user. Notice the following about the code for the first page of the wizard:

- Some tags, including `<apex:pageBlock>`, can take an optional `<apex:facet>` child element that controls the header or footer of the component. The order in which the facet tag appears in the `<apex:pageBlock>` body doesn't matter because it includes a `name` attribute that identifies where the element should be placed. In this page of the wizard, the facet tag defines the **Next** button that appears in the footer of the `pageBlock` area.

- An `<apex:commandButton>` tag represents a user control that executes a method in the controller class. In this page of the wizard, the **Next** button calls the `step2()` method in the controller, which returns a `PageReference` to the next step of the wizard. Command buttons must appear in a form, because the form component itself is responsible for refreshing the page display based on the new `pageReference`.

```
<apex:facet name="footer">
  <apex:commandButton action="{!step2}" value="Next"
                     styleClass="btn"/>
</apex:facet>
```

- An `<apex:panelGrid>` tag organizes a set of data for display. Similar to a table, it simply takes a number of columns and then places all child elements in successive cells, in left-to-right, top-to-bottom order. For example, in the Account Information area of this page, the "Account Name" label is in the first cell, the input field for `Account Name` is in the second cell, the "Account Site" label is in the third cell, and the input field for `Account Site` is in the fourth.

```
<apex:panelGrid columns="2">
  <apex:outputLabel value="Account Name" for="accountName"/>
  <apex:inputField id="accountName" value="{!account.name}"/>
  <apex:outputLabel value="Account Site" for="accountSite"/>
  <apex:inputField id="accountSite" value="{!account.site}"/>
</apex:panelGrid>
```

- The `value` attribute on the first `<apex:inputField>` tag in the preceding code excerpt assigns the user's input to the name field of the account record that's returned by the `getAccount()` method in the controller.
- The `<apex:outputLabel>` and `<apex:inputField>` tags can be bound together when the `id` attribute value on `<apex:inputField>` tag matches the `for` attribute value on `<apex:outputLabel>`. Binding these tags together improves the user experience because it provides special behavior in the Web page. For example, clicking on the label puts the cursor in the associated input field. Likewise, if the input is a checkbox, it toggles the checkmark.

On page 2 of the wizard, data about the opportunity is gathered from the user. Notice the following about the code for the second page of the wizard:

- Because this page displays two buttons in the `pageBlock` footer, they're wrapped in an `<apex:outputPanel>` tag. This tag needs to be used because `<apex:facet>` expects only one child component.

   Note: You also must use an `<apex:panelGroup>` tag within an `<apex:panelGrid>` if you want to place more than one component into a single cell of the grid.

- Although the code for placing the `Close Date`, `Stage`, and `Role for Contact` fields on the form is the same as the other fields, the `<apex:inputField>` tag examines the data type of each field to determine how to display it. For example, clicking in the `Close Date` text box brings up a calendar from which users can select the date.

On page 3 of the wizard, the user can choose to save the changes or cancel. Notice that the third page of the wizard simply writes text to the page with `<apex:outputText>` tags.

See Also

- *Using Query String Parameters in a Visualforce Page* on page 139
- *Building a Table of Data in a Visualforce Page* on page 31
- *Building a Form in a Visualforce Page* on page 33
- *Using AJAX in a Visualforce Page* on page 141

Creating a Custom Visualforce Component

Problem

You want to use the same functionality on multiple Visualforce pages, but there isn't a standard component to do it.

Solution

You can create a custom component and use that on your Visualforce page. The following custom component allows your users to easily increase or decrease a value on the page. First, create the component, and then add it to a Visualforce page.

To create a custom component:

1. In Salesforce click **Setup ➤ Develop ➤ Components**.
2. Click **New**.
3. In the `Label` text box, enter `Add or Subtract Values`.
4. In the `Name` text box, enter `addSubValue`.
5. In the `Description` text box, enter `Increase or decrease a value`.
6. In the `Body` text box, enter the following Visualforce markup:

```
<apex:component>

<-- Attribute Definitions -->
  <apex:attribute name="myvalue"
   description="Default value for the component."
   type="Integer" required="true"/>
  <apex:attribute name="max"
```

```
      description="Maximum value"
      type="Integer" required="true"/>
      <apex:attribute name="min"
      description="Minimum value"
      type="Integer" required="true"/>

<!- JavaScript definitions -->
  <script>
    funtion increment(valueId) {
      if(document.getElementById(valueId).value < {!max})
        {
          document.getElementById(valueId).value++;
        }
      else
        {
          alert("You can't increase the number above " + {!max});
        }
    }

    function decrement(valueId) {
      if(document.getElementById(valueId).value >{!min})
        {
          document.getElementById(valueId).value--;
        }
      else
        {
          alert("You can't decrease the number below " + {!min});
        }
    }
  </script>

<!-- Custom Component Definition -->
<table cellspacing='0' cellpadding='0'>
 <tr>
  <td rowspan="2">
   <apex:inputText value="{!myvalue}" size="4" id="theValue"/>
  </td>
  <td>
   <div onclick="increment('{!$Component.theValue}');">&#9650;</div>
  </td>
 </tr>
 <tr>
  <td>
   <div onclick="decrement('{!$Component.theValue}');">&#9660;</div>
  </td>
 </tr>
</table>
</apex:component>
```

7. Click **Save**.

To add your new component to a page:

1. Click **SetupDevelop** ➤ **Pages**.
2. Click **New**.

3. In the name field, enter `testAddSub`.

4. Optionally enter a label and description.

5. In the editor, enter the following markup:

```
<apex:page>
  <apex:pageBlock title="Increase or Decrease the Number Displayed">
    <apex:form>
      <c:addSubValue myvalue="10" min="0" max="15"/>
    </apex:form>
  </apex:pageBlock>
</apex:page>
```

6. Click **Save**.

When you open the page in a browser, you will be see something like the following:

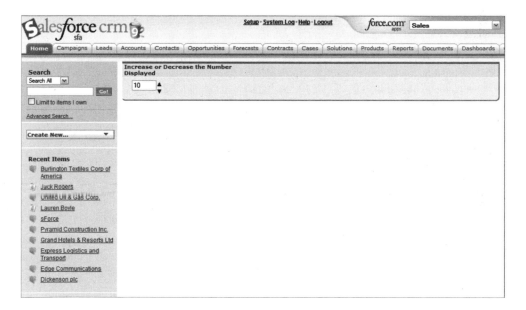

Click the up or down arrow to increase or decrease the number displayed. If you try to change it to a value lower than 0 or greater than 15, an error message displays in a popup dialog.

Discussion

This solution illustrates how you can mix Visualforce, HTML, and JavaScript within a custom component. This combination allows you to create very powerful custom components. To really make this component useful, you can bind the value to a field (like the number of employees on an account) and update that field when your user submits the form.

The name of a custom component can only contain alphanumeric characters, start with a letter, and must be unique from all other components in your organization.

The description of a custom component appears in the component reference with other standard component descriptions. If your custom component includes `apex:attribute` components, the description will be included in the component reference as well.

A single component can hold up to 1 MB of text, or approximately 1,000,000 characters.

When working on a custom component, you can click **Quick Save** to save your changes and continue editing your component.

The Visualforce markup must be valid before you can save your component.

Overriding a Standard Page

Problem

You want to override what happens when a user clicks a tab in Salesforce, such as the Account or Contact tab.

Solution

To override a standard object tab:

1. Create a Visualforce page called `accountOverride`.

   a. Click **SetupDevelop ➤ Pages**.
   b. Click **New**.
   c. In the label field, enter `Override the Account Home Page`.
   d. In the name field, enter `accountOverride`.
   e. In the description, enter `This page will display for all users`.
   f. In the editor, enter the following markup:

```
<apex:page standardController="Account" recordSetVar="accounts"

           tabStyle="Account">
  <apex:form>
    <apex:pageBlock>
      <apex:pageBlockTable value="{!accounts}" var="a">
        <apex:column value="{!a.name}"/>
        <apex:column value="{!a.lastmodifieddate}"/>
        <apex:column value="{!a.owner.alias}"/>
      </apex:pageBlockTable>
    </apex:pageBlock>
    <apex:panelGrid columns="2">
      <apex:commandLink action="{!previous}">
        Previous
      </apex:commandlink>
      <apex:commandLink action="{!next}">
```

```
        Next
      </apex:commandlink>
    </apex:panelGrid>
  </apex:form>
</apex:page>
```

    a. Click **Save**.

2. Set the page level security to allow all users to view the page.

    a. Click **Security** for the page you just created.

    b. Select all the profiles in the Available Profiles list and click **Add** to add them to the Enabled Profiles list.

    c. Click **Save**.

3. Create an override that directs users to your new page.

    a. Click **Setup ➤ Customize ➤ Accounts ➤ Buttons and Links**.

    b. In the Standard Buttons and Links list, click **Override** for the Accounts Tab.

    c. Set the content type to **Visualforce Page**.

    d. From the **Content Name** drop-down list, select **accountOverride**.

    e. Click **Save**.

Discussion

Overriding a tab overrides what a user sees when he or she clicks on the tab. Overriding a standard button overrides its functionality in all parts of the Salesforce user interface. For example, if you override a **New** button for contacts, it overrides the **New** button on the Contacts tab, the **New** button on any Contacts related list, and the **Contact** option in the Create New drop-down list in the sidebar.

You can override the home tab for all standard and custom objects.

See Also

- *Overriding a Standard Button* on page 27
- *Dynamically Updating a Page* on page 48

Dynamically Updating a Page

Problem

You have fields on a page in your Salesforce application that you only want displayed when the user has made a specific selection. In this example, you want to capture specific information about a lost opportunity. During the normal progression of a deal, there is no reason to display a field called `Reason Lost`. You want this field to display only when the `Stage` moves to `Closed Lost`. In addition to the `Reason Lost` field, you would like a required lookup field that contains competitors names, so that the user can specify which competitor won the deal.

Solution

Using Visualforce, you can create a page that updates just a portion of that page based on a changed value.

Because you're merely extending the existing behavior of the Force Platform, you don't need to create a controller (an Apex class).

Some Visualforce components are AJAX aware and allow you to add AJAX behaviors to a page without having to write any JavaScript. One of the most widely used AJAX behaviors is a *partial page update*, in which only a specific portion of a page is updated following some user action, rather than a reload of the entire page. The simplest way to implement a partial page update is to use the `reRender` attribute on a Visualforce component.

This example creates two new fields for Opportunity: `Primary Competitor` and `Reason Lost`. After you create the fields, you need to create a Visualforce page that uses these fields with an existing opportunity.

To create the new fields:

1. In Salesforce click **Setup ➤ Customize ➤ Opportunities ➤ Fields**.
2. In Opportunity Custom Fields & Relationships, click **New**.
3. Select `Lookup Relationship` and click **Next**.
4. For `Related To` select Account and click **Next**.
5. In the `Field Label` text box, enter `Primary Competitor`.
6. In the `Field Name` text box, enter `Primary_Competitor`.
7. Add a brief description in the **Description** text box, and what should display as help text in the **Help Text** text box as a best practice.
8. Click **Next**.
9. In Enterprise, Unlimited, and Developer Editions, accept the default field-level security and click **Next**.
10. Use the default values to make the field appear on all page layouts, and click **Next**.

11. Use the default value for the related list label, and accept the defaults for all the page layouts where the related list appears.
12. Click **Save and New** so you can immediately create the second field.
13. Select Text Area (Long) and click **Next**.
14. In the Field Label text box, enter Reason Lost.
15. In the Field Name text box, enter Reason_Lost.
16. Add a brief description in the **Description** text box, and what should display as help text in the **Help Text** text box as a best practice.
17. Click **Next**.
18. Use the default values and click **Next** for field-level security, adding the reference to page layouts, and adding custom related lists.
19. Click **Save**.

To create the Visualforce page:

1. In Salesforce click **Setup ➤ Develop ➤ Pages**.
2. Click **New**.
3. In the Label text box, enter Dynamic Opportunity Edit.
4. In the Name text box, enter opportunityEdit.
5. In the Description text box, enter Dynamically edit an opportunity.
6. In the Body text box, delete the existing Visualforce markup and enter the following instead:

```
<apex:page standardController="Opportunity" sidebar="false">
  <apex:sectionHeader title="Edit Opportunity"
                      subtitle="{!opportunity.name}"/>
  <apex:form >
    <apex:pageBlock title="Edit Opportunity" id="thePageBlock"
                    mode="edit">
      <apex:pageMessages />
      <apex:pageBlockButtons >
        <apex:commandButton value="Save" action="{!save}"/>
        <apex:commandButton value="Cancel" action="{!cancel}"/>
      </apex:pageBlockButtons>
      <apex:actionRegion >
        <apex:pageBlockSection title="Basic Information"
                               columns="1">
          <apex:inputField value="{!opportunity.name}"/>
          <apex:pageBlockSectionItem >
            <apex:outputLabel value="Stage"/>
            <apex:outputPanel >
              <apex:inputField value="{!opportunity.stageName}">
                <apex:actionSupport event="onchange"
                                    rerender="thePageBlock"
                                    status="status"/>
              </apex:inputField>
              <apex:actionStatus startText="applying value..."
                                 id="status"/>
            </apex:outputPanel>
```

```
            </apex:pageBlockSectionItem>
            <apex:inputField value="{!opportunity.amount}"/>
            <apex:inputField value="{!opportunity.closedate}"/>
          </apex:pageBlockSection>
      </apex:actionRegion>
      <apex:pageBlockSection title="Closed Lost Information"
            columns="1"
            rendered="{!opportunity.stageName == 'Closed Lost'}">
          <apex:inputField
              value="{!opportunity.Primary_Competitor__c}"
              required="true"/>
          <apex:inputField value="{!opportunity.Reason_Lost__c}"/>
      </apex:pageBlockSection>
    </apex:pageBlock>
  </apex:form>
</apex:page>
```

7. Click **Save**.

To test the Visualforce page:

1. Find the ID for an opportunity record:

   a. Click the Opportunities tab and find an opportunity that hasn't been closed.

   b. Click the name of that opportunity. In the URL, the ID of the opportunity record follows the name of the instance of Salesforce your organization uses. For example, in the following URL, `https://na3.salesforce.com/006D000000C4V1N`, `006D000000C4V1N` is the ID of an opportunity record.

2. Call the page by using the following URL:

   `https://salesforce_instance/apex/opportunityEdit?id=ID`

   Substitute the instance of Salesforce that you use, such as `na3.salesforce.com`, for `salesforce_instance`. Substitute the opportunity record ID you found in the previous step for `ID`. For example, `https://na3.salesforce.com/apex/opportunityEdit?id=006D000000C4V1D`.

Your page should resemble the following:

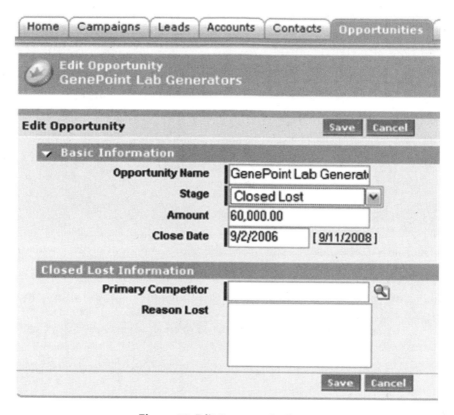

Figure 10: Edit Opportunity Page

Discussion

Note that the Basic Information portion of the page (the top page block) is contained in an
`<apex:actionRegion>` tag:

```
<apex:actionRegion >

   <apex:inputField value="{!opportunity.name}"/>
. . .
   <apex:inputField value="{!opportunity.stageName}">
. . .
   <apex:inputField value="{!opportunity.amount}"/>
. . .
   <apex:inputField value="{!opportunity.closedate}"/>

. . .
</apex:actionRegion>
```

The `<apex:actionRegion>` tag encapsulates which components should be processed by the
Force Platform server when the AJAX partial page update request to rerender the page is made.
Because these fields are in an action region, they do not get passed to the server until the user

clicks **Save**: all the data is still in memory. This is important when you have field dependencies. For example, once the user specifies Closed Lost, the `Primary Competitor` field becomes required. If the updated field information was sent back to the server before the user could update the field, you would receive an error about the required field.

When a user changes the value of `Stage` to Closed Lost, a message displays stating "applying value. . ." This message is generated by the following markup in the Visualforce page.

```
<apex:inputField value="{!opportunity.stageName}">
  <apex:actionSupport event="onchange"
                      rerender="thePageBlock"
                      status="status"/>
</apex:inputField>

<apex:actionStatus startText="applying value..." id="status"/>
```

The input field is `opportunity.stageName`, the event is `onchange`, and the status is `status`. This is bound to the `<apex:actionStatus>` tag by the ID `status`.

In addition to controlling the message that displays, this input field also controls the rendering of the page. If the field changes, this field specifies that a component named `thePageBlock` should be rerendered. The entire page is contained in an `<apex:pageBlock>` tag with the ID `thePageBlock`:

```
<apex:pageBlock title="Edit Opportunity" id="thePageBlock" mode="edit">
```

Toward the bottom of the Visualforce page markup is an `<apex:pageBlockSection>`section. This section is only rendered when the `opportunity.stageName` field has been set to Closed Lost:

```
<apex:pageBlockSection title="Closed Lost Information"
      columns="1"
      rendered="{!opportunity.stageName == 'Closed Lost'}">
  <apex:inputField value="{!opportunity.Primary_Competitor__c}"
                   required="true"/>
  <apex:inputField value="{!opportunity.Reason_Lost__c}"/>
</apex:pageBlockSection>
```

See Also

- *Using AJAX in a Visualforce Page* on page 141
- *Overriding a Page for Some, but not All, Users* on page 53

Overriding a Page for Some, but not All, Users

Problem

Some of your users should use a custom Visualforce page, while others should use a standard Salesforce page.

Solution

To override the Account tab with a Visualforce page for most of your users, but send users with the "System Administrator" profile to the standard Salesforce Account home page:

1. Create a Visualforce page called `conditionalAccountOverride`.

   a. Click **Setup ➤ Develop ➤ Pages**.

   b. Click **New**.

   c. In the label field, enter `Override the Account Page for Most Users`.

   d. In the name field, enter `accountOverride`.

   e. In the description, enter `This page will display for all users, except System Administrators, when they click the Account tab`.

   f. In the editor, enter the following markup:

   ```
   <apex:page action=
     "{!if($Profile.Name !='System Administrator',
       null,
       urlFor($Action.Account.Tab, $ObjectType.Account,
       null, true))}"
     standardController="Account"
     recordSetVar="accounts"
     tabStyle="Account">

     <!-- Replace with your markup -->
     This page replaces your Account home page for
     all users except Administrators.
   </apex:page>
   ```

   g. Click **Save**.

2. Set the page level security to allow all users to view the page.

   a. Click **Security** for the page you just created.

   b. Select all the profiles that will be using this page in the Available Profiles list and click **Add** to add them to the Enabled Profiles list.

"Overriding a Page for Some, but not All, Users" contributed by Jill Wetzler, Member of Technical Staff, for salesforce.com

       c. Click **Save**.

3. Create an override that directs users to your new page.

       a. Click **Setup ➤ Customize ➤ Accounts ➤ Buttons and Links**.

       b. In the Standard Buttons and Links list, click **Override** for the Accounts Tab.

       c. Set the content type to **Visualforce Page**.

       d. From the **Content Name** drop-down list, select **conditionalAccountOverride**.

       e. Click **Save**.

Discussion

This solution uses the `action` attribute on the `apex:page` component to test the user's profile. Using the `action` attribute is a good way to ensure an action is taken when the page loads.

If instead of limiting the standard page to a particular group of users, you want to limit the override to a particular group of users, such as all "Marketing Users" and "Solution Managers," you need to create a controller extension.

To override the Account tab with a custom Visualforce page only for users with the "Marketing User" or the "Solution Manager" profile:

1. Create a Visualforce page called `standardAcctPage`.

       a. Click **Setup ➤ Develop ➤ Pages**.

       b. Click **New**.

       c. In the label field, enter `Override the Account Page for Most Users`.

       d. In the name field, enter `standardAcctPage`.

       e. In the description, enter `This page will display for all users, except Marketing Users and Solution Managers, when they click the Account tab`.

       f. In the editor, enter the following markup:

```
<apex:page standardController="account"
           extensions="overrideCon"
           action="{!redirect}">
  <apex:detail/>
</apex:page>
```

This page overrides your current Account home page. It uses a controller extension to test the user profile. If the user is a "Marketing User" or "Solution Manager," they are redirected to a different page.

2. Using the procedure in step 1, create a second Visualforce page called `customAcctPage`:

```
<apex:page standardController="account">
  <h1>Override Account page for two profiles</h1>
  <apex:detail />
</apex:page>
```

This is the page that only the "Marketing Users" and "Solutions Managers" will see. They only get to this page through redirection.

3. Grant access to both pages for all profiles.

   a. Click **Security** for the each of the pages you just created.
   b. Select all the profiles that will be using this page in the Available Profiles list and click **Add** to add them to the Enabled Profiles list.
   c. Click **Save**.

4. Create a controller extension called `overrideCon`.

   a. Click **Setup ➤ Develop ➤ Apex Classes**.
   b. Click **New**.
   c. In the editor, add the following content:

```
public class overrideCon {
   String recordId;

public overrideCon(ApexPages.StandardController
       controller) {recordId = controller.getId();}

public PageReference redirect() {
   Profile p = [select name from Profile where id =
               :UserInfo.getProfileId()];
   if ('Marketing User'.equals(p.name)
       || 'Solution Manager'.equals(p.name))
       {
        PageReference customPage =
Page.customAccountPage;
        customPage.setRedirect(true);
        customPage.getParameters().put('id', recordId);
        return customPage;
       } else {
          return null; //otherwise stay on the same page

       }
     }
}
```

   d. Click **Save**.

5. Create an override that directs users to the `standardAcctPage` page when they click on the Accounts tab.

a. Click **Setup ➤ Customize ➤ Accounts ➤ Buttons and Links**.
b. In the Standard Buttons and Links list, click **Override** for the Accounts Tab.
c. Set the content type to **Visualforce Page**.
d. From the **Content Name** drop-down list, select **standardAcctPage**.
e. Click **Save**.

When a user clicks on the Account tab, if their profile is "Marketing User" or "Solution Manager" the controller extension will automatically redirect them to the `customAcctPage`.

See Also

- For more information about page level security and creating home page overrides, see the Salesforce online help.
- For more information about creating page overrides, see *Overriding a Standard Button* on page 27.
- For more information about creating controller extensions, see Custom Controllers and Controller Extensions in the Visualforce Developer Guide.

Creating Tabbed Accounts

Problem

In Salesforce, all the information for an account displays on a single page. If there's a lot of information, you might end up doing a lot of scrolling. You'd like a different way to display the information for accounts.

Solution

Using a Visualforce page, you can make each section for an account display in a tab, such as contacts, opportunities, and so on.

To create a tabbed view for account, first you have to create a Visualforce page. Then you have to override the standard account view to use the page.

To create the Visualforce page:

1. In Salesforce click **Setup ➤ Develop ➤ Pages**.
2. Click **New**.
3. In the `Label` text box, enter `Tabbed Account View`.

"Creating Tabbed Accounts" contributed by Matthew Friend, Senior Technical Sales Engineer, for salesforce.com

4. In the `Name` text box, enter `tabbedAccount`.

5. In the `Description` text box, enter `Displays account information in tabs`.

6. In the `Body` text box, delete the existing Visualforce markup and enter the following instead:

```
<apex:page standardController="Account" showHeader="true"
          tabStyle="account" >
  <apex:tabPanel switchType="client"
                 selectedTab="tabdetails"
                 id="AccountTabPanel">
    <apex:tab label="Details" name="AccDetails"
              id="tabdetails">
      <apex:detail relatedList="false" title="true"/>
    </apex:tab>
    <apex:tab label="Contacts" name="Contacts"
              id="tabContact">
      <apex:relatedList subject="{!account}"
                        list="contacts" />
    </apex:tab>
    <apex:tab label="Opportunities" name="Opportunities"
              id="tabOpp">
      <apex:relatedList subject="{!account}"
                        list="opportunities" />
    </apex:tab>
    <apex:tab label="Open Activities" name="OpenActivities"

              id="tabOpenAct">
      <apex:relatedList subject="{!account}"
                        list="OpenActivities" />
    </apex:tab>
    <apex:tab label="Notes and Attachments"
              name="NotesAndAttachments"
              id="tabNoteAtt">
      <apex:relatedList subject="{!account}"
                        list="NotesAndAttachments" />
    </apex:tab>
  </apex:tabPanel>
</apex:page>
```

7. Click **Save**.

To override the standard account view:

1. Click **Setup ➤ Customize ➤ Accounts ➤ Buttons and Links**.
2. In the Standard Buttons and Links related list, click **Override** next to View.
3. For **Content Type** select Visualforce Page.
4. For **Content Name** select tabbedAccount.
5. Click **Save**.

Discussion

To see your changes, select the Account tab, then select an account to view. Across the top of the page you should see a list of tabs: Details, Contacts, Opportunities, Open Activities and Notes and Attachments.

The tabbed display looks like the following:

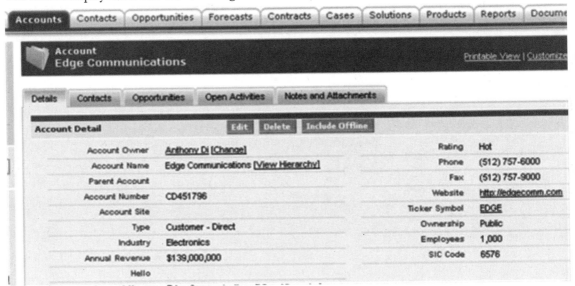

Figure 11: Account Detail Page Displayed as Tabbed View

See Also

- *Overriding a Standard Page* on page 46
- *Overriding a Standard Button* on page 27
- *Adding CSS to Visualforce Pages* on page 58

Adding CSS to Visualforce Pages

Problem

You want to set your pages apart by changing color, font, or other display options on the page.

Solution

Add CSS markup to your page, then have the appropriate component refer to it.

This example expands *Creating Tabbed Accounts* on page 56.

The following Visualforce page markup is from *Creating Tabbed Accounts* on page 56. It creates tabs to display account information.

```
<apex:page standardController="Account" showHeader="true"
          tabStyle="account" >
  <apex:tabPanel switchType="client" selectedTab="tabdetails"
                 id="AccountTabPanel">
    <apex:tab label="Details" name="AccDetails" id="tabdetails">
      <apex:detail relatedList="false" title="true"/>
    </apex:tab>
    <apex:tab label="Contacts" name="Contacts" id="tabContact">
      <apex:relatedList subject="{!account}" list="contacts" />
    </apex:tab>
    <apex:tab label="Opportunities" name="Opportunities"
              id="tabOpp">
      <apex:relatedList subject="{!account}"
                        list="opportunities" />
    </apex:tab>
    <apex:tab label="Open Activities" name="OpenActivities"
              id="tabOpenAct">
      <apex:relatedList subject="{!account}"
                        list="OpenActivities" />
    </apex:tab>
    <apex:tab label="Notes and Attachments"
              name="NotesAndAttachments" id="tabNoteAtt">
      <apex:relatedList subject="{!account}"
                        list="NotesAndAttachments" />
    </apex:tab>
  </apex:tabPanel>
</apex:page>
```

One thing you may notice about this page is that all of the tabs display in the same color. When you select a tab, it does not change color. Adding the following CSS markup to the Visualforce page causes the color of the active tab to change when the user selects it.

To add CSS markup to the page:

1. In Salesforce click **Setup ➤ Develop ➤ Pages**.
2. Click **Edit** next to the page `tabbedAccount`.
3. Add this code immediately following the `<apex:page>` tag. This Visualforce page markup defines the colors for the active tab and inactive tabs, as CSS:

```
<style>
  .activeTab {background-color: #236FBD; color:white;
      background-image:none}
  .inactiveTab {background-color: lightgrey; color:black;
              background-image:none}
</style>
```

4. Replace the existing `<apex:tabPanel>` markup with the following:

```
<apex:tabPanel switchType="client" selectedTab="tabdetails"
               id="AccountTabPanel" tabClass="activeTab"
               inactiveTabClass="inactiveTab">
```

This code sets values for the following:

- `tabClass` attribute: specifies the style class used to display a tab when it is active.
- `inactiveTabClass` attribute: specifies the style class used to display a tab when it is inactive.

5. Click **Save**.

Here is the complete updated Visualforce page markup:

```
<apex:page standardController="Account" showHeader="true"
     tabStyle="account" >
   <style>
      .activeTab {background-color: #236FBD; color:white;
         background-image:none}
      .inactiveTab { background-color: lightgrey; color:black;
         background-image:none}
   </style>
   <apex:tabPanel switchType="client" selectedTab="tabdetails"
                  id="AccountTabPanel" tabClass='activeTab'
                  inactiveTabClass='inactiveTab'>
      <apex:tab label="Details" name="AccDetails" id="tabdetails">
         <apex:detail relatedList="false" title="true"/>
      </apex:tab>
      <apex:tab label="Contacts" name="Contacts" id="tabContact">
         <apex:relatedList subject="{!account}" list="contacts" />
      </apex:tab>
      <apex:tab label="Opportunities" name="Opportunities"
               id="tabOpp">
         <apex:relatedList subject="{!account}"
                           list="opportunities" />
      </apex:tab>
      <apex:tab label="Open Activities" name="OpenActivities"
               id="tabOpenAct">
         <apex:relatedList subject="{!account}"
                           list="OpenActivities" />
      </apex:tab>
      <apex:tab label="Notes and Attachments"
               name="NotesAndAttachments" id="tabNoteAtt">
         <apex:relatedList subject="{!account}"
                           list="NotesAndAttachments" />
      </apex:tab>
   </apex:tabPanel>
</apex:page>
```

The tabbed display with colored tabs looks like the following:

Figure 12: Account Detail Page Displayed as Tabbed View

See Also

- *Creating Tabbed Accounts* on page 56
- *Overriding a Standard Page* on page 46

Editing Multiple Records Using a Visualforce List Controller

Problem

You need to edit a set of records at the same time. A standard detail page, though, only allows you to edit one record at a time.

Solution

Create a Visualforce page using a *standard list controller*. The standard list controller enables you to create Visualforce pages that can display or act on a set of records.

To create a Visualforce page using a standard list controller to edit a list of opportunities:

1. In Salesforce click **Setup ➤ Develop ➤ Pages**.
2. Click **New**.
3. In the `Label` text box, enter `Multiple opportunity edit`.

4. In the `Name` text box, enter `multOppEdit`.

5. In the `Description` text box, enter `Edit multiple opportunity records in a set`.

6. In the `Body` text box, delete the existing Visualforce markup and enter the following instead:

```
<apex:page standardController="Opportunity"
           recordSetVar="opportunities"
           tabStyle="Opportunity" sidebar="false">
  <apex:form >
    <apex:pageBlock >
      <apex:pageMessages />
      <apex:pageBlockButtons >
        <apex:commandButton value="Save"
                            action="{!save}"/>
      </apex:pageBlockButtons>
      <apex:pageBlockTable value="{!opportunities}"
                           var="opp">
        <apex:column value="{!opp.name}"/>
        <apex:column headerValue="Stage">
          <apex:inputField value="{!opp.stageName}"/>
        </apex:column>
        <apex:column headerValue="Close Date">
          <apex:inputField value="{!opp.closeDate}"/>
        </apex:column>
      </apex:pageBlockTable>
    </apex:pageBlock>
  </apex:form>
</apex:page>
```

7. Click **Save**.

Call the page by using the following URL:

```
https://salesforce_instance/apex/multOppEdit
```

Substitute `salesforce_instance` for the instance of Salesforce that you use, such as `na3.salesforce.com`. For example, `https://na3.salesforce.com/apex/multOppEdit`.

Your page should resemble the following:

Figure 13: Editing Multiple Opportunities on a Single Page

Discussion

Using a standard list controller is very similar to using a standard controller. First you set the `standardController` attribute on the `<apex:page>` component. This specifies the type of records that you want to access. Then set the `recordSetVar` attribute on the same component. This indicates that you're using a standard set controller.

```
<apex:page standardController="Opportunity"
           recordSetVar="opportunities"
           tabStyle="Opportunity"
           sidebar="false">
```

The `recordSetVar` attribute not only indicates that the page uses a list controller, it indicates the variable name of the record collection. This variable is then used to access data in the record collection.

```
<apex:pageBlockTable value="{!opportunities}" var="opp">
```

In this example, two fields, `Stage` and `Close Date` are displayed for edit in the table. They each form a column in the table:

```
<apex:pageBlockTable value="{!opportunities}" var="opp">
    <apex:column value="{!opp.name}"/>
    <apex:column headerValue="Stage">
        <apex:inputField value="{!opp.stageName}"/>
    </apex:column>
    <apex:column headerValue="Close Date">
        <apex:inputField value="{!opp.closeDate}"/>
    </apex:column>
</apex:pageBlockTable>
```

See Also

- *Building a Table of Data in a Visualforce Page* on page 31

- *Creating a Wizard with Visualforce Pages* on page 35

Registering a Custom Domain for Your Force Platform Site

Problem

You want to use a branded top-level domain name for your public Force Platform site—without exposing the `force.com` domain in the URL.

Solution

With Force Platform Sites, you can register a branded top-level domain name for your public site. When users visit your site, they see only the URL that you registered, and not the Force Platform domain. For example, if you registered `http://www.mycompany.com` with a domain name registrar, all site traffic is redirected from that domain to your Force Platform domain. Users see only `http://www.mycompany.com` in the browser's address bar.

To enable Force Platform Sites, contact your salesforce.com representative.

 Note: Branded, top-level domains are not supported for Developer Edition and Developer Sandboxes. SSL is supported, but if org-wide security settings are enabled, and the site-level override is not enabled, branded domains revert to `prefix.secure.force.com` on customer login.

To use a branded top-level domain for your public site:

1. Register your Force Platform domain.

   a. Click **Setup ➤ Develop ➤ Sites**.

   b. Enter a unique name for your Force Platform domain. The name is case-sensitive. Only alphanumeric characters are allowed. Salesforce.com recommends using your company's name or a variation, such as "mycompany."

       Caution: You cannot modify your Force Platform domain name after you have registered it.

   c. Click **Check Availability** to confirm that the domain name you entered is unique. If it is not unique, you are prompted to change it.

   d. Read and accept the Force Platform Sites Terms and Use by selecting the checkbox.

e. Click **Register My Force.com Domain**. After you accept the Terms and Use and register your Force Platform domain, the change is tracked in your organization's setup audit trail.

This domain is used for all of your sites, even if you use a branded domain.

2. Register your branded, top-level domain name with a domain name registrar, such as GoDaddy.com. For this example, let's say you registered www.acme.com. Once you register the domain, you can also register subdomain names, such as support.acme.com, partners.acme.com, developers.acme.com.

3. Create CNAME records with your registrar to point your top-level domain and your subdomains to your Force Platform domain. In this example, create CNAME records to point from:

   - acme.com to acme.force.com
   - support.acme.com to acme.force.com
   - partners.acme.com to acme.force.com
   - acmeideas.com to acme.force.com

 Note: If you choose to create a branded top-level domain or subdomain through a domain name registrar, the CNAME record that you provide to that registrar must be your Force Platform domain name and not the site URL. For example, if you entered "mycompany" when registering your Force Platform domain, the CNAME must be mycompany.force.com, not the full value of the site URL.

4. Create your site and associate your branded domain or subdomain:

   a. Click **Setup ➤ Develop ➤ Sites**.
   b. Click **New**.
   c. On the Site Edit page, define the site and enter your branded domain or subdomain in the Custom Web Address field. This field determines which branded domain or subdomain is associated with each site.
   d. Click **Save**.

Discussion

By registering a top-level domain through a domain name registrar and associating it with your site, you can create a completely branded experience for your users. With Force Platform sites and Visualforce pages, you can customize the look and feel, the branding, and public security settings for each of your sites.

See Also

Customizing the Look and Feel of Your Force Platform Site on page 68

Using Force Platform Site-Specific Merge Fields

Problem

You want to create one Visualforce "About Us" page to be used for several public sites, so you can't hard-code site-specific values like site URL, site email address, and site template. You want the "About Us" page to conditionally display links for registration and login, and connect the "Contact Us" link to each respective site's designated email address.

Solution

Take advantage of the available merge fields when creating the Visualforce pages used for your public sites. By using merge fields, the same Visualforce page can be used for multiple sites.

 Note: To enable Force Platform Sites, contact your salesforce.com representative. The Force Platform Sites feature is available as Developer Preview in Developer Edition. See Force Platform Sites Considerations for more information.

The following merge fields are available:

Expression	Description
{!$Site.Name}	Returns the API name of the current site
{!$Site.Domain}	Returns the Force Platform domain name for your organization
{!$Site.CustomWebAddress}	Returns the value of the `Custom Web Address` field for the current site
{!$Site.OriginalUrl}	Returns the current domain name displayed in the browser's address bar
{!$Site.CurrentSiteUrl}	Returns the value of the site URL for the current request
{!$Site.LoginEnabled}	Returns TRUE if the current site is associated with an active login-enabled Customer Portal; otherwise returns FALSE
{!$Site.RegistrationEnabled}	Returns TRUE if the current site is associated with an active self-regitration-enabled Customer Portal; otherwise returns FALSE
{!$Site.IsPasswordExpired}	Returns TRUE if the currently logged-in user's password is expired
{!$Site.AdminEmailAddress}	Returns the value of the `Site Contact` field for the current site
{!$Site.Prefix}	Returns the path of the `Default Web Address` for the current site

Expression	Description
{!$Site.Template}	Returns the value of the `Site Template` field for the current site
{!$Site.ErrorMessage}	Returns error IDs or handled error messages thrown by the application
{!$Site.ErrorDescription}	Returns the Apex exception error description

In the following example, Visualforce page uses the `{!$Site.Template}`, `{!$Site.AdminEmailAddress}`, `{!$Site.LoginEnabled}`, and `{!$Site.RegistrationEnabled}` merge fields (shown in bold).

```
<apex:page showHeader="false" title="About Us">
<!-- This page uses the template associated with the site.
     No need to hardcode the template name. -->
  <apex:composition template="{!$Site.Template}">
    <apex:define name="body">
      <apex:form>
        <apex:outputPanel layout="block">
          <apex:panelGrid columns="1">
            <apex:outputText value="About Us text goes here"/>
            <apex:outputText value="..."/>
            <apex:outputText value="..."/>

<!-- The contact email address is dynamically populated with the
     current site's contact email address. -->
            <apex:panelGroup id="Contact">
              <apex:outputText value="Contact us by email at:"/>
              <apex:outputLink value=
                "mailto:{!$Site.AdminEmailAddress}">
                company@acme.com</apex:outputLink>
            </apex:panelGroup>

<!-- The Login Panel group is rendered if the current site
     is login-enabled. -->
            <apex:panelGroup id="Login" rendered=
                "{!$Site.LoginEnabled}">
              <apex:outputText value="Existing User? "/>
              <apex:outputLink value="{!$Page.SiteLogin}"> Login to
                Acess your Account</apex:outputLink>
            </apex:panelGroup> <apex:outputText value="..."/>
            <apex:outputText value="..."/>
            <apex:outputText value="..."/>

<!-- The Register Panel group is rendered if the Customer Portal
     associated with the current site is registration-enabled. -->
            <apex:panelGroup id="Register" rendered=
                "{!$Site.RegistrationEnabled}">
              <apex:outputText value="New User?"/>
              <apex:outputLink value="{!$Page.SiteRegister}">
```

```
                    Register to get an Account</apex:outputLink>
          </apex:panelGroup>
        </apex:panelGrid>
      </apex:outputPanel>
    </apex:form>
  </apex:define>
</apex:composition>
</apex:page>
```

Discussion

Force Platform Sites takes advantage of the power and flexibility of Visualforce. With the out-of-box merge fields and additional expressions available, you can more easily create feature-rich site pages across multiple sites.

Customizing the Look and Feel of Your Force Platform Site

Problem

Your Force Platform site is up and running, but the pages don't have your company's look and feel. The public sees the standard Salesforce beige and blue. You want to use your company's logo and stylesheet.

Solution

The default sample pages are all branded with the Force Platform look and feel, but you can upload your own logo and stylesheet as static resources and reference them from the site template. The site template controls the layout and branding for your entire site.

 Note: To enable Force Platform Sites, contact your salesforce.com representative. The Force Platform Sites feature is available as Developer Preview in Developer Edition. See Force Platform Sites Considerations for more information.

To brand your site with your logo, colors, and layouts:

1. First, assign the template for your site:

    a. Click **Setup ➤ Develop ➤ Sites**.
    b. Click **Edit**.
    c. Use the lookup field to find and select SiteTemplate for the `Site Template` field.
    d. Click **Save**.

2. Next, upload your stylesheet and company logo as static resources:

    a. Click **Setup ➤ Develop ➤ Static Resources**.

    b. For each static resource:

        a. Click **New**.

        b. Enter the name and description, and browse to the file to upload. In this example, the stylesheet is named SiteCSS and the logo is named Logo.

        c. Set the **Cache Control** setting to Public. Static resources with private cache control do not show up in sites.

        d. Click **Save**.

3. Now modify the SiteHeader to display your company's logo (Logo) and use your company's stylesheet:

    a. Click **Setup ➤ Develop ➤ Components**.

    b. Click **Edit** next to the SiteHeader component.

    c. Replace the following line:

```
<apex:image url="{!$Site.Prefix}
   {!$Label.site.img_path}/force_logo.gif"
   style="align: left;" alt="Salesforce"
   width="233" height="55" title="Salesforce"/>
```

    with this new line:

```
<apex:image id="logo" value="{!$Resource.Logo}"/>
```

    d. Add the following line after `<apex:stylesheet value="{!$Resource.SiteCSS}"/>`:

```
<apex:stylesheet value="{!$Resource.SiteCSS}"/>
```

    e. Click **Save**.

4. Browse to your site's URL to see your company logo and style.

Discussion

Enable and customize the Visualforce site template and its components to control the design of your sites. Because the site template can reference other components and static resources, you can change the look and feel of your site with just a few modifications.

See Also

Registering a Custom Domain for Your Force Platform Site on page 64

Integrating Your Force Platform Site with Google Analytics

Problem

You want to be able to track page views and see usage and visitor analysis for your public Force Platform site so that you can improve its usability and targeted content.

Solution

Force Platform Sites allows you to leverage other Internet services via mash-ups or direct integration. Google Analytics offers a free analytics service with dozens of reports to help you track, among other things, your site's visitors and the performance of your marketing campaigns.

 Note: To enable Force Platform Sites, contact your salesforce.com representative. The Force Platform Sites feature is available as Developer Preview in Developer Edition. See Force Platform Sites Considerations for more information.

To integrate with Google Analytics:

1. Go to `http://www.google.com/analytics/sign_up.html` and follow the instructions to register for a Google Analytics account.

    Note: For the `Website's URL` field, enter the full URL for your site. For example, if you registered `acme.force.com` as your Force Platform domain name, and created a partner site on that domain, your full URL might be `http://acme.force.com/partners`.

2. Copy the JavaScript Tracking Code you receive from Google Analytics.
3. Keeping the Google Analytics window open, open another browser window and do the following:

   a. Click **Setup ➤ Develop ➤ Sites**.
   b. Click the site label link for your site. This takes you to the Site Details page.
   c. On the Site Pages related list, click the **Site Template** link.
   d. Click **Edit**.
   e. Paste the JavaScript Tracking Code, as directed, into the Visualforce page for your site template.

4. Click **Continue** in the Google analytics window.
5. Click the **Check Status** link to start the tracking process.

    Note: It may take up to 24 hours to initially collect data for your site. Check your Google Analytics account the next day and click the **View Report** link. You will see the analytics dashboard for your site, from which you can drill down to several detailed reports.

Discussion

The more you understand the usage and traffic patterns for your public site, the more you can fine-tune the site to improve both the quality of the content and the user experience. Take advantage of Force Platform Sites Visualforce technology, which allows you to integrate with powerful Internet applications and services, such as Google Analytics.

Adding a Feed to Your Force Platform Site

Problem

Your Force Platform site is up and running, and you'd like to add a feed that shows your users up to the last 20 accounts added to your Salesforce organization.

Solution

Define a feed and add it to a Visualforce page in your site. Users can then click an icon to subscribe to the feed.

 Note: To enable Force Platform Sites, contact your salesforce.com representative. The Force Platform Sites feature is available as Developer Preview in Developer Edition. See Force Platform Sites Considerations for more information.

Before you start, make sure that sites are enabled and that you have set up a site as described in the Salesforce online help, including setting the public access settings and enabling feeds for your site.

To create a feed and add it to a Visualforce page in your site:

1. Click **Setup ➤ Develop ➤ Sites** to display the list of sites created for your organization.
2. Click the name of the site where you want to add a feed. Click the `Site Label` link, not the `Site URL` link.
3. In the Syndication Feeds detail area, click **New** and enter the following values:
   - `Name: LatestAccounts`
   - `Description: Up to the last 20 accounts added to our organization.`
   - `Query: SELECT Name from Account`
   - `Mapping ft: "test", fa:"Mysti", et:"Account", ec:Name`
   - `Max Cache Age Seconds: 600`
4. Click **Save**, then click **Back to Site Detail** to return to the sites detail page.

5. Click **Preview** next to **LatestAccounts** to test the feed to ensure it delivers the information you expect. The preview page displays what the feed will display to users, and provides a link to the site where the feed will be displayed.

6. After the feed is created and tested, add a link to the feed in your Visualforce page by adding the following markup:

```
<A HREF="/xml/services/LatestAccounts">Latest Accounts</A>
```

The path assumes your page is located in the base directory of the site. You may have to adjust the path if it is not.

7. Now users who visit the page can click the link **Latest Accounts** and subscribe to the feed.

Discussion

The feed created here is very simple. You can write much more complex SOQL queries for the feed to tailor the information for your users. For example, the following query would report up the last five accounts created later than yesterday:

```
SELECT Name from Account where CreatedDate < Yesterday LIMIT 5
```

The SOQL query defines what information is collected, but the mapping determines what information is displayed in the feed itself, using elements of the ATOM protocol. For an explanation of the elements, see "Defining Syndication Feeds" in the Salesforce online help. This topic also explains some of the limitations placed on SOQL for feeds queries. These limits are in place to ensure good performance.

It's important that you set public access settings for objects properly. Because the feed issues queries as the site guest user, you must assign the correct public access settings to the profile for that guest user, or queries may return either not enough information or information about objects that you don't wish to share with the guest user. Similarly, you must set sharing rules appropriately. Instructions for setting the public access settings and sharing rules are provided in the Salesforce online help.

Feeds support the use of bind variables in both the query definition and mapping. At run time, the value of the bind variable is passed in the URL. More information about bind variables is provided in the Salesforce online help.

See Also

- *Visualforce Developer's Guide*
- *Customizing the Look and Feel of Your Force Platform Site* on page 68
- *Registering a Custom Domain for Your Force Platform Site* on page 64
- *Using Force Platform Site-Specific Merge Fields* on page 66
- *Integrating Your Force Platform Site* on page 70

Using Dynamic Apex

Problem

You want to write Apex scripts that use standard sObjects, then you want to package your code so other organizations can download it from Force Platform AppExchange. In addition, you want your code to work regardless of the standard objects available on the organization that downloads your package.

Solution

Dynamic Apex enables developers to create more flexible applications by providing them with the ability to do the following:

- Access information about sObjects in general and the fields of an sObject.

  Describe information for an sObject includes whether that type of sObject supports operations like create or undelete, the sObject's name and label, the sObject's fields and child objects, and so on. The describe information for a field includes whether the field has a default value, whether it is a calculated field, the type of the field, and so on.

   Note: Describe information provides information only about *objects* in an organization, not individual records.

- Write SOQL queries, SOSL queries, and DML that are *dynamic*; that is, you don't have to know all the names, objects, or parameters when you first write the code.

  Dynamic SOQL and SOSL queries provide the ability to execute SOQL or SOSL as a string at runtime, while *dynamic DML* provides the ability to create a record dynamically and then insert it into the database using DML. Using dynamic SOQL, SOSL, and DML, an application can be tailored precisely to the organization, as well as the user's permissions. This can be useful for applications that are installed from Force Platform AppExchange.

   Note: Because this recipe uses the development mode of Visualforce, be sure you have enabled it. To enable Visualforce development mode, click **Setup ➤ My personal Information ➤ Personal Information**, and click **Edit.** Select the Development Mode checkbox, and then click **Save**.

This recipe demonstrates using describe information for an organization. It uses a Visualforce page for displaying the information.

1. Create the Apex class that the Visualforce page uses to populate a dropdown with a list of all the sObjects available in the organization. Click **Setup ➤ Develop ➤ Apex Classes**, then click **New**.

2. Copy and paste the following into the **Body** text field for the class:

```
public class Describer {

    private Map <String, Schema.SObjectType> schemaMap =
            Schema.getGlobalDescribe();
    public List <Pair> fields {get; set;}
    public List <SelectOption> objectNames
            {public get; private set;}
    public String selectedObject {get; set;}

// Intialize objectNames and fields
    public Describer() {
        objectNames = initObjNames();
        fields = new List<Pair>();

    }
// Populate SelectOption list  -
// find all sObjects available in the organization
    private List<SelectOption> initObjNames() {
        List<SelectOption> objNames =
            new List<SelectOption>();
        List<String> entities =
            new List<String>(schemaMap.keySet());
        entities.sort();
        for(String name : entities)
            objNames.add(new SelectOption(name,name));
        return objNames;
    }

    // Find the fields for the selected object
    public void showFields() {
        fields.clear();
        Map <String, Schema.SObjectField> fieldMap =

schemaMap.get(selectedObject).getDescribe().fields.getMap();

        for(Schema.SObjectField sfield : fieldMap.Values()){
            schema.describefieldresult dfield =
                sfield.getDescribe();
            Pair field = new Pair();
            field.key = dfield.getname();
            fields.add(field);
        }
    }


    public class Pair {
        public String key {get; set;}
        public String val {get; set;}
    }
}
```

3. To create the Visualforce page, enter the following URL in your browser's address bar:

4. `http://MySalesforceInstance/apex/DescribePage`

Where *MySalesforceInstance* is the URL for your Salesforce organization. For example, if your organization uses `na3.salesforce.com`, enter `http://na3.salesforce.com/apex/DescribePage`.

5. Click **Create page DescribePage** to create the page.

6. At the bottom of the page, click **Page Editor**.

7. Select all the text automatically generated for the page, and replace it with the following:

```
<apex:page Controller="Describer">

<apex:form id="Describe">

    <apex:pageBlock id="block2" >

        <apex:pageblockbuttons location="top" >

            <apex:commandButton
             value="Get Describe Object Fields"
             action="{!showFields}"/>

        </apex:pageblockbuttons>

        <apex:pageblocksection >

            <apex:selectList value="{!selectedObject}" size="1">

                <apex:selectOptions value="{!objectNames}"/>

            </apex:selectList>

        </apex:pageblocksection>

        <apex:pageblocksection
             id="fieldList" rendered=
             "{!not(isnull(selectedObject))}">

            <apex:panelBar items="{!fields}" var="fls">

                <apex:panelBarItem label="{!fls.key}"/>

            </apex:panelBar>

        </apex:pageblocksection>

    </apex:pageBlock>

</apex:form>

</apex:page>
```

Discussion

The controller first populates the dropdown with the list of sObjects. When a user clicks the **Get Describe Object Fields** button on the Visualforce page, the controller populates the `<apex:panelbar>` on the Visualforce page with the names of all the fields associated with that sObject.

See Also

Using Properties in Apex on page 143

Chapter 2

Managing Workflow and Approvals

Your organization operates more efficiently with standardized internal procedures and automated business processes. Use workflow rules and approval processes to automate them. Not only do you save time, but you enforce consistency across your business practices.

Build workflow rules to trigger actions, such as email alerts, tasks, field updates, and outbound messages based on time triggers, criteria, or formulas. Use approval processes to automate all of your organization's approvals, from simple to complex.

Managing Large Opportunities Using Time-Based Workflow

Problem

You want to create a workflow rule to send an email alert when an opportunity with an amount greater than $1,000,000 is created, as well as 30 days before, 15 days before, and 5 days after the opportunity close date. After the close date, you want to assign a task to the opportunity owner to update the deal.

Solution

Create a workflow rule with multiple time triggers to send email alerts based on the criteria you specify. In this example, the rule criteria are that the opportunity must have a value greater than $1,000,000 and must not be closed. First we'll create the workflow rule, then define the immediate and time-dependent workflow actions.

1. Create a new workflow rule.

   a. Click **Setup ➤ Create ➤ Workflow & Approvals ➤ Workflow Rules**.
   b. Click **New Rule**.
   c. Select Opportunity.
   d. Enter the name and description, then select `When a record is created, or when a record is edited and did not previously meet the rule criteria`.
   e. Under Rule Criteria, select `Run this rule if the following` and choose **criteria are met**.
   f. Define the rule to fire when `Opportunity: Amount greater than 1,000,000` and `Opportunity: Closed equals FALSE`.
   g. Click **Save & Next**.

2. Add an immediate workflow action to send an email alert when an opportunity meets the above criteria.

   a. Click **Add Workflow Action** and select **New Email**.
   b. Define the workflow alert by providing the description, selecting the email template, and adding the recipients. In this example, the recipient might be the VP of Sales role. To find the right VP, select **Role** in the `Search` menu and click **Find**.
   c. Click **Save**.

3. Create time triggers for large opportunities nearing their close dates, as well as one for missed opportunities.

   a. Click **Add Time Trigger** in the Time-Dependent Workflow Actions section of the Edit Workflow Rule page.

    b. Set a time trigger for 30 days before `Opportunity: Close Date` and click **Save**.

    c. Set a time trigger for 15 days before `Opportunity: Close Date` and click **Save**.

    d. Set a time trigger for 5 days after `Opportunity: Close Date` and click **Save**.

4. Add actions to each time trigger.

    a. Under Time-Dependent Workflow Actions, click **Add Workflow Action** and select **New Email** for each of the three time triggers. Define the alerts by providing descriptions, selecting appropriate email templates, and adding recipients.

- For the 30 days before time trigger, the recipient might be the VP of Sales role.
- For the 15 days before time trigger, the recipient might be the record owner.
- For the 5 days after time trigger, the recipient might be the Executive Sponsor for the Sales team.

    b. Click **Save** for each workflow action.

    c. Click **Add Workflow Action** and select **New Task** for the 5 days after time trigger.

        a. Assign the task of updating the deal to the opportunity owner.

        b. Set the due date to `Rule Trigger Date` plus 1 day.

        c. Select the `Notify Assignee` option.

        d. Set `Status` and `Priority`, and add any comments.

    d. Click **Save**.

5. Return to the Workflow Rule detail page and click **Activate** to activate the rule.

Discussion

You want to be able to track large opportunities closely. Proactively manage your opportunities using workflow rules with multiple time triggers. As the close date approaches for a large deal, automatic workflow actions, like email alerts, increase the visibility to executives who can then take the necessary actions to close the deal. Time-dependent actions can also be used to remind management to review lost deals after the close date to determine the causes of failure, and to learn what to do next time to ensure success.

See Also

Managing Lost Opportunities Using Workflow on page 80

Managing Lost Opportunities Using Workflow

Problem

You want to create a workflow rule to send an email alert when an opportunity with an amount greater than $1,000,000 is closed and lost.

Solution

Create a workflow rule to send email alerts based on the formula you specify. In this example, the rule criteria are that the opportunity must have a value greater than $1,000,000 and `Stage` changes from Proposal/Price Quote to Closed Lost. First we'll create the workflow rule, then define the immediate workflow actions.

1. Create a new workflow rule.

    a. Click **Setup** ➤ **Create** ➤ **Workflow & Approvals** ➤ **Workflow Rules**.

    b. Click **New Rule**.

    c. Select Opportunity.

    d. Enter the name and description, then select `Every time a record is created or edited`.

    e. Under Rule Criteria, select `Run this rule if the following` and choose **formula evaluates to true**.

    f. Add the following formula to the formula field:

    ```
    AND(
    ISPICKVAL(StageName,"Closed Lost"),
    ISPICKVAL(PRIORVALUE(StageName),"Proposal/Price Quote"),
    Amount > 1000000
    )
    ```

    g. Click **Check Syntax** to ensure there were no mistakes, then click **Save & Next**.

2. Add an immediate workflow action to send an email alert when an opportunity meets the above criteria.

    a. Click **Add Workflow Action** and select **New Email**.

    b. Define the workflow alert by providing the description, selecting the email template, and adding the recipients. In this example, the recipient might be the VP of Sales role. To find the right VP, select **Role** in the `Search` menu and click **Find**.

    c. Click **Save**.

3. Return to the Workflow Rule detail page and click **Activate** to activate the rule.

Discussion

If you lose a large opportunity, you want to know why. Using a workflow rule with a formula for the rule criteria, you can track specific field value changes using sophisticated formula functions, such as ISPICKVAL and PRIORVALUE. When a large opportunity is lost, automatic workflow actions, like email alerts, notify key people in your organization so that they can investigate what went wrong, and learn what to do next time to ensure success.

See Also

Managing Large Opportunities Using Time-Based Workflow on page 78

Using Workflow to Notify Case Contact for Priority Cases

Problem

You want to create a workflow rule to send an email alert to the case contact when you receive a high priority case for accounts that have a Platinum service-level agreement (SLA).

Solution

Create a workflow rule to send email alerts based on the criteria you specify. In this example, the rule criteria are that the case priority is high and the account SLA is platinum. First we'll create the workflow rule, then define the immediate workflow actions.

1. Create a new workflow rule.

   a. Click **Setup ➤ Create ➤ Workflow & Approvals ➤ Workflow Rules**.
   b. Click **New Rule**.
   c. Select Case.
   d. Enter the name and description, then select `Only when a record is created`.
   e. Under Rule Criteria, select `Run this rule if the following` and choose **criteria are met**.
   f. Define the rule to fire when `Case: Priority equals HIGH` and `Account: SLA equals PLATINUM`.

2. Add an immediate workflow action to send an email alert to the case contact when a case meets the above criteria.

   a. Click **Add Workflow Action** and select **New Email**.
   b. Define the workflow alert by providing the description, selecting the email template, and adding the recipients. In this example, the recipient is the case contact.

    c. Click **Save**.

3. Return to the Workflow Rule detail page and click **Activate** to activate the rule.

Discussion

When a high priority account files a case, you want to know right away. Use a workflow rule with an automatic email alert to notify the right people so that they can take care of your highest priority customers. Workflow email alerts can be used to notify anyone inside or outside of your organization—they don't have to be Salesforce users.

Using Workflow to Add Account Names to Opportunity Names

Problem

You want to create a workflow rule to enforce a consistent naming standard for opportunities. The opportunity name for any opportunity that does not include the associated account name changes to *Account Name: Opportunity Name*.

Solution

Create a workflow rule to evaluate all opportunity names based on the formula you specify. If the name does not include the associated account name, it will be added. First we'll create the workflow rule, then define the immediate actions.

1. Create a new workflow rule.

    a. Click **Setup ➤ Create ➤ Workflow & Approvals ➤ Workflow Rules**.
    b. Click **New Rule**.
    c. Select the Opportunity object.
    d. Enter the name and description, then select `When a record is created, or when a record is edited and did not previously meet the rule criteria`.
    e. Under Rule Criteria, select `Run this rule if the following` and choose **formula evaluates to true**.
    f. Add the following formula to the formula field:

```
NOT(CONTAINS(Name, Account.Name))
```

    g. Click **Check Syntax** to ensure there were no mistakes, then click **Save & Next**.

2. Add an immediate workflow action to update the `Opportunity Name` field when an opportunity meets the above criteria.

      a. Click **Add Workflow Action** and select **New Field Update**.

      b. Define the workflow field update by providing the name and description and selecting the `Field to Update`. In this example, select `Opportunity Name`.

      c. Under Text Options, select `Use a formula to set the new value` and specify the following formula:

```
Account.Name & ": " & Name
```

      d. Click **Save**.

3. Return to the Workflow Rule detail page and click **Activate** to activate the rule.

Discussion

You want to be able to enforce consistency across your business practices. Using a workflow rule with a formula for the rule criteria, you can set standard naming conventions for opportunities or other objects. Formulas can span multiple objects and, when used with field updates within a workflow rule, can be a powerful tool for enforcing company standards.

Requiring Parallel Approvals for Large Campaigns

Problem

You want to create an approval process to route all approval requests to the Director of Marketing, route all approved requests $25,000 or greater to two designated Vice Presidents (VPs) for unanimous approval, and finally, send all requests, regardless of size, to the Director of Finance for final approval. Requests under $25,000 that are approved by the Director of Marketing should skip the two VPs and go directly to the Director of Finance.

Solution

Create a three-step approval process based on the criteria you specify. In this example, all requests are sent to the Director of Marketing, approved requests under $25,000 skip the VPs approval step and go directly to the Director of Finance; and approved requests $25,000 or greater are sent to the VPs for parallel approval. Both must approve the request.

First we'll create the approval process, then define the approval steps and final approval/rejection actions.

1. Create a new approval process.

      a. Click **Setup ➤ Create ➤ Workflow & Approvals ➤ Approval Processes**.

    b. From the `Manage Approval Processes For` drop-down list, select the object type for this approval process. For this example, select **Campaign**.

    c. Click **Create New Approval Process** and select **Use Standard Setup Wizard**.

    d. Enter the `Process Name` and `Description` for your new approval process, then click **Next**.

    e. From the `Use this approval process if the following` drop-down list, select **criteria are met**.

    f. Define the rule to fire when `Status not equal to Completed, Aborted` and `Budgeted Cost not equal to 0`.

    g. Click **Next**.

    h. Leave the default selections for Step 3, then click **Next**.

    i. For the `Approval Assignment Email Template`, find and select the appropriate template, then click **Next**.

    j. Leave the default selections for Step 5, but select the `Display approval history information...` option, then click **Next**.

    k. By default, only the record owner—Campaign Owner, in this example—is listed under `Allowed Submitters`. Add any other users, groups, or roles that are allowed to submit requests for approval. Select the `Allow submitters to recall approval requests` option to enable the recall feature for the submitter.

        Note: Admin users can recall approval requests, regardless of this setting. This option only enables recall for the user submitting the approval request.

    l. Click **Save**.

    m. Select `Yes, I'd like to create an approval step now`, then click **Go**.

2. Create the first approval step.

    a. If you're not already on the New Approval Step page, click **New Approval Step** in the Approval Steps section of the Approval Process detail page.

    b. Enter the name and description. Let's call this step "Marketing Approval." Click **Next**.

    c. For the step criteria, select `All records should enter this step`. Click `Next`.

    d. Select `Automatically assign to approver(s)`, choose **User**, and find and select the user you want. In this example, the first approver is a Director of Marketing. Since there is only one approver for this step, leave the default for the `When multiple approvers are selected:` setting. You can also allow the approver's delegate to approve the request.

    e. Click **Save**.

    f. Select the `No, I'll do this later...` option and click **Go**.

3. Create the second approval step.

    a. Click **New Approval Step** in the Approval Steps section of the Approval Process detail page.

    b. Enter the name and description. Let's call this step "Large Budget Approval." Click **Next**.

    c. For the step criteria, select `Enter this step if the following` and choose **criteria are met**.

    d. Set the criteria as `Budgeted Cost greater or equal 25000`.

    e. Select `Automatically assign to approver(s)`, choose **User**, and find and select the user you want. In this example, the first approver is the first VP.

    f. Click **Add Row**

    g. Choose **User**, and find and select the user you want. In this example, the first approver is the second VP.

    h. Select the `Require UNANIMOUS approval from all selected approvers` option.

    i. Under Reject Behavior, select the `Perform ONLY the rejection actions for this step and send the approval request back to the most recent approver. (Go Back 1 Step)` option. If either of the VPs rejects the request, it gets sent back to the Marketing Approval step.

    j. Click **Save**.

    k. Select the `No, I'll do this later...` option and click **Go**.

4. Create the third approval step.

    a. Click **New Approval Step** in the Approval Steps section of the Approval Process detail page.

    b. Enter the name and description. Let's call this step "Finance Approval." Click **Next**.

    c. For the step criteria, select `All records should enter this step`.

    d. Select `Automatically assign to approver(s)`, choose **User**, and find and select the user you want. In this example, the approver is the Director of Finance.

    e. Under Reject Behavior, select the `Perform all rejection actions for this step AND all final rejection actions. (Final Rejection)` option.

    f. Click **Save**.

    g. Select the `No, I'll do this later...` option and click **Go**.

5. Go back and edit Step 2.

    a. Click **Edit** next to Step 2.

    b. Click **Next** to go to the Specify Step Criteria page of the wizard.

    c. For the `else` option, select **go to next step**. Approved requests less than $25,000 are sent directly to the Finance Approval step, skipping the Large Budget Approval step.

    d. Click **Save**.

 Note: You have to create Step 3 before you can set the `else` option. This option isn't enabled for the last step of an approval process.

6. Add final approval actions for the approval process.

    a. Click **Add New**, then select **Email** in the Final Approval Actions section of the Approval Process detail page.

    b. Add a description.

    c. For the `Email Template`, find and select a template to use for the approval message.

    d. For the `Search` field, select **Owner** .

    e. Select Campaign Owner and click **Add**. On approval, the campaign owner receives email notification.

    f. Click **Save**.

7. Add final rejection actions for the approval process.

    a. Click **Add New**, then select **Email** in the Final Rejection Actions section of the Approval Process detail page.

    b. Add a description.

    c. For the `Email Template`, find and select a template to use for the rejection message.

    d. For the `Search` field, select **Owner**.

    e. Select Campaign Owner and click **Add**. On rejection, the campaign owner receives email notification.

    f. Click **Save**.

8. Return to the Approval Process detail page and click **Activate** to activate the approval process.

Discussion

Automating your company's campaign budget approval process enforces your best business practices. Use a single approval process to manage multiple conditions and approval requirements. Requiring multiple, unanimous approvals enforces stricter standards for large budget approvals, while the option to skip certain approval steps streamlines the process. Using parallel approvals and the "else" option, you can create sophisticated processes to match your complex business needs.

Using a Matrix-Based Dynamic Approval Process

Problem

You want to be able to create a single criteria-based approval process to route opportunity discount approval requests to designated approvers, based on the requester's region and the opportunity's account type.

Solution

The Dynamic Approval Routing application, available for free on Force Platform AppExchange, provides a sample solution that automates an opportunity discount approval process based on region and account type, and routes opportunities through three required levels of approval. The Dynamic Approval Routing application comes packaged with the necessary custom object, validation rule, Apex class, and Apex triggers and tests. The package also comes with documentation on how to customize the application to fit your needs.

To take advantage of dynamic approvals, do the following:

1. Go to Force Platform AppExchange and install the Dynamic Approval Routing application.

    Note: For Developer Edition organizations, or any organizations with fewer than three users, select the **Ignore Apex test failures** checkbox before installing the package. Otherwise, the Apex test fails and the installation does not succeed.

2. Once installation is complete, click All Tabs, then click **Customize My Tabs**. Add the Approval Routing Rules tab to the Selected Tabs list.
3. Customize the following fields' picklist values to match your organization.

   - `Owner Region`—Custom picklist field on the User object to model the opportunity owner's region. Set the region for all opportunity owners.
   - `Account Type`—Custom picklist field on the Opportunity object to model the account type associated with the opportunity. Set the account type for all opportunities.

    Note: You may have to enable the `Owner Region` and `Account Type` fields in the Page Layouts for Users and Opportunities, respectively.

4. Create an Approval Routing Rule for each combination of region and account type.

   a. Select the `Account Type` and `Owner Region` for the rule. The `Routing Key`, a composite key based on the `Account Type` and `Owner Region` fields, is created automatically.

   b. For each rule, select approvers for `Level1`, `Level2`, and `Level3`, the custom user lookup fields used to model the levels of authorization. Approvers for all opportunities are assigned according to the submitter's region and the opportunity's type.

5. Create the approval process for opportunity discounts.

   a. Click **Setup ➤ Create ➤ Workflow & Approvals ➤ Approval Processes**.

   b. From the `Manage Approval Processes For` drop-down list, select the object type for this approval process. For this example, select **Opportunity**.

   c. Click **Create New Approval Process** and select **Use Standard Setup Wizard**.

   d. Enter the `Process Name` (Opportunity Discount Approval) and `Description` for your new approval process, then click **Next**.

   e. From the `Use this approval process if the following` drop-down list, select **criteria are met**.

   f. Define the rule to fire when `Closed equals False`.

   g. Click **Next**.

   h. Leave the `Next Automated Approver Determined By` set at **None**, but select the `Administrators OR the currently assigned approver can edit records during the approval process` option, then click **Next**.

   i. Leave the `Approval Assignment Email Template` blank, then click **Next**.

   j. Select the fields you want to display on the approval page, click the `Display approval history information...` option, then click **Next**.

   k. By default, only the record owner—Opportunity Owner, in this example—is listed under `Allowed Submitters`. Leave this setting.

   l. Click **Save**.

       Note: The approval process described here is a generic one. You can create any approval process you want to use the Approval Routing Rules you defined in the Dynamic Approval Routing custom object.

6. Create the three approval steps to correspond to the `Level1`, `Level2`, and `Level3` approver fields defined in the Approval Routing Rule.

a. From the Approval Process Detail page, click **New Approval Step**.
b. Name the steps `Level 1 Approval`, `Level 2 Approval`, `Level 3 Approval`.
c. For the step criteria, select `All records should enter this step`.
d. Select `Automatically assign to approver(s)` and choose **Related User**.
e. Find and select Level1, Level2, and Level3 for your three steps, respectively.
f. Click **Save**.

Once you become more familiar with how these routing rules work, you can design data-driven approval routing for all approval processes involving multiple routing criteria.

Discussion

In previous Salesforce releases, implementing a solution for an organization with multiple account types and regions would require multiple approval processes: one for each combination of region and account type. As the numbers of account types and regions grow, the number of approval processes required jump significantly. For example, if you had two account types and three regions, you would need six approval processes; if you had 10 account types and five regions, you would need to create and maintain 50 approval processes.

By leveraging the Dynamic Approval Routing application, which uses a custom object, validation rules, and Apex code, you can create a single data-driven approval process to handle your most complex approval processes.

Sending Outbound Messages with Workflow

Problem

You want to send an outbound message to an external Web service when records are created or updated in Salesforce.

Solution

Set up a workflow rule to send the outbound message, generate the WSDL document for the message, and then set up a listener in your language of choice.

"Sending Outbound Messages with Workflow" contributed by Markus Spohn, Director of Product Management, Integration, for salesforce.com

For the following example, we'll revisit our sample Recruiting application. We'll set up a message to a legal services provider if a visa is required before a candidate can start his or her new job:

1. Set up a workflow rule that triggers an outbound message.

    a. Click **Setup ➤ Create ➤ Workflow & Approvals ➤ Workflow Rules** and create a new workflow rule that fires when a candidate is created, or when a candidate is edited and did not previously meet the rule's criteria. Set the criteria for the rule to be "Visa Required equals True."

    b. Add an outbound message workflow action:

        a. In the Immediate Workflow Actions area, click **Add Workflow Action ➤ New Outbound Message**.

        b. Enter a name and description for the outbound message.

        c. Specify the `Endpoint URL` for the recipient of the message. Salesforce sends a SOAP message to this endpoint, which is the Web service listener that will consume the outbound message.

        d. Select a Salesforce user whose security settings will control the data that's visible for the message.

        e. Select `Include Session ID` if you want the Salesforce `sessionId` included in the message. You should include it if you intend to make API calls and you don't want to include a username and password in the body of your message (which is far less secure than sending the `sessionId`).

        f. Select the field values that you want included in the outbound message.

        g. Click **Save**.

    c. Activate the workflow rule by returning to the Workflow Rule detail page and clicking **Activate**.

2. Generate the WSDL document for your outbound message: Return to the Outbound Message detail page by clicking **Setup ➤ Create ➤ Workflow & Approvals ➤ Outbound Messagaes** and selecting the name of the outbound message. Then click **Click for WSDL**. This file is bound to the outbound message and contains the instructions about how to reach the endpoint service and what data is sent to it. Save the file to your local machine.

3. Build a listener for the outbound message. This Web service endpoint has to conform to the definition of the WSDL file. For example, to build a listener using .NET:

    a. Run `wsdl.exe/serverInterfaceleads.wsdl` with .NET 2.0. This generates `NotificationServiceInterfaces.cs`, which defines the notification interface.

    b. Create a class that implements `NotificationServiceInterfaces.cs`.

While there are a number of ways to do this, one simple way is to compile the interface to a .dll first (.dlls must be in the `bin` directory in ASP.NET):

```
mkdir bin csc /t:library /out:bin\nsi.dll
NotificationServiceInterfaces.cs
```

Then write an ASMX-based Web service that implements this interface. For example, a very simple implementation in `MyNotificationListener.asmx` might be:

```
<%@WebService class="MyNotificationListener"
            language="C#"%>
class MyNotificationListener : INotificationBinding
{
    public notificationsResponse
            notifications(notifications n)
    {
        notificationsResponse r =
            new notificationsResponse();
        r.Ack = true;
        return r;
    }
}
```

c. Deploy the service by creating a new virtual directory in IIS for the directory that contains `MyNotificationListener.asmx`.

You can test that the service is deployed by viewing the service page with a browser. For example, if you create a virtual directory named `salesforce`, navigate to

`http://localhost/salesforce/MyNotificationListener.asmx.`

Discussion

Although this recipe only outlines the procedure for a .NET-based solution using IIS, the process for other Web services-enabled languages and tools is similar. Note that your listener must meet the following requirements:

- It must be reachable from the public Internet.
- If it uses SSL, it must use one of the following ports:

  ◊ 80: this port only accepts HTTP connections

  ◊ 443: this port only accepts HTTPS connections

  ◊ 7000-10000: these ports accept HTTP or HTTPS connections

- If it requires client certificates, you must have the current Salesforce client certificate available at **Setup ➤ Develop ➤ API**.

- The common name (CN) of the listener's certificate must match the domain name for your endpoint's server, and the certificate must be issued by a Certificate Authority trusted by the Java 2 Platform, Standard Edition 5.0 (JDK 1.5).

See Also

- *Tracking Outbound Messages from Workflow* on page 92
- *Sending Messages from Apex*
- "Outbound Messaging" in the *Force Platform Web Services API Developer's Guide* at `www.salesforce.com/us/developer/docs/api/index_CSH.htm#sforce_api_om_outboundmessaging.htm`
- The "Creating an Outbound Messaging Notification Service with CSharp and .Net Framework 2.0" whitepaper at `wiki.apexdevnet.com/index.php/Creating_an_Outbound_Messaging_Notification_Service_with_CSharp_and_.Net_Framework_2.0`

Tracking Outbound Messages from Workflow

Problem

You want to track the status of the outbound messages that have been sent to external servers as a result of a workflow rule.

Solution

Click **Setup ➤ Monitoring ➤ Outbound Messages**.

Alternatively, click **Setup ➤ Create ➤ Workflow & Approvals ➤ Outbound Messages**, and then click **View Message Delivery Status**. From this page you can:

- View the status of your outbound messages, including the total number of attempted deliveries
- View the action that triggered the outbound message by clicking any workflow or approval process action ID
- Click **Retry** next to a message to immediately re-deliver the message
- Click **Del** next to a message to permanently remove the outbound message from the queue

See Also

- *Sending Outbound Messages with Workflow* on page 89

"Tracking Outbound Messages from Workflow" contributed by Markus Spohn, Director of Product Management, Integration, for salesforce.com

- "Outbound Messaging" in the *Force Platform Web Services API Developer's Guide* at `www.salesforce.com/us/developer/docs/api/index_CSH.htm#sforce_api_om_outboundmessaging.htm`
- The "Creating an Outbound Messaging Notification Service with CSharp and .Net Framework 2.0" whitepaper at `wiki.apexdevnet.com/index.php/Creating_an_Outbound_Messaging_Notification_Service_with_CSharp_and_.Net_Framework_2.0`

Chapter 3

Searching and Querying Data

Truly useful, cloud computing business apps include business logic and processes that help companies run their businesses efficiently. As we've mentioned, the Force Platform gives you the power to write code and develop components to incorporate business logic, such as data validation, into your app. Pretty much any business process you write for your app will require your code to search, query, and examine sets of records upon which the business process will operate. So what's the best way to do that?

In this chapter, you'll learn how to examine your app's objects, relationships, and fields in a graphical way. You'll also learn the difference between SOQL and SOSL and how to use them to construct queries that examine sets of records in your app. Then you'll see how to use SOQL to query related objects using their relationship associations and how to filter your queries by a relative date or the division of a record. Finally, you'll use the AJAX toolkit to query your data in a command-line environment. These examples and best practices are a great way to get started developing your own queries to manipulate the data in ways that are unique to your app.

You can use the recipes in this chapter without setting up the Force Platform API, because the tools you'll use are already set up for you. But all the query techniques you learn here can be used if you do work with the API. For more information, see *Chapter 6: Integrating Applications with the API and Apex* on page 195.

Using the Force Platform Explorer to Examine Your Data Model

Problem

You want to browse through the fields, attributes, and relationships of every object in your Salesforce organization, and you're on a Windows platform.

Solution

Use the Force Platform Explorer, an open-source C#.Net client application available on Developer Force. Force Platform Explorer is a lightweight, .NET-based tool that lets you browse the schema within your organization, edit data values, and build and test SOQL and SOSL queries While the Force Platform IDE and AJAX Tools include a lightweight version of this handy application, the stand-alone .NET version of Force Platform Explorer includes more functionality, including the ability to test SOSL statements, view documents, and update database values. To download it, go to
`wiki.apexdevnet.com/index.php/Apex_Explorer`.

After installing the Force Platform Explorer, open the application and log in by clicking the **Login** button and entering your standard Salesforce username and password. At this point the Force Platform Explorer issues a `describeGlobal()` call to the API to populate the interactive list of objects in the right sidebar.

 Tip: The permissions associated with your login affect the visibility of objects and fields in the Force Platform Explorer. Be sure that your login has access to the data you need to explore—a user with the "Modify All Data" permission typically works best.

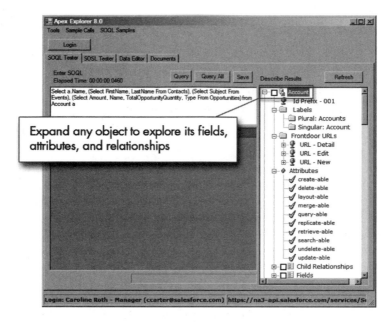

Figure 14: The Force Platform Explorer

Once you've logged in, you can expand any object to explore its fields, attributes, and relationships. For example, the following information is available if you expand the Account object:

Id Prefix

> The first three characters of the Salesforce ID for records of this object type. For example, the ID of any account record always starts with 001. Likewise, contact records always start with 003.

Labels

> The labels that are used to display this object in both singular and plural form.

Frontdoor URLs

> The URLs that can be used to reach detail, edit, and list pages for the object in a Web browser. See *Creating a Custom Detail Page Button* on page 23.

Attributes

> A list of actions that you can perform on the object. See www.salesforce.com/us/developer/docs/api/index_CSH.htm# sforce_api_calls_describesobjects_describesobjectresult.htm .

Child Relationships

> The relationships that have been defined on other objects that reference this object as the "one" side of a one-to-many relationship. For example,

if you expand the Child Relationships node under the Account object, contacts, opportunities, and tasks are included in this list.

> **Note:** Relationships that are defined on this object so that it represents the "many" side of a one-to-many relationship (for example, the Parent Account relationship on the Account object) are included in the list of fields.

Fields

The fields that are available on this object. These, too, have associated attributes, relationships, a label, and a field type that you can expand for more information. For example, if you expand the Account object's `CreatedById` field:

- **Attributes** indicate what actions can be performed on the field. For example, `CreatedById` can't be created, updated, or set to null because it is `defaulted on create`. However, it can be used in SOQL query filters and to sort a list of records.
- **CreatedBy** represents the name of the relationship that's used to access the user record to which `CreatedById` refers. For example, you can use `CreatedBy.<fieldName>` to select User data in SOQL queries.
- **label** specifies the label that's used to display the field in Salesforce.
- **Type** indicates the type of field, including its length, number of digits, and precision. For this example, `CreatedById` is a reference field because it represents a lookup relationship to the User object.

> **Note:** Standard objects are listed by their standard names, even if you've renamed them.

Discussion

If you want to connect to a different instance of Salesforce, such as your Developer Sandbox or a pre-release instance, click **Tools ➤ Options**, and set the domain name of the `Endpoint` to the appropriate server. For example, if you wanted to point to a sandbox organization, change:

```
https://www.salesforce.com/services/Soap/u/14.0
```

To:

```
https://test.salesforce.com/services/Soap/u/14.0
```

You can also use the `Endpoint` parameter to change to a different version of the API. For example, to have the Force Platform Explorer use Version 14 of the API, change your `Endpoint` to:

```
https://www.salesforce.com/services/Soap/u/14.0
```

See Also

- *Constructing SOQL and SOSL Queries in the Force Platform Explorer* on page 102
- *Using SoqlXplorer to Examine Your Data Model* on page 99

Using SoqlXplorer to Examine Your Data Model

Problem

You want to browse through the fields, attributes, and relationships of every object in your Salesforce organization, and you're on the Mac OS X platform.

Solution

For Mac users, SoqlXplorer is a great counterpart to the Force Platform Explorer for Windows. SoqlXplorer provides metadata exploration, a SOQL query tester, and a graphical schema view for examining object relationships (a piece of functionality that's only available on the Mac OS X platform!). Download SoqlXplorer from Simon Fell's PocketSOAP website at `www.pocketsoap.com/osx/soqlx`. After the download automatically extracts itself, drag the SoqlXplorer icon to your Applications folder to complete the installation.

After installing SoqlXplorer, open the application and log in by entering your standard Salesforce username and password and specifying the server to which you want to connect. Choose www.salesforce.com to connect to the normal production servers, or test.salesforce.com to connect to a sandbox organization.

After you click **Login**, SoqlXplorer issues a `describeGlobal()` call to the API to populate the interactive list of objects in the right sidebar.

You can expand any object to explore its fields and relationships. To view attributes for an object, toggle the **Details** button to On in the bottom right corner of the window. If you select an object field, the **Details** popup shows properties for the field instead.

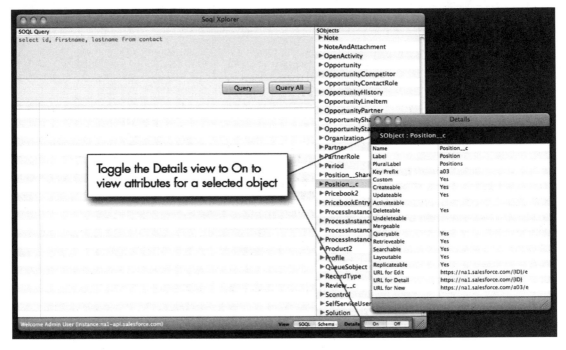

Figure 15: Viewing Object Attributes in SoqlXplorer

Two views are available in the main window: SOQL and Schema.

- Use **SOQL** view to open a SOQL query editor where you can construct and execute SOQL queries. The queries you write use syntax-highlighting to improve legibility, and you can double-click an object's name to automatically build a query that selects all available fields. You can also double-click any result data to copy and paste it elsewhere.

- Use **Schema** view to open an interactive entity relationship diagram (ERD) of the objects in your organization. Select any object in the right sidebar to view that object's parent relationships (in blue) and child relationships (in orange). You can expand the fields of any object by clicking the + toggle button in the upper right corner of any object, and you can double-click an object to move it to the center of the view.

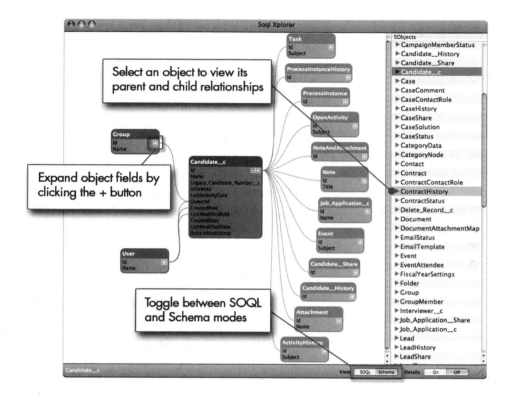

Figure 16: Schema View in SoqlXplorer

 Tip: Simon Fell frequently adds new functionality to SoqlXplorer. To automatically check for updates, click **SoqlXplorer ➤ Preferences** and select `Check for updates at startup`.

See Also

- *Constructing SOQL and SOSL Queries in the Force Platform Explorer* on page 102
- *Using the Force Platform Explorer to Examine Your Data Model* on page 96

Choosing Between SOQL and SOSL

Problem

You know that the platform supports Salesforce Object Query Language (SOQL) and Salesforce Object Search Language (SOSL), but you don't know what the difference is between the two, or when to use one over the other.

Solution

A SOQL query is the equivalent of a SELECT clause in a SQL statement. Use SOQL with a `query()` call when:

- You know in which objects or fields the data resides
- You want to retrieve data from a single object or from multiple objects that are related to one another
- You want to count the number of records that meet particular criteria
- You want to sort your results as part of the query
- You want to retrieve data from number, date, or checkbox fields

A SOSL query is a programmatic way of performing a text-based search. Use SOSL with a `search()` call when:

- You don't know in which object or field the data resides and you want to find it in the most efficient way possible
- You want to retrieve multiple objects and fields efficiently, and the objects may or may not be related to one another
- You want to retrieve data for a particular division in an organization with Divisions, and you want to find it in the most efficient way possible

 Tip: Although SOQL was previously the only one of the two query languages that allowed condition-based filtering with WHERE clauses, as of the Summer '07 release SOSL supports this functionality as well.

See Also

- *Constructing SOQL and SOSL Queries in the Force Platform Explorer* on page 102
- *Finding Search Data Based on Division* on page 110
- "Salesforce Object Query Language (SOQL)" at
www.salesforce.com/us/developer/docs/api/index_CSH.htm#sforce_api_calls_soql.htm
- "Salesforce Object Search Language (SOSL)" at
www.salesforce.com/us/developer/docs/api/index_CSH.htm#sforce_api_calls_sosl.htm

Constructing SOQL and SOSL Queries in the Force Platform Explorer

Problem

You want to construct a SOQL or SOSL query, but you don't want to type all the object and field names by hand.

Solution

Use the Force Platform Explorer to build and test SOQL and SOSL queries with point-and-click functionality. Building SOQL and SOSL queries in the Force Platform Explorer saves you time if you're learning SOQL and SOSL syntax, or if you're looking for an easy way to test queries before implementing them in an s-control or integration.

 Note: This recipe describes how to create SOQL and SOSL queries in the Force Platform Explorer, but other metadata explorer tools such as SoqlXplorer for Mac OS X, or the SOQL Explorer in the Force Platform IDE work in a similar manner.

After logging in to the Force Platform Explorer, the Describe Results pane displays an interactive list of selectable fields for each object in your Salesforce organization. Selecting one or more fields from this pane automatically creates a SOQL query in the SOQL Tester pane on the left.

For example, the following screenshot shows a SOQL query that was automatically generated after selecting the `MailingCity` and `MailingState` fields of the Contact object.

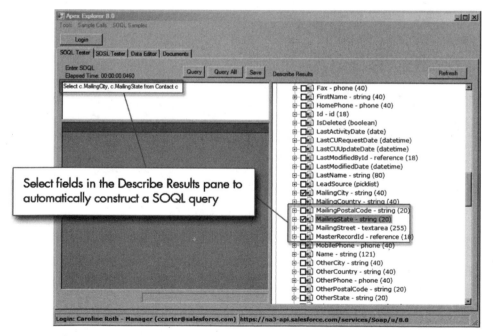

Figure 17: Constructing SOQL Queries in the Force Platform Explorer

- If you want to include a field from a related object in a query, expand the `Child Relationships` element under the parent object, expand the child object you want to query, and then expand its `Child Fields`. You can add a child field to your query just by selecting its checkbox.

- If you want to filter the results by any additional values, enter the WHERE clause for the SOQL query by hand.

Once the query is constructed, click **Query** to execute it against the database. Results appear in the lower pane.

If you want to save the query for future use, click **Save** and enter a label. Saved queries are stored in **SOQL Samples ➤ Saved Queries**.

The Force Platform Explorer also allows you to construct SOSL queries in the same way:

1. In the SOSL Tester tab enter a Search Query according to the same rules that you use for entering queries in the search text box in the Salesforce user interface. For example, *acme**, or *jerry g*.
2. In the Search Group drop-down list, specify whether you want to search all possible fields or restrict your search to just name, email, or phone fields.
3. Optionally, specify the objects and fields that you want returned by your SOSL query in the Return Field Spec text area. For example:

```
Lead(Name, Phone ORDER BY Name DESC), Contact(Name, Phone WHERE
    createddate = THIS_FISCAL_QUARTER)
```

4. Click **Send Request**.

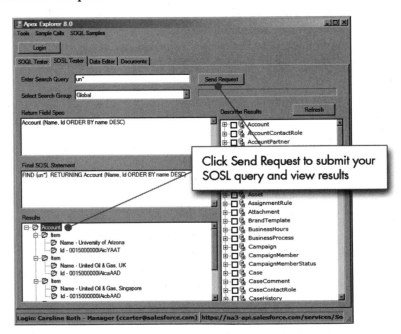

Figure 18: Constructing SOSL Queries in the Force Platform Explorer

See Also

- *Choosing Between SOQL and SOSL* on page 101
- "Salesforce Object Query Language (SOQL)" at
  www.salesforce.com/us/developer/docs/api/index_CSH.htm#sforce_api_calls_soql.htm
- "Salesforce Object Search Language (SOSL)" at
  www.salesforce.com/us/developer/docs/api/index_CSH.htm#sforce_api_calls_sosl.htm

Querying Multiple Related Objects Using Relationship Queries

Problem

You want to use as few SOQL queries as possible to access data from multiple related objects.

Solution

Use SOQL relationship syntax to pull data from related records in a single query.

For each of the following examples, the child object is the object on which the relationship field (the foreign key) is defined, and the parent is the object that the child references:

Basic Child-to-Parent (Foreign Key) Traversal

To traverse a relationship from a child to a parent, use standard dot notation off the name of the relationship. For example, this SOQL query retrieves information about contacts from the Contact object, along with the name of each contact's related account (the parent object):

```
SELECT Id, LastName, FirstName, Account.Name
FROM Contact
```

Account is the name of the relationship that's defined by the AccountId lookup field on the Contact object. Using dot notation, this SOQL query retrieves the Name field on the account that is related through the Account relationship.

Expanded Child-to-Parent (Foreign Key) Traversal

Child-to-parent traversals can extend up to five levels from the original root object. For example, the last selected field in this SOQL statement extends two levels from the root contact record by retrieving the name of the parent account on the account associated with the contact:

```
SELECT Id, LastName, FirstName, Account.Name,
    Account.Parent.Name
FROM Contact
```

Basic Parent-to-Child (Aggregate) Traversal

To traverse a relationship from a parent to a set of children, use a nested query. For example, this SOQL query retrieves opportunities and the opportunity products associated with each opportunity:

```
SELECT Id, Name, Amount,
       (SELECT Quantity, UnitPrice, TotalPrice
        FROM OpportunityLineItems)
FROM Opportunity
```

Using the nested query, we're specifying that for each opportunity we want the respective set of OpportunityLineItem records that are related through the OpportunityLineItems child relationship.

Combined Child-to-Parent and Parent-to-Child Traversal

Foreign key and aggregate traversals can also be combined in a single query. For example:

```
SELECT Id, Name, Account.Name,
       (SELECT Quantity, UnitPrice, TotalPrice,
               PricebookEntry.Name,
               PricebookEntry.Product2.Family
        FROM OpportunityLineItems)
FROM Opportunity
```

See Also

- *Constructing SOQL and SOSL Queries in the Force Platform Explorer* on page 102
- "Relationship Queries" at www.salesforce.com/us/developer/docs/api/index_CSH.htm#sforce_api_calls_soql_relationships.htm
- "Salesforce Object Query Language (SOQL)" at www.salesforce.com/us/developer/docs/api/index_CSH.htm#sforce_api_calls_soql.htm

Finding a Contact, Lead, or Person Account

Problem

You want to write a query to find a person, but you don't know whether this person is stored as a lead, as a contact, or as a person account.

Solution

Perform the search with one SOSL query, rather than multiple SOQL queries. For example:

- To look for *Joe* in all searchable text fields in the system, and return the IDs of the records where *Joe* is found in a case-insensitive search:

```
FIND {Joe}
```

- To look for all email fields that start with *jo* or end in *acme.com*, and return the IDs of the records where those fields are found:

```
FIND {"jo*" OR "*acme.com"}
IN EMAIL FIELDS
```

 Tip: If you know you're looking for a name, an email address, or a phone number, it's more efficient to narrow your search scope to only name fields, email fields, or phone fields, respectively, rather than searching every field.

- To look for the name *Joe Smith* or *Joe Smythe* in the name field on a lead or contact only, and return the name and phone number of any matching record that was also created in the current fiscal quarter:

```
FIND {"Joe Smith" OR "Joe Smythe"}
IN NAME FIELDS
RETURNING
    lead(name, phone WHERE createddate = THIS_FISCAL_QUARTER),
    contact(name, phone WHERE createddate = THIS_FISCAL_QUARTER)
```

If you want to search for records based on a query string that was entered by a user, first escape any special characters that were entered by the user, and then construct the appropriate SOSL string. For example, the following JavaScriptl searches leads, contacts, and accounts for any instance of a record named "Phil Degauss":

```
<html>
<head>
<script src="/soap/ajax/10.0/connection.js"></script>
<script type="text/javascript">
function init() {
    var who = "phil degauss";

    // These special characters must be preceded by a backslash
    // before they can be used in a SOSL query.
    who = who.replace(/([\&\|\!\(\)\{\}\[\]\^~\:\\\+\-])/g, "\\$1");

    var sstr = "find {" + who + "} in NAME FIELDS RETURNING " +
               "Lead (id, firstname, lastname), " +
               "Contact(id, firstname, lastname), " +
               "Account(id, name)";

    // Issue the SOSL query using the AJAX Toolkit.
    var sr = sforce.connection.search(sstr);
    var m = document.getElementById('main');

    // Write out the results.
```

```
    if (sr) {
        var list = sr.getArray('searchRecords');
        for (var i = 0; i < list.length; i++ ) {
            m.innerHTML += "<p>Search results : " +
            list[i].toString();
        }
    } else {
        m.innerHTML += "<p>No search results";
    }
}
</script>
</head>

<body onload="init();">
<div id="main"></div>
</body>
</html>
```

Discussion

You can make this solution even more robust by making use of the * wildcard character. For example, the solution here only searches for exact matches of the name "Phil Degausse." If you wanted this solution to also return a record named "Philip Degausse," or "Phil Degaussey," modify the user's search string by appending * after each token in the string:

```
var who = "phil* degauss*";
```

Note that it's still important to maintain the space between the two names, so that each token phil* and degauss* will match individual name fields in the objects that are queried.

See Also

- *Choosing Between SOQL and SOSL* on page 101
- "Salesforce Object Search Language (SOSL)" at www.salesforce.com/us/developer/docs/api/index_CSH.htm#sforce_api_calls_sosl.htm

Retrieving Data Based on a Relative Date

Problem

You want to retrieve records based on a relative date, such as "before last year" or "during the next fiscal quarter."

Solution

Use a date literal in the WHERE clause of your SOQL or SOSL statement. For example:

- This SOQL statement returns all opportunities that closed yesterday:

```
SELECT Id FROM Opportunity WHERE CloseDate = YESTERDAY
```

- This SOQL statement returns all opportunities that closed prior to the beginning of the last fiscal quarter:

```
SELECT Id FROM Opportunity WHERE CloseDate < LAST_FISCAL_QUARTER
```

- This SOQL statement returns all opportunities with a close date that is more than 15 days away:

```
SELECT Id FROM Opportunity WHERE CloseDate > NEXT_N_DAYS:15
```

Discussion

When you specify a date in a SOQL or SOSL query, it can be a specific date or dateTime field, or it can be an expression that uses a date literal—a keyword that represents a relative range of time such as last month or next year. To construct an expression that returns date or dateTime values within the range, use =. To construct an expression that returns date or dateTime values that fall on either side of the range, use > or <.

Salesforce provides date literals such as YESTERDAY, TODAY, LAST_WEEK, NEXT_WEEK. For a complete list, including examples and range definitions, see "Date Formats and Date Literals" in the *Force Platform Web Services API Developer's Guide* at
www.salesforce.com/us/developer
/docs/api/index_CSH.htm#sforce_api_calls_soql_select_dateformats.htm:

Remember that date and dateTime field values are stored as Greenwich Mean Time (GMT) or Coordinated Universal Time (UTC). When one of these values is returned in Salesforce, it's automatically adjusted for the time zone specified in your organization preferences.

See Also

- *Constructing SOQL and SOSL Queries in the Force Platform Explorer* on page 102
- "Salesforce Object Query Language (SOQL)" at www.salesforce.com/us/developer /docs/api/index_CSH.htm#sforce_api_calls_soql.htm
- "Salesforce Object Search Language (SOSL)" at www.salesforce.com/us/developer /docs/api/index_CSH.htm#sforce_api_calls_sosl.htm

Finding Search Data Based on Division

Problem

You want to retrieve data for a particular division.

Solution

Use the `WITH` clause in a SOSL query to filter on division before any other filters are applied. Although you can also filter on an object's `Division` field within a `WHERE` clause, using `WITH` is more efficient because it filters all records based on division before applying other filters. For example:

```
FIND {test} RETURNING Account (id where name like 'Smith'),
                      Contact (id where name like 'Smith')
            WITH DIVISION = 'Global'
```

Notice that the `WITH` clause filters based on the `Division` name field, rather than its ID. If you filter on division in a `WHERE` clause, you need to use the division ID instead.

See Also

- *Constructing SOQL and SOSL Queries in the Force Platform Explorer* on page 102
- "Salesforce Object Query Language (SOQL)" at `www.salesforce.com/us/developer/docs/api/index_CSH.htm#sforce_api_calls_soql.htm`
- "Salesforce Object Search Language (SOSL)" at `www.salesforce.com/us/developer/docs/api/index_CSH.htm#sforce_api_calls_sosl.htm`

Previewing Query Results

Problem

Your solution gives users a chance to build a query or set up a filter for a query that you've already written. You want to offer users a preview of what data is returned from their query, including the total number of records that are returned.

Solution

Run two SOQL queries: one that uses `COUNT()` to return the total number of records that will be returned, and one that uses `LIMIT` to quickly return 25 random records that match the query.

Discussion

If your solution allows a user to build a query or set up a filter for an existing query, there's a chance that the user might execute a long-running query that uses `query()` or `queryMore()` in a loop. This query could easily take a lot longer than the user expects.

To avoid this issue, it's a good idea to give users a preview of their query results if the result set is going to be greater than 1,000 records, including the total number of records that will be returned and a sample of what the resulting data will look like. You can then prompt them with a question such as, "Are you sure?" before proceeding with the full query.

Although running the normal `query()` call returns the total result size, it also returns a batch of up to 2,000 records, depending on your configured batch size. If you want your application to be faster, it's a good idea to run a `COUNT()` query and a `LIMIT` query instead.

For example, the following SOQL query returns the total number of accounts in the organization, without any filters. You can use this value in a prompt to the user to ask if they're sure they want to proceed with the query:

```
SELECT COUNT() FROM Account
```

Then you can use the following SOQL query to return a random subset of the total data to the user. The user might decide that he or she requires additional fields before the full query should run:

```
SELECT Name, BillingCity FROM Account LIMIT 25
```

See Also

- *Implementing the Query/Query More Pattern* on page 206
- *Constructing SOQL and SOSL Queries in the Force Platform Explorer* on page 102
- "Salesforce Object Query Language (SOQL)" at www.salesforce.com/us/developer/docs/api/index_CSH.htm#sforce_api_calls_soql.htm

Sorting Query Results

Problem

You've issued a SOQL or SOSL query and want the results sorted by the value of one or more fields.

Solution

Use the ORDER BY clause in your SOQL or SOSL statement to efficiently receive results in the order that you prefer.

 Note: You can't use the ORDER BY clause in any Apex query if it also uses locking. Those query results, however, are always ordered by ID.

For example, this SOQL query:

```
SELECT Name FROM Contact ORDER BY FirstName
```

Returns a list of contacts sorted alphabetically by first name:

- Andy Young
- Ashley James
- Jack Bond
- Jill Jazzy
- Stella Pavlov
- Zebidiah Jazzy

This SOQL query:

```
SELECT Name FROM Contact ORDER BY LastName DESC,
                              FirstName DESC
```

Returns a list of contacts sorted in reverse-alphabetical order by last name and then in reverse-alphabetical order by first name:

- Andy Young
- Stella Pavlov
- Zebidiah Jazzy
- Jill Jazzy
- Ashley James
- Jack Bond

This SOSL query:

```
FIND {Ja*} RETURNING Contact (Name ORDER BY LastName)
```

Returns a list of contacts that include "Ja" in the name, sorted alphabetically by last name:

- Jack Bond
- Ashley James
- Jill Jazzy

- Zebidiah Jazzy

This SOSL query:

```
FIND {Ja*} RETURNING Contact (Name ORDER BY LastName,
                                          FirstName DESC),
                 Lead (Name ORDER BY FirstName)
```

Returns a list of contacts and leads that include "Ja" in the name, where contacts are sorted alphabetically by last name and then reverse-alphabetically by first name, and where leads are sorted alphabetically by first name:

- (Contact) Jack Bond
- (Contact) Ashley James
- (Contact) Zebidiah Jazzy
- (Contact) Jill Jazzy
- (Lead) Jack Rodgers
- (Lead) Tom Jamison

Discussion

ORDER BY is the best solution for sorting because the Force Platform server does the work and your code doesn't need to do anything else after receiving the data.

You can sort your query results by any of the specified object's fields that is not a long text area or multi-select picklist field, even if the field is not one of the query fields that you want returned.

 Note: If you attempt to sort by a long text area or multi-select picklist field, you'll receive a "malformed query" error message.

The ORDER BY clause for SOQL and SOSL includes a number of features:

- Sort by Multiple Fields

  You can sort your query by multiple fields, so that records that have the same value for the first field are then ordered by the value of a second field. For example, the following query returns contacts sorted first by LastName and then by FirstName:

```
SELECT Name FROM Contact ORDER BY LastName,
                                  FirstName
```

- Sort in Ascending and Descending Order

You can specify whether values should be sorted in ascending or descending order by adding the modifiers ASC or DESC to any sort field. For example, the following query returns contacts in reverse-alphabetical order:

```
SELECT Name FROM Contact ORDER BY LastName DESC,
                              FirstName DESC
```

When this value is not specified, results are sorted in ascending order by default.

- Sort Null Values

  You can also specify whether null values should be sorted at the beginning (FIRST) or end (LAST) of the list of results. For example, the following query places null values at the end of a list of contact mailing cities and states that's organized by state in reverse-alphabetical order:

```
SELECT MailingCity, MailingState FROM Contact
                    ORDER BY MailingState DESC NULLS LAST
```

ORDER BY always follows the WHERE clause in a SOQL or SOSL statement. For example:

```
SELECT Name FROM Contact WHERE Name like 'Ja%'
                ORDER BY LastName, FirstName
```

 Note: SOQL query sorting is case insensitive. If you require case sensitive sorting, you'll need to implement this in your own code.

See Also

- *Choosing Between SOQL and SOSL* on page 101
- *Constructing SOQL and SOSL Queries in the Force Platform Explorer* on page 102
- "Salesforce Object Query Language (SOQL)" at www.salesforce.com/us/developer/ docs/api/index_CSH.htm#sforce_api_calls_soql.htm
- "Salesforce Object Search Language (SOSL)" at www.salesforce.com/us/developer/ docs/api/index_CSH.htm#sforce_api_calls_sosl.htm

Viewing Tags

Problem

You want to use the API to see all the tags that are available in an organization.

Solution

Perform the search on the `TagDefiniton` object to retrieve multiple tags.

The following call will return a list of the public tags in alphabetic order:

```
sforce.connection.query("SELECT Name FROM TagDefinition WHERE Type =
'Public' ORDER BY Name");
```

An example response might be:

- Great Lakes
- Manager
- Midwest
- Northeast
- Northwest
- Senior Manager
- Southeast
- Southwest
- Staff
- Team Lead

Discussion

Querying `TagDefinition` does not indicate how many times a tag is being used, nor on what type of record. To find this information, see *View Records with Tags* on page 115

See Also

- *Updating Tag Definitions* on page 232
- "TagDefinition" in the *Force Platform Web Services API Developer's Guide* at http://www.salesforce.com/us/developer/docs/api/Content/sforce_api_objects_tagdefinition.htm

View Records with Tags

Problem

You want to generate a list of records that use the same public tag.

Solution

You can retrieve a list of records with a particular tag by calling queries on specific tag objects.

For instance, to retrieve a list of all contacts tagged as Staff and all contacts tagged as Great Lakes, execute the following in the AJAX Toolkit or your own client application:

```
var staffContactResults = sforce.connection.query("SELECT ItemId FROM
 ContactTag WHERE Name = 'Staff'");
var greatLakesContactResults = sforce.connection.query("SELECT ItemId
 FROM ContactTag WHERE Name = 'Great Lakes'");
```

Another example: to find all contacts tagged as both Staff and Great Lakes, use the following query to form a result array with any null rows dropped:

```
var ReturnedContacts = sforce.connection.query("SELECT Name, Id, (SELECT
 ItemId, Name, Id FROM Tags WHERE Name = 'Staff' OR Name = 'Great
Lakes') FROM Contact");
var TagArray = new Array();
var arraySize = 0;
for (var i = 0; i < ReturnedContacts.size; i++)
{
  if (ReturnedContacts.records[i].Tags != null)
  {
   TagArray[arraySize] = ReturnedContacts.records[i].Tags;
   arraySize++;
  }
}
```

See Also

- "TagDefinition" in the *Force Platform Web Services API Developer's Guide* at
  www.salesforce.com/us/developer/docs/api/index_CSH.htm#sforce_api_objects_tagdefinition.htm
- *The AJAX Toolkit Developer's Guide* at
  www.salesforce.com/us/developer/docs/ajax/index.htm

Writing Shorter Queries Using Outer Joins

Problem

You'd like to write short, simple queries similar to an outer join in SQL. For example, "retrieve all the IDs for accounts whose opportunities are all closed."

Solution

Use IN or NOT IN to write simple queries that exploit Salesforce support of semi-joins and anti-joins in SOQL.

For example, if you want to find the account IDs for all accounts where there is a lost opportunity associated to the account, use a semi-join:

```
SELECT Id, Name
FROM Account
WHERE Id IN
(SELECT AccountId FROM Opportunity WHERE StageName = 'Closed Lost')
```

If you want to find the account IDs for all accounts that have no open opportunities, use an anti-join query:

```
SELECT Id
FROM Account
WHERE Id NOT IN (SELECT AcountId FROM Opportunity
  WHERE IsClosed = false
)
```

You can write nested queries using relationships. For example, if you want to find opportunity IDs and their related line items if the line item value is greater than $10,000, issue a query similar to the following:

```
SELECT Id, (SELECT Id from OpportunityLineItem)
FROM Opportunity
WHERE Id IN (
  SELECT OpportunityId FROM OpportunityLineItem
    WHERE totalPrice > 10000
)
```

Discussion

Because semi-joins and anti-joins can potentially use a lot of resources during calculation, salesforce.com enforces some limits on these types of queries. For more information, see Semi-Joins with IN and Anti-Joins with NOT IN in the *Force Platform API Developer's Guide*.

See Also

Constructing SOQL and SOSL Queries in the Force Platform Explorer on page 102

Chapter 4

Displaying Data and Modifying Data Actions

After using recipes in previous chapters that help you modify the look and feel of Salesforce or inspect existing data, you may wish to modify how specific data is presented, or change the behavior of data actions. Use the recipes in this chapter to explore the Force Platform: change how confidential information is displayed, change the default behavior of bulk processing of records, handling of duplicate records, and many other data display or data action modifications.

- Controlling Recursive Triggers
- Comparing Queries Against Trigger.old and Trigger.new
- Preventing Duplicate Records from Saving
- Creating a Child Record When a Parent Record is Created
- Using System.runAs in Test Methods

Creating a Many-to-Many Relationship

Problem

You want to model a many-to-many relationship between objects in which each record of one object can be related to many records of the other object, and vice versa. For example, a customer case can require many bug fixes, and a bug fix can resolve multiple customer cases.

Note: This recipe has been provided by salesforce.com Training & Certification and is drawn from the expert-led training courses available around the world. Salesforce.com training courses provide an opportunity to get hands-on experience with the Force Platform and Salesforce applications as well as to prepare you to become Salesforce.com Certified. Register for a course at `www.salesforce.com/training`.

Solution

Relate the two objects using a *custom junction object*, and customize the junction object related lists and reports. A custom junction object is an object with two master-detail relationships. Its purpose is to create an association between two other objects. For example, a many-to-many relationship between bugs and cases uses a custom junction object called BugCaseAssociation to associate the Bug and Case objects.

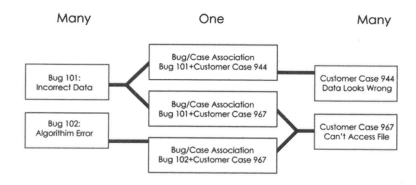

Figure 19: A Many-to-Many Relationship Between Bugs and Customer Cases

To create the junction object:

1. Click **Setup ➤ Create ➤ Objects**.
2. Click **New Custom Object**.
3. In the custom object wizard, consider these tips specifically for junction objects:

- Name the object with a label that indicates its purpose, such as `BugCaseAssociation`.
- For the `Record Name` field, use the auto-number data type.
- Do not launch the custom tab wizard before clicking **Save**. Junction objects do not need a tab.

To create the two master-detail relationships:

1. Verify that the two objects you want to relate to each other already exist. For example, you may want to relate the standard case object to a custom bug object.
2. On the junction object, create the first master-detail relationship field. In the custom field wizard:

   a. Choose `Master-Detail Relationship` as the field type.

   b. Select one of the objects to relate to your junction object. For example, select `Case`.

   The first master-detail relationship you create on your junction object becomes the *primary* relationship. This affects the following for the junction object records:

   - Look and feel: The junction object's detail and edit pages use the color and any associated icon of the primary master object.
   - Record ownership: The junction object records inherit the value of the `Owner` field from their associated primary master record. Because objects on the detail side of a relationship do not have a visible `Owner` field, this is only relevant if you later delete both master-detail relationships on your junction object.
   - Division: If your organization uses divisions to segment data, the junction object records inherit their division from their associated primary master record. Similar to the record ownership, this is only relevant if you later delete both master-detail relationships.

   c. Select a `Sharing Setting` option. For master-detail relationship fields, the `Sharing Setting` attribute determines the sharing access that users must have to a master record in order to create, edit, or delete its associated detail records.

   d. For the `Related List Label` that will display on the page layout of the master object, do not accept the default. Change this to use the name of the other master object in your many-to-many relationship. For example, change this to `Bugs` so users will see a Bugs related list on the case detail page.

3. On the junction object, create the second master-detail relationship. In the custom field wizard:

    a. Choose `Master-Detail Relationship` as the field type.

    b. Select the other desired master object to relate to your junction object. For example, select `Bug`.

    The second master-detail relationship you create on your junction object becomes the *secondary* relationship. If you delete the primary master-detail relationship or convert it to a lookup relationship, the secondary master object becomes primary.

    c. Select a `Sharing Setting` option. For master-detail relationship fields, the `Sharing Setting` attribute determines the sharing access that users must have to a master record in order to create, edit, or delete its associated detail records.

    d. For the `Related List Label` that will display on the page layout of the master object, do not accept the default. Change this to use the name of the other master object in your many-to-many relationship. For example, change this to `Cases` so users will see a Cases related list on the bug detail page.

To customize the fields that display in the junction object related list on each master object page layout:

1. Edit the page layout of each master object that is related to the junction object. For example, to modify the BugCaseAssociations related list for case records, edit the page layout for cases at **Setup ➤ Customize ➤ Cases ➤ Page Layouts**.
2. Select the related list you want to modify and click **Edit Properties** to open the related list popup window. For example, on cases the BugCaseAssociations related list was renamed to Bugs, so select the Bugs related list.
3. Add the fields to display in the related list. You can add fields from the junction object itself, but more importantly, you can add fields from the other master object.

    Each field is prefixed with its object name in the popup window. In the related list itself, only fields from the junction object are prefixed with the object name; fields from the other master object are not.

 Note: The junction object related list does not include an icon on the master record's detail pages because the junction object does not have a custom tab. If you make a tab for the junction object, the icon is included.

Discussion

For a many-to-many relationship in Salesforce, each master object record displays a related list of the associated junction object records. To create a seamless user experience, you can change the name of the junction object related list on each of the master object page layouts to have the name of the other master object. For example, you might change the BugCaseAssociations related list to `Cases` on the bugs page layout and to `Bugs` on the cases page layout. You can further customize these related lists to display fields from the other master object.

Review the following considerations before creating many-to-many relationships between objects:

- Junction object records are deleted when either associated master record is deleted. If both associated master records are deleted, the junction object record is deleted permanently and cannot be restored.
- Sharing access to a junction object record is determined by a user's sharing access to both associated master records and the `Sharing Setting` option on the relationship field. For example, if the sharing setting on both parents is Read/Write, then the user must have Read/Write access to *both* parents in order to have Read/Write access to the junction object.
- In a many-to-many relationship, a user cannot delete a parent record if there are more than 200 junction object records associated with it *and* if the junction object has a roll-up summary field that rolls up to the other parent. To delete this object, manually delete junction object records until the count is fewer than 200.
- Roll-up summary fields that summarize data from the junction object can be created on both master objects.
- Formula fields and validation rules on the junction object can reference fields on both master objects.
- You can define Apex triggers on both master objects and the junction object.
- A junction object cannot be on the master side of another master-detail relationship.
- Junction objects cannot be on the subscriber side of a Salesforce to Salesforce connection.
- You cannot create a many-to-many self relationship, that is, the two master-detail relationships on the junction object cannot have the same master object.

Many-to-many relationships provide two standard report types that join the master objects and the junction object. The report types are:

- "Primary master with junction object and secondary master" in the primary master object's report category
- "Secondary master with junction object and primary master" in the secondary master object's report category

The order of the master objects in the report type is important. The master object listed first determines the scope of records that can be displayed in the report.

You can create custom reports based on these standard report types. In addition, you can *create custom report types* to customize which related objects are joined in the report.

See Also

- "Considerations for Relationships" in the Salesforce online help

- "Customizing Page Layouts" in the Salesforce online help
- "What is a Custom Report Type?" in the Salesforce online help

Storing and Displaying Confidential Information

Problem

You want to store employee Social Security numbers as encrypted data as required by government regulations or industry standards. Only select certain users should be able to view the entire social security number; all other users should only be able to view the last four digits. In addition, you want to ensure that users enter the numbers in the standard social security number format, including the dashes after the third and fifth digits.

Solution

On the standard user object, create an encrypted custom field to store the user's Social Security number. Set the field's Mask Type attribute to hide the first five digits of the social security number, and add field-level help to inform users of the required format. Then, create a validation rule that uses the REGEX() function to verify that the value of the custom field is in the correct format. Finally, create a new custom profile that allows a select group of users to the see the Social Security numbers unmasked.

 Note: To enable encrypted fields for your organization, contact salesforce.com Customer Support.

1. Define the encrypted custom field.

   a. Click **Setup ➤ Customize ➤ Users ➤ Fields**.

   b. In the User Custom Fields related list, click **New**.

   c. Select Text (Encrypted), and click **Next**.

   d. In the Field Label field, enter Social Security Number.

   e. In the Length field, enter 11. This allows the field to accept all nine digits of the Social Security number plus the dashes after the third and fifth digits.

   f. In the Description field, enter Encrypted Social Security Number field.

   g. In the Help Text field, enter information to help your users understand what value to type. For example, Enter your Social Security number. Remember to include dashes after the third and fifth digits.

   h. In the Mask Type field, select Social Security Number. This option hides the first five digits (it hides the first 7 characters) and displays the last four. Only users with profiles that have the "View Encrypted Data" permission selected are able to view all nine digits of the Social Security number.

   i. In the `Mask Character` field, select the character, either an asterisk (*) or an X, to use for hidden characters.

   j. Click **Next**.

   k. In Enterprise, Unlimited, and Developer Editions, set the field-level security to determine whether the field should be visible or read only for specific profiles. These settings determine whether or not the field itself is visible, but do not affect whether or not the user sees the masked or full Social Security number. You will specify the type of masking when you create the custom profile.

   l. Click **Next**.

   m. Leave the `Add Field` and `User Layout` checkboxes selected.

   n. Click **Save**.

2. Create the validation rule.

   a. Click **Setup ➤ Customize ➤ Users ➤ Validation Rules**.

   b. Click **New**.

   c. In the `Rule Name` field, enter `Social Security Number Format Check`.

   d. In the `Description` field, enter `Validates that the Social Security Number is in the correct format`.

   e. Enter the following error condition formula:

```
NOT(
OR(
LEN (Social_Security_Number__c) = 0,
REGEX( Social_Security_Number__c ,
"[0-9]{3}-[0-9]{2}-[0-9]{4}")
)
)
```

   f. Click **Check Syntax** to make sure the syntax is correct.

   g. In the `Error Message` field, enter a message that appears if the user enters a Social Security number in an invalid format. For example, the message might read: `The Social Security number you entered is not in the correct format. The correct format is 999-99-9999.`

   h. In the `Error Location` field, specify whether you want the error message you entered above to appear at the top of the page or next to the field. If you choose `Field`, select the `Social Security Number` field in the adjacent drop-down list.

   i. Click **Save**.

3. Create the custom profile.

a. Click **Setup** ➤ **Manage Users** ➤ **Profiles**.

b. Click **New**.

c. Select an existing profile to copy.

d. Name the new custom profile.

e. Click **Save**.

f. Click **Edit**.

g. In the General User Permissions section, select the `View Encrypted Data` checkbox. This allows users with this profile to see the complete value of encrypted fields instead of the masking characters.

h. Click **Save**.

4. Assign the new custom profile to the users allowed to view the encrypted data.

Discussion

Government regulations and industry standards require many companies to use encryption to protect their most sensitive employee and customer data. Encrypted custom fields can help companies comply with these regulations. Salesforce encrypts these fields with 128-bit keys and uses the AES (Advanced Encryption Standard) algorithm which has been adopted as an encryption standard by the U.S. government. Encrypted custom fields should only be used when regulations require encryption because they involve additional processing and have search-related limitations.

To further protect the confidentiality of encrypted custom field values, Salesforce requires you to specify a mask type for each encrypted field you create. Character masking lets you hide the characters in encrypted field values, allowing users to see the full value of an encrypted custom field only if their profile has the "View Encrypted Data" permission. If your company uses parts of confidential data, such as the last four digits of a person's Social Security or credit card number, to verify the identity of customers, configure your encrypted custom fields to use a mask type that reveals only the those digits, such as the `Last Four Characters Clear` mask type.

In addition to ensuring your data's confidentiality, you also want to ensure its accuracy. Validation rules improve the quality of your data by verifying that the data a user enters in a record meets the standards you specify before the user can save the record. A validation rule contains a formula expression that evaluates the data in one or more fields and returns a value of "True" or "False." If the validation rule returns "True," Salesforce lets the user save the record; otherwise, Salesforce displays an error message.

The validation rule in this recipe uses the `REGEX()` function, which compares the custom field to a regular expression. A regular expression is a string used to describe a format of a string according to certain syntax rules. Salesforce regular expression syntax is based on Java Platform SE 6 syntax; however, backslash characters (\) must be changed to double backslashes (\\) because backslash is an escape character in Salesforce.

See Also

- *Validating Data Based on Fields in Other Records* on page 136
- "About Validation Rules" in the Salesforce online help
- "Operators and Functions" in the Salesforce online help
- "About Encrypted Custom Fields" in the Salesforce online help

Averaging Aggregated Data

Problem

You want to calculate the average value of a numeric field on a set of detail records in a master-detail relationship.

 Note: This recipe has been provided by salesforce.com Training & Certification and is drawn from the expert-led training courses available around the world. Salesforce.com training courses provide an opportunity to get hands-on experience with the Force Platform and Salesforce applications as well as to prepare you to become Salesforce.com Certified. Register for a course at `www.salesforce.com/training`.

Solution

Create two roll-up summary fields: one that sums a numeric field on a detail record and another that counts the number of detail records. Then use a formula field that divides the first roll-up summary field by the second.

To illustrate this example, we'll look at the Job Application and Review objects in the sample Recruiting application. The Job Application object is the master in a master-detail relationship with the Review object. The Review object has a 1-5 rating system. We want to display the average rating on the job application.

To create the first roll-up summary field:

1. Click **Setup ➤ Create ➤ Objects**.
2. Click **Job Application**.
3. In the Custom Fields & Relationships related list, click **New**.
4. Select the `Roll-Up Summary` data type, and click **Next**.
5. In the `Field Label` field, enter `Total Rating`. Once you move your cursor, the `Field Name` text box should be automatically populated with Total_Rating.
6. Click **Next**.
7. In the `Summarized Object` drop-down list, choose Reviews.
8. Under Select Roll-Up Type, select `SUM`.

9. In the `Field to Aggregate` drop-down list, select **Rating**.
10. Leave `All records should be included in the calculation` selected, and click **Next**.
11. Configure the remaining field-level security and page layout settings as desired.
12. Click **Save**.

To create the second roll-up summary field:

1. Click **Setup ➤ Create ➤ Objects**.
2. Click **Job Application**.
3. In the Custom Fields & Relationships related list, click **New**.
4. Select the `Roll-Up Summary` data type, and click **Next**.
5. In the `Field Label` field, enter `Number of Reviews`. Once you move your cursor, the `Field Name` text box should be automatically populated with Number_of_Reviews.
6. Click **Next**.
7. In the `Summarized Object` drop-down list, choose Reviews.
8. Under Select Roll-Up Type, select `COUNT`.
9. Leave `All records should be included in the calculation` selected, and click **Next**.
10. Configure the remaining field-level security and page layout settings as desired.
11. Click **Save**.

To create the formula field:

1. Click **Setup ➤ Create ➤ Objects**.
2. Click **Job Application**.
3. In the Custom Fields & Relationships related list, click **New**.
4. Select the `Formula` data type, and click **Next**.
5. In the `Field Label` field, enter `Average Rating`. Once you move your cursor, the `Field Name` text box should be automatically populated with Average_Rating.
6. Select the `Number` formula return type and click **Next**.
7. Enter the following formula:

```
IF(Number_of_Reviews__c > 0, Total_Rating__c /
Number_of_Reviews__c, 0)
```

8. Click **Next**.
9. Configure the remaining field-level security and page layout settings as desired.
10. Click **Save**.

Discussion

Roll-up summary fields let you easily display values from a set of detail records. Use roll-up summary fields to display the total number of detail records, the sum of all the values in a detail record field, or the highest or lowest value of a detail field.

Before you begin working with roll-up summary fields, note that they are only available on the master object in a master-detail relationship.

When working with merge fields in formulas, use the IF function to ensure that the formula field displays correctly even if they have an invalid value. (For example, an invalid value may occur if the formula divides by zero.) The IF function in this recipe ensures that the formula displays a value when there are one or more reviews, and displays a zero if there are no reviews; otherwise, the formula field might display #Error.

See Also

- *Blocking Record Creation with Cross-Object Validation Rules* on page 133
- "About Roll-Up Summary Fields" in the Salesforce online help
- "Useful Advanced Formula Fields" in the Salesforce online help
- "Considerations for Relationships" in the Salesforce online help

Displaying Fields from a Related Record on a Detail Page

Problem

You want to show field values from a related object on a detail page.

Solution

Use a cross-object formula field to retrieve and display the field values from a related object.

To illustrate this example, we'll look at the Review object in the sample Recruiting application. The Review object is the detail record of the Job Application object. The Job Application object has lookup relationships to the Position and Candidate objects. Using cross-object formulas, we will display the title of the related position and the name of the related candidate on each review record.

1. Click **Setup ➤ Create ➤ Objects**.
2. Click **Review**.
3. In the Custom Fields & Relationships related list, click **New**.
4. Select the Formula data type, and click **Next**.

5. In the `Field Label` field, enter `Position`. Once you move your cursor, the `Field Name` text box should be automatically populated with Position.

6. Select the `Text` formula return type and click **Next**.

7. Click the Advanced Formula tab.

 Note: You can create cross-object formulas only on the Advanced Formula tab.

8. Click the **Insert Field** button.

9. Select `Review` > in the first column. The second column displays all of the Review object's fields as well as its related objects, which are denoted by a greater-than (>) sign .

10. Select `Job Application` > in the second column. The third column displays the fields of the Job Application object.

11. Select `Position>` in the third column. The fourth column displays the fields of the Position object.

   Be sure that you select `Position` > (with the greater-than sign) and not `Position`. The one with the greater-than sign is the Position object, while the one without the greater-than sign is the `Position` lookup field on the Job Application object.

12. Choose `Position Title` in the fourth column.

13. Click **Insert**.

   Your formula now looks like this:

```
Job_Application__r.Position__r.Name
```

14. Click **Next**.

15. Configure the remaining field-level security and page layout settings as desired.

16. Click **Save**.

The Review object now displays the value of the `Position Title` field from the related position record. Next, create a cross-object formula field on the Review object that displays the first and last names of the candidate being reviewed, and we'll use the `HYPERLINK` function so that users can access the candidate's record by clicking the formula field.

1. Click **Setup ➤ Create ➤ Objects**.

2. Click **Review**.

3. In the Custom Fields & Relationships related list, click **New**.

4. Select the `Formula` data type, and click **Next**.

5. In the `Field Label` field, enter `Candidate`. Once you move your cursor, the `Field Name` text box should be automatically populated with Candidate.

6. Select the `Text` formula return type and click **Next**.

7. Click the Advanced Formula tab.
8. From the `Functions` list, double-click `HYPERLINK`.
9. Delete `url` from the `HYPERLINK` function you just inserted, but leave your cursor there.
10. Click the **Insert Field** button, select `Review >`, `Job Application >`, `Candidate >`, `Record ID`, and click **Insert**.
11. Delete `friendly_name` from the `HYPERLINK` function, but leave your cursor there.
12. Click the **Insert Field** button, select `Review >`, `Job Application >`, `Candidate >`, `First Name`, and click **Insert**.
13. Enter a space, click the **Insert Operator** button, and choose Concatenate.
14. Enter another space, then type a blank space enclosed in quotes:

    ```
    " "
    ```

    This appends a blank space after the first name of the candidate.
15. Enter a space, click the **Insert Operator** button, and choose Concatenate once more to add a second ampersand in your formula.
16. Click the **Insert Field** button, select `Review >`, `Job Application >`, `Candidate >`, and `Last Name`, then click **Insert**.
17. Delete `[ target ]` from the `HYPERLINK` function. This is an optional parameter that isn't necessary for our formula field.
18. Click **Check Syntax** to check your formula for errors.

    Your finished formula should look like this:

    ```
    HYPERLINK( Job_Application__r.Candidate__r.Id ,
    Job_Application__r.Candidate__r.First_Name__c & " " &
    Job_Application__r.Candidate__r.Last_Name__c )
    ```

19. Click **Next**.
20. Configure the remaining field-level security and page layout settings as desired.
21. Click **Save**.

Discussion

Cross-object formulas are formulas that span two or more objects by referencing merge fields from related records. They are available anywhere you can use formulas except for default values and summary reports. Use them in calculations or simply to display fields from related objects on detail pages, list views, related lists, and reports.

Each formula can reference up to five related objects, and can span to an object that is five relationships away. For example, consider the following formula we created in the first set of solution steps:

```
Job_Application__r.Position__r.Name
```

This formula spans two relationships: first it spans to the review's related job application (`Job_Application__r`), then to the job application's related position (`Position__r`). The formula ultimately references the position's title (`Name`) on the Position object. Notice that each part of the formula is separated by a period, and that the relationship names consist of the related object followed by `__r`.

In the second cross-object formula field we created, we used the Concatenate (&) operator to join two separate fields (`First_Name__c` and `Last_Name__c`) and inserted a space between them. We also used the `HYPERLINK` function, which lets you to create a hyperlink to any URL or record in Salesforce. Note that the label of the hyperlink can differ from the URL itself, which is especially useful when working with a cross-object formula field that displays a value that a user will want to click. In this recipe, we used the `HYPERLINK` function to let users conveniently access the candidate's record by clicking the `Candidate's Name` field on the Review object.

See Also

- *Validating Data Based on Fields in Other Records* on page 136
- *Averaging Aggregated Data* on page 128
- *The Sample Recruiting App* on page 3
- "About Formulas" in the Salesforce online help
- "Useful Advanced Formula Fields" in the Salesforce online help
- "Formulas: How Do I..." in the Salesforce online help
- "Operators and Functions" in the Salesforce online help

Blocking Record Creation with Cross-Object Validation Rules

Problem

You want to prevent a subset of users from saving a record if certain conditions exist on a related record.

For example, the Recruiting app has the following custom objects:

- Employment Website Information about the cost of posting a position on a particular employment website, such as Monster.com, and the budget the company has allocated for posting on that website.
- Position An open employment opportunity in the company.
- Job Posting A custom junction object between the Employment Website and Position objects that represents a single posting on an employment website.

You want to prevent users from creating a Job Posting record if the record will cause the company to go over its budget for an employment website unless the position was created by the CEO.

 Note: This recipe has been provided by salesforce.com Training & Certification and is drawn from the expert-led training courses available around the world. Salesforce.com training courses provide an opportunity to get hands-on experience with the Force Platform and Salesforce applications as well as to prepare you to become Salesforce.com Certified. Register for a course at `www.salesforce.com/training`.

Solution

Create a cross-object validation rule on the Job Posting object that references one roll-up summary field and two currency fields on the Employment Website object.

Create the roll-up summary field.

1. Click **Setup ➤ Create ➤ Objects**.
2. Click **Employment Website**.
3. In the Custom Fields & Relationships related list, click **New**.
4. Select the `Roll-Up Summary` data type, and click **Next**.
5. In the `Field Label` field, enter `Current Number of Posts`. Once you move your cursor, the `Field Name` text box should be automatically populated with Current_Number_of_Posts.
6. Click **Next**.
7. In the `Summarized Object` drop-down list, choose Job Postings.
8. Under Select Roll-Up Type, select `COUNT`.
9. Leave `All records should be included in the calculation` selected, and click **Next**.
10. Configure the remaining field-level security and page layout settings as desired.
11. Click **Save**.

Create the currency field that stores the price per post.

1. Click **Setup ➤ Create ➤ Objects**.
2. Click **Employment Website**.
3. In the Custom Fields & Relationships related list, click **New**.
4. Select the `Currency` data type, and click **Next**.
5. In the `Field Label` field, enter `Price Per Post`. Once you move your cursor, the `Field Name` text box should be automatically populated with Price_Per_Post.
6. In the `Length` field, enter `7`.
7. In the `Decimal Places` field, enter `2`.
8. Click **Next**.

9. Configure the remaining field-level security and page layout settings as desired.
10. Click **Save**.

Create the currency field that stores the maximum budget.

1. Click **Setup ➤ Create ➤ Objects**.
2. Click **Employment Website**.
3. In the Custom Fields & Relationships related list, click **New**.
4. Select the `Currency` data type, and click **Next**.
5. In the `Field Label` field, enter `Maximum Budget`. Once you move your cursor, the `Field Name` text box is automatically populated with Maximum_Budget.
6. In the `Length` field, enter `7`.
7. In the `Decimal Places` field, enter `2`.
8. Click **Next**.
9. Configure the remaining field-level security and page layout settings as desired.
10. Click **Save**.

Create the validation rule.

1. Click **Setup ➤ Create ➤ Objects**.
2. Click **Job Posting**.
3. In the Validation Rules related list, click **New**.
4. In the `Rule Name` field, enter `Max Posts`.
5. Enter the following error condition formula:

```
(
Position__r.CreatedBy.UserRole.Name
   <>
"CEO"
)
&&
(
Employment_Website__r.Current_Number_of_Posts__c
   *
Employment_Website__r.Price_Per_Post__c
)
   >
(
Employment_Website__r.Maximum_Budget__c
   -
Employment_Website__r.Price_Per_Post__c
)
```

6. In the `Error Message` field, enter `You have exceeded the budget for posting on this employment website.`
7. In the `Error Location` field, select `Top of Page`.
8. Click **Save**.

Discussion

The first part of the validation rule formula spans to the Positions object to verify that the user who created the position is not the CEO. This gives users the flexibility of going over budget on job postings for positions that the CEO has created.

The second part of the validation rule formula spans to the Employment Website object to retrieve three values that are essential to the calculation. First, the formula references the roll up summary field to count how many Job Posting records have been saved for the associated Employment Website record. Then the formula references the currency field that stores the price per post, and multiplies this value by the job record count to anticipate what the total amount spent on this website will be if the job posting is saved. Finally, the formula references the currency field that stores the maximum budget, and subtracts the price per post from this value. Subtracting the price per post from the maximum budget compensates for the fact that Salesforce cannot determine if the record exceeds the budget until after the record is saved.

See Also

- *Validating Data Based on Fields in Other Records* on page 136
- *Averaging Aggregated Data* on page 128
- *The Sample Recruiting App* on page 3
- "About Validation Rules" in the Salesforce online help
- "About Roll-Up Summary Fields" in the Salesforce online help
- "Useful Advanced Formula Fields" in the Salesforce online help
- "Considerations for Relationships" in the Salesforce online help

Validating Data Based on Fields in Other Records

Problem

You want to validate a candidate's ZIP code before saving a candidate record.

Solution

On the Candidate object in the Recruiting app, create a validation rule that uses the VLOOKUP() function to verify the value of the ZIP Code field against a list of valid ZIP codes stored on a custom object.

1. Create a custom object called ZIP Code with the following settings:

Field	Value
Label	ZIP Code

Field	Value
Plural Label	ZIP Codes
Object Name	ZIP_Code
Description	Represents a ZIP code
Context-Sensitive Help Setting	Open the standard Salesforce Help & Training window
Record Name	ZIP Code
Data Type	Text
Allow Reports	No
Allow Activities	No
Track Field History	No
Deployment Status	Deployed
Add Notes & Attachments related list to default page layout	No
Launch New Custom Tab Wizard after saving this custom object	Yes

2. Add the following custom fields to the ZIP code object:

Field Label	Data Type
City	Text (Length: 20)
Latitude	Number
Longitude	Number
State	Text (Length: 20)
State Abbreviation	Text (Length: 2)

3. Create a validation rule on the Candidate object that uses the following formula:

```
LEN(ZIP_Code__c) > 0 &&
(Country__c = "USA" || Country__c = "US") &&
VLOOKUP(
$ObjectType.ZIP_Code__c.Fields.City__c,
$ObjectType.ZIP_Code__c.Fields.Name,
LEFT(ZIP_Code__c,5))
```

```
<> City__c
)
```

Set the `Error Message` to `The ZIP Code you entered is incorrect.`

4. Download the compressed file from http://zips.sourceforge.net. It contains the United States zip codes in Comma-Separated Values (CSV) file format. Extract its contents.

5. Click **Setup ➤ Data Management ➤ Data Loader ➤ Download the Data Loader**.

6. Follow the on-screen instructions to download and install the Data Loader.

7. Use the Data Loader to load the CSV file data into Salesforce.

    a. Launch the Data Loader.

    b. Click **Insert**.

    c. Enter your Salesforce username and password, and click **Login**.

    d. After Salesforce verifies your login credentials, click **Next**.

    e. A popup window appears that displays the record count. Click **OK**.

    f. Select ZIP Code (ZIP_Code_c) and click **Next**.

    g. Click **Create or Edit a Map**.

    h. Map the Salesforce fields to the fields in the CSV file by dragging the Salesforce fields from the top table to the bottom table.

    i. Click **OK**.

    j. Click **Next**.

    k. Click **Finish**.

    l. A popup appears that asks if you want to create new records. Click **Yes**.

Discussion

The `VLOOKUP()` function returns a value by looking up a related value on a custom object. In this recipe, the validation rule uses the `VLOOKUP()` function to search the `Name` field on all the ZIP code records. It searchesuntil it finds one that matches the value of the `ZIP Code` field on the candidate record that the user is trying to save. After finding the matching ZIP code record, the `VLOOKUP()` function checks the record's `City` field to see if it is not equal to the `City` field on the candidate record. If the search for a matching ZIP code record is unsuccessful, or if the values of the `City` fields on either record do not match, the validation rule prevents the candidate record from being saved, and returns the message `The ZIP Code you entered is incorrect.`

See Also

- "About Validation Rules" in the Salesforce online help
- *Storing and Displaying Confidential Information* on page 125
- "Operators and Functions" in the Salesforce online help

- *The Sample Recruiting App* on page 3
- "Useful Advanced Formula Fields" in the Salesforce online help

Using Query String Parameters in a Visualforce Page

Problem

You want to read and set query string parameters in a Visualforce page, either in a custom controller or in the page itself.

Solution

The way to read and set query string parameters depends on whether you access them from a custom controller or directly from a Visualforce page.

To read a query string parameter:

- If you're writing a custom controller, use the `ApexPages` global object variable and `currentPage()` and `getParameters()` methods to get query string parameters. For example, to get the value of the name query parameter in the URL: `https://na1.salesforce.com/001/e?name=value`, use the following line in your custom controller:

```
String value = ApexPages.currentPage().getParameters().get('name');
```

- If you're editing a page, use the `$PageContext` global variable in a merge field.

  For example, suppose you want to add the Open Activities related list to an account detail page, but instead of showing the account's activities, you want to show the activities of a specified contact. To specify the contact, the following page looks for a query string parameter for the contact's ID under the name `relatedId`:

```
<apex:page standardController="Account">
    <apex:pageBlock title="Hello {!$User.FirstName}!">
        You belong to the {!account.name} account.<br/>
        You're also a nice person.
    </apex:pageBlock>
    <apex:detail subject="{!account}" relatedList="false"/>
    <apex:relatedList list="OpenActivities"
                   subject="{!$CurrentPage.parameters.relatedId}"/>
</apex:page>
```

For this related list to render in a saved page, valid account and contact IDs must be specified in the URL. For example, if `001D000000HRgU6` is the account ID and `003D0000000OXDIx` is the contact ID, use the URL

```
https://na3.salesforce.com/apex/MyFirstPage?id=001D000000HRgU6&
relatedId=003D0000000XDIx.
```

To set a query string parameter:

- If you're writing a custom controller, use the `setParameters()` method with `ApexPages.currentPage()` to add a query parameter in a test method. For example:

```
String key = 'name';
String value = 'Caroline';
ApexPages.currentPage().setParameters().put(key, value);
```

 Note: The `setParameters()` method is only valid inside test methods.

- If you're editing a page, you can either construct a URL manually:

```
<apex:outputLink value="http://google.com/search?q={!account.name}">

    Search Google
</apex:outputLink>
```

Or you can use the `<apex:param>` tag as a child tag to write cleaner code:

```
<apex:outputLink value="http://google.com/search">
    Search Google
    <apex:param name="q" value="{!account.name}"/>
</apex:outputLink>
```

 Note: In addition to `<apex:outputLink>`, `<apex:param>` can be a child of other tags such as `<apex:include>` and `<apex:commandLink>`.

See Also

Using AJAX in a Visualforce Page

Problem

You want to use AJAX in a Visualforce page so that only part of the page needs to be refreshed when a user clicks a button or link.

Solution

Use the `reRender` attribute on an `<apex:commandLink>` or `<apex:commandButton>` tag to identify the component that should be refreshed. When a user clicks the button or link, only the identified component and all of its child components are refreshed.

For example, the following page shows a list of contacts. When a user clicks the name of a contact, only the area below the list refreshes, showing the details for the contact:

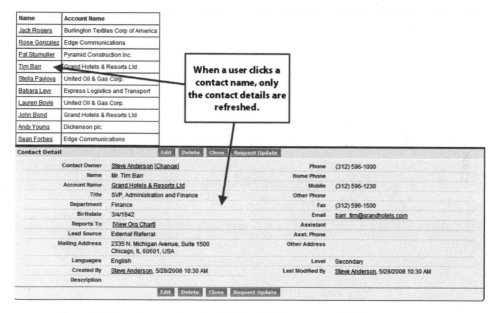

Figure 20: Developers Can Use Embedded AJAX to Refresh Part of a Page

The following markup defines the page from the previous example:

```
<apex:page controller="contactController" showHeader="true"
          tabStyle="Contact">
  <apex:form>
    <apex:dataTable value="{!contacts}" var="c"
                    cellpadding="4" border="1">
      <apex:column>
        <apex:facet name="header"><b>Name</b></apex:facet>
        <apex:commandLink reRender="detail">{!c.name}
```

```
        <apex:param name="id" value="{!c.id}"/>
      </apex:commandLink>
    </apex:column>
    <apex:column>
      <apex:facet name="header"><b>Account Name</b></apex:facet>
      {!c.account.name}
    </apex:column>
  </apex:dataTable>
  </apex:form>
  <apex:outputPanel id="detail">
    <apex:detail subject="{!contact}" title="false"
              relatedList="false"/>
    <apex:relatedList list="ActivityHistories"
                    subject="{!contact}"/>
  </apex:outputPanel>
</apex:page>
```

Notice the following about the markup for this page:

- Setting the reRender attribute of the <apex:commandLink> tag to 'detail' (the id value for the <apex:outputPanel> tag) means that only the output panel component is refreshed when a user clicks the name of a contact.

- The <apex:param> tag sets the id query parameter for each contact name link to the ID of the associated contact record.

- In the <apex:column> tags, an <apex:facet> tag is used to add the header row. Facets are special child components of some tags that can control the header, footer, or other special areas of the parent component. Even though the columns are in an iteration component (the data table), the facets only display once, in the header for each column.

- In the <apex:outputPanel> tag, the details for the currently-selected contact are displayed without the detail section title or complete set of related lists; however, we can add individual related lists with the <apex:relatedList> tag.

The following markup defines the Apex controller class for the page. It includes two methods: one to return a list of the ten most recently modified contacts and one to return a single contact record based on the id query parameter of the page URL:

```
public class contactController {

    // Return a list of the ten most recently modified contacts
    public List<Contact> getContacts() {
        return [SELECT Id, Name, Account.Name, Phone, Email
                FROM Contact
                ORDER BY LastModifiedDate DESC LIMIT 10];
    }

    // Get the 'id' query parameter from the URL of the page.
    // If it's not specified, return an empty contact.
    // Otherwise, issue a SOQL query to return the contact from the
    // database.
    public Contact getContact() {
        Id id = System.currentPageReference().getParameters().get('id');
```

```
        return id == null ? new Contact() : [SELECT Id, Name
                                              FROM Contact
                                              WHERE Id = :id];
    }
}
```

See Also

- *Using Query String Parameters in a Visualforce Page* on page 139
- *Building a Table of Data in a Visualforce Page* on page 31
- *Building a Form in a Visualforce Page* on page 33
- *Creating a Wizard with Visualforce Pages* on page 35

Using Properties in Apex

Problem

You want to create a page that captures input from users, and that input spans multiple sObjects.

Solution

Use a Visualforce page with a custom Apex controller, and give it properties to represent the input fields from Accounts and Contacts.

1. Create a custom controller with a simple `getName` method.

   a. Click **Setup ➤ Develop ➤ Apex Classes**.
   b. Click **New**.
   c. In the editor, add the following content:

   ```
   /*
    * This class is the controller for the
    * NewCustomer VisualForce page.
    * It uses properties to hold values entered
    * by the user.  These values
    * will used to construct multiple SObjects.
    */
   public class Customer {

   // Add properties here

       /* Required method in a VisualForce controller */
       public String getName() {
           return 'Customer';
       }
   ```

```
// Add methods here
// Add queries here
}
```

    d. Click **Quick Save**.

2. Update the controller by replacing the line `// Add properties here` with the following Apex properties:

```
public String companyName {get; set;}
public Integer numEmployees {get; set;}
public String streetAddress {get; set;}
public String cityAddress {get; set;}
public String stateAddress {get; set;}
public String postalCodeAddress {get; set;}
public String countryAddress {get; set;}
public String department {get; set;}
public String email {get; set;}
public String phone {get; set;}
public String firstName {get; set;}
public String lastName {get; set;}
public String title {get; set;}
```

3. Click **Quick Save**.

4. Update the controller by replacing the line `// Add methods here` with the following method for saving the property values to a new pair of Account and Contact objects:

```
/*
 * Takes the values entered by the user in the VisualForce

 * page and constructs Account and Contact sObjects.
 */
public void save() {
    Account a = new Account(
        Name = companyName,
        NumberOfEmployees = numEmployees,
        ShippingStreet = streetAddress,
        ShippingCity = cityAddress,
        ShippingState = stateAddress,
        ShippingPostalCode = postalCodeAddress,
        ShippingCountry = countryAddress);

    insert a;

    Contact c = new Contact(
        FirstName = firstName,
        LastName = lastName,
        Account = a,
        Department = department,
        Email = email,
        Phone = phone,
        Title = title,
        MailingStreet = streetAddress,
```

```
            MailingCity = cityAddress,
            MailingState = stateAddress,
            MailingPostalCode = postalCodeAddress,
            MailingCountry = countryAddress);

        insert c;
    }
```

5. Click **Quick Save**.

6. Update the controller by replacing the line `// Add queries here` with queries for displaying Accounts and Contacts related lists:

```
    /* Used for the Account list at the end of the
       VisualForce page
    */
    public List<Account> getAccountList() {
        return [select name, numberofemployees from account];
    }

    /* Used for the Contact list at the end of the
       VisualForce page
    */
    public List<Contact> getContactList() {
        return [select name, title, department, email, phone
                from contact];
    }
```

7. Click **Save**.

8. Click **SetupDevelop ➤ Pages**.

9. Click **New**.

10. In the name field, enter `newCustomerEntry`.

11. Optionally enter a label and description.

12. In the editor, enter the following markup:

```
<apex:page controller="Customer">
    <apex:form >
        <apex:pageBlock title="New Customer Entry">
            <p>First Name:
                <apex:inputText value="{!firstName}"/></p>
            <p>Last Name:
                <apex:inputText value="{!lastName}"/></p>
            <p>Company Name:
                <apex:inputText value="{!companyName}"/></p>
            <p># Employees:
                <apex:inputText value="{!numEmployees}"/></p>
            <p>Department:
                <apex:inputText value="{!department}"/></p>
            <p>Email:
                <apex:inputText value="{!email}"/></p>
            <p>Phone:
                <apex:inputText value="{!phone}"/></p>
```

```
            <p>Title:
               <apex:inputText value="{!title}"/></p>
            <p>Address</p>
            <p>Street:
               <apex:inputText value="{!streetAddress}"/></p>
            <p>City:
               <apex:inputText value="{!cityAddress}"/></p>
            <p>State:
               <apex:inputText value="{!stateAddress}"/></p>
            <p>Zip:
               <apex:inputText
                value="{!postalCodeAddress}"/></p>
            <p>Country:
               <apex:inputText value="{!countryAddress}"/></p>


            <p><apex:commandButton action="{!save}"
               value="Save New Customer"/></p>
         </apex:pageBlock>
      </apex:form>
   <!-- Add related lists here -->
</apex:page>
```

13. Click **Quick Save**.

14. Update the page by replacing `<!-- Add related lists here -->` with the following markup to displays the related lists from the queries:

```
   <apex:pageBlock title="Accounts">
      <apex:pageBlockTable value="{!accountList}" var="acct">

         <apex:column value="{!acct.Name}"/>
         <apex:column value="{!acct.NumberOfEmployees}"/>
      </apex:pageBlockTable>
   </apex:pageBlock>
   <apex:pageBlock title="Contacts">
      <apex:pageBlockTable value="{!contactList}" var="item">

         <apex:column value="{!item.Name}"/>
         <apex:column value="{!item.Phone}"/>
         <apex:column value="{!item.Title}"/>
         <apex:column value="{!item.Department}"/>
         <apex:column value="{!item.Email}"/>
      </apex:pageBlockTable>
   </apex:pageBlock>
```

15. Click **Save**.

16. Call the page by using the following URL:

`https://salesforce_instance/apex/newCustomerEntry.`

Discussion

You want to ask the user to enter information about a new customer. The fields are used to create both a new account and a new contact associated with that account. Using a Visualforce page lets you present whatever user interface you want, using HTML and Visualforce markup; however, each standard controller in Visualforce corresponds to a single sObject type, such as Account or Contact. To work with more than on sObject type, you need to use a custom controller.

When using a Apex custom controller, the easiest way to do to access data on exposed by the controller is to use Apex properties. The syntax for Apex properties is similar to C# properties. Java-style bean properties (with getters and setters that you create for each property) also work; however, the property syntax used above is much more readable, and makes it easier to distinguish the controller's properties from its actions.

Queries in a custom controller can be used to present data to the user. In this example, queries are used to create two tables that mimic related lists.

Since the form is simple HTML, you can modify it to your style either using HTML or Visualforce components.

Note that when you add a new customer and click **Save**, the account and contact information is displayed in the related lists on the page.

See Also

- *Creating a Child Record When a Parent Record is Created* on page 160
- *Using Dynamic Apex* on page 73

Mass Updating Contacts When an Account Changes

Problem

You want to update the address of all contacts associated with an account whenever the account's address changes.

Solution

Write a trigger in Apex that updates associated contacts when an account is updated. For example:

```
trigger updateContactsOnAddressChange on Account
                                  (before update) {

    // The map allows us to keep track of the accounts that have
```

```
    // new addresses
    Map<Id, Account> acctsWithNewAddresses = new Map<Id, Account>();

    // Trigger.new is a list of the Accounts that will be updated
    // This loop iterates over the list, and adds any that have new
    // addresses to the acctsWithNewAddresses map.
    for (Integer i = 0; i < Trigger.new.size(); i++) {
        if (   (Trigger.old[i].ShippingCity != Trigger.new[i].
                                                ShippingCity)
            || (Trigger.old[i].ShippingCountry != Trigger.new[i].
                                                ShippingCountry)
            || (Trigger.old[i].ShippingPostalCode != Trigger.new[i].
                                                ShippingPostalCode)
            || (Trigger.old[i].ShippingState != Trigger.new[i].
                                                ShippingState)
            || (Trigger.old[i].ShippingStreet != Trigger.new[i].
                                                ShippingStreet))  {
            acctsWithNewAddresses.put(Trigger.old[i].id,
                                    Trigger.new[i]);
        }
    }

    List<Contact> updatedContacts = new List<Contact>();

    //Here we can see two syntatic features of Apex:
    //  1) iterating over an embedded SOQL query
    //  2) binding an array directly to a SOQL query with 'in'

    for (Contact c : [SELECT id, accountId, MailingCity,
                            MailingCountry, MailingPostalCode,
                            MailingState, MailingStreet
                    FROM contact
                    WHERE accountId
                        in :acctsWithNewAddresses.keySet()]) {
      Account parentAccount = acctsWithNewAddresses.get(c.accountId);

      c.MailingCity = parentAccount.ShippingCity;
      c.MailingCountry = parentAccount.ShippingCountry;
      c.MailingPostalCode = parentAccount.ShippingPostalCode;
      c.MailingState = parentAccount.ShippingState;
      c.MailingStreet = parentAccount.ShippingStreet;

      // Rather than insert the contacts individually, add the
      // contacts to a list and bulk insert it. This makes the
      // trigger run faster and allows us to avoid hitting the
      // governor limit on DML statements
      updatedContacts.add(c);
    }
    update updatedContacts;
}
```

See Also

Bulk Processing Records in a Trigger

Problem

You're new to writing triggers, and when you write one for bulk processing, it often runs into Apex governor limits.

Solution

For efficient bulk processing, it's critical that triggers execute a constant number of database queries, regardless of how many records are being processed. Instead of looping over individual records in the `Trigger.old` or `Trigger.new` lists, use maps to organize records based on their ID or another identifying field, and use sets to isolate distinct records.

For example, consider the following lead deduplication trigger, which rejects any new or updated lead that has a duplicate email address:

- The trigger first uses a map to store the updated leads with each lead's email address as the key.
- The trigger then uses the set of keys in the map to query the database for any existing lead records with the same email addresses. For every matching lead, the duplicate record is marked with an error condition.

```
trigger leadDuplicatePreventer on Lead
                         (before insert, before update) {

   Map<String, Lead> leadMap = new Map<String, Lead>();
   for (Lead lead : System.Trigger.new) {

       // Make sure we don't treat an email address that
       // isn't changing during an update as a duplicate.
       if ((lead.Email != null) &&
               (System.Trigger.isInsert ||
               (lead.Email !=
                   System.Trigger.oldMap.get(lead.Id).Email))) {

           // Make sure another new lead isn't also a duplicate
           if (leadMap.containsKey(lead.Email)) {
               lead.Email.addError('Another new lead has the '
                                   + 'same email address.');
           } else {
```

"Bulk Processing Records in a Trigger" contributed by Steve Fisher, Senior Vice President of the Platform Division for salesforce.com

```
                   leadMap.put(lead.Email, lead);
         }
      }
   }

   // Using a single database query, find all the leads in
   // the database that have the same email address as any
   // of the leads being inserted or updated.
   for (Lead lead : [SELECT Email FROM Lead
                     WHERE Email IN :leadMap.KeySet()]) {
      Lead newLead = leadMap.get(lead.Email);
      newLead.Email.addError('A lead with this email '
                           + 'address already exists.');
   }
}
```

See Also

- *Preventing Duplicate Records from Saving* on page 154 contains further discussion of the Apex trigger in this recipe.
- *Controlling Recursive Triggers* on page 150

Controlling Recursive Triggers

Problem

You want to write a trigger that creates a new record as part of its processing logic; however, that record may then cause another trigger to fire, which in turn causes another to fire, and so on. You don't know how to stop that recursion.

Solution

Use a static variable in an Apex class to avoid an infinite loop. Static variables are local to the context of a Web request (or test method during a call to runTests()), so all triggers that fire as a result of a user's action have access to it.

For example, consider the following scenario: frequently a Salesforce user wants to follow up with a customer the day after logging a call with that customer. Because this is such a common use case, you want to provide your users with a helpful checkbox on a task that allows them to automatically create a follow-up task scheduled for the next day.

You can use a `before insert` trigger on Task to insert the follow-up task, but this, in turn, refires the `before insert` trigger before the follow-up task is inserted. To exit out of this recursion, set a static class boolean variable during the first pass through the trigger to inform the second trigger that it should not insert another follow-up task:

Note: For this Apex script to work properly, you first must define a custom checkbox field on Task. In this example, this field is named `Create_Follow_Up_Task__c`.

The following code defines the class with the static class variable:

```
public class FollowUpTaskHelper {

    // Static variables are local to the context of a Web request
    // (or testMethod during a runTests call)
    // Therefore, this variable will be initialized as false
    // at the beginning of each Web request which accesses it.

    private static boolean alreadyCreatedTasks = false;


    public static boolean hasAlreadyCreatedFollowUpTasks() {
        return alreadyCreatedTasks;
    }

    // By setting the variable to true, it maintains this
    // new value throughout the duration of the request
    // (or testMethod)
    public static void setAlreadyCreatedFollowUpTasks() {
        alreadyCreatedTasks = true;
    }


    public static String getFollowUpSubject(String subject) {
        return 'Follow Up: ' + subject;
    }

}
```

The following code defines the trigger:

```
trigger AutoCreateFollowUpTasks on Task (before insert) {

    // Before cloning and inserting the follow-up tasks,
    // make sure the current trigger context isn't operating
    // on a set of cloned follow-up tasks.
    if (!FollowUpTaskHelper.hasAlreadyCreatedFollowUpTasks()) {

        List<Task> followUpTasks = new List<Task>();

        for (Task t : Trigger.new) {
            if (t.Create_Follow_Up_Task__c) {

                // False indicates that the ID should NOT
                // be preserved
                Task followUpTask = t.clone(false);
                System.assertEquals(null, followUpTask.id);
```

```
                 followUpTask.subject =

FollowUpTaskHelper.getFollowUpSubect(followUpTask.subject);
             if (followUpTask.ActivityDate != null) {
                 followUpTask.ActivityDate =
                     followUpTask.ActivityDate + 1; //The day after
             }
             followUpTasks.add(followUpTask);
         }
     }
     FollowUpTaskHelper.setAlreadyCreatedFollowUpTasks();
     insert followUpTasks;
   }
}
```

The following code defines the test methods:

```
// This class includes the test methods for the
// AutoCreateFollowUpTasks trigger.

public class FollowUpTaskTester {
    private static integer NUMBER_TO_CREATE = 4;
    private static String UNIQUE_SUBJECT =
                                  'Testing follow-up tasks';

    static testMethod void testCreateFollowUpTasks() {
        List<Task> tasksToCreate = new List<Task>();
        for (Integer i = 0; i < NUMBER_TO_CREATE; i++) {
            Task newTask = new Task(subject = UNIQUE_SUBJECT,
                    ActivityDate = System.today(),
                    Create_Follow_Up_Task__c = true );
            System.assert(newTask.Create_Follow_Up_Task__c);
            tasksToCreate.add(newTask);
        }

        insert tasksToCreate;
        System.assertEquals(NUMBER_TO_CREATE,
                          [select count()
                           from Task
                           where subject = :UNIQUE_SUBJECT
                           and ActivityDate = :System.today()]);

        // Make sure there are follow-up tasks created
        System.assertEquals(NUMBER_TO_CREATE,
            [select count()
             from Task
             where subject =
             :FollowUpTaskHelper.getFollowUpSubject(UNIQUE_SUBJECT)
             and ActivityDate = :System.today()+1]);
    }

    static testMethod void assertNormalTasksArentFollowedUp() {
        List<Task> tasksToCreate = new List<Task>();
        for (integer i = 0; i < NUMBER_TO_CREATE; i++) {
            Task newTask = new Task(subject=UNIQUE_SUBJECT,
```

```
                                    ActivityDate = System.today(),
                                    Create_Follow_Up_Task__c = false);
            tasksToCreate.add(newTask);
        }

        insert tasksToCreate;
        System.assertEquals(NUMBER_TO_CREATE,
                        [select count()
                         from Task
                         where subject=:UNIQUE_SUBJECT
                         and ActivityDate =:System.today()]);

        // There should be no follow-up tasks created
        System.assertEquals(0,
                [select count()
                 from Task
                 where subject=
                 :FollowUpTaskHelper.getFollowUpSubject(UNIQUE_SUBJECT)

                 and ActivityDate =:(System.today() +1)]);
    }

}
```

See Also

- *Bulk Processing Records in a Trigger* on page 149
- *Comparing Queries Against Trigger.old and Trigger.new* on page 153

Comparing Queries Against Trigger.old and Trigger.new

Problem

You're writing a `before update` or `before delete` trigger and need to issue a SOQL query to get related data for records in the `Trigger.new` and `Trigger.old` lists.

Solution

Correlate records and query results with the `Trigger.newMap` and `Trigger.oldMap` ID-to-SObject maps.

For example, the following trigger uses `Trigger.oldMap` to create a set of unique IDs (`Trigger.oldMap.keySet()`). The set is then used as part of a query to create a list of job applications associated with the candidates being processed by the trigger. For every job application returned by the query, the related candidate is retrieved from `Trigger.oldMap` and prevented from being deleted.

```
trigger candidateTrigger on Candidate__c (before delete) {
    for (Job_Application__c jobApp : [SELECT Candidate__c
                                      FROM Job_Application__c
                                      WHERE Candidate__c
                                      IN :Trigger.oldMap.keySet()]) {

        Trigger.oldMap.get(jobApp.Candidate__c).addError(
                'Cannot delete candidate with a job application');

    }
}
```

Discussion

It's a better practice to use `Trigger.newMap` and `Trigger.oldMap` because you can't assume that directly querying the `Trigger.new` and `Trigger.old` lists will return the same number of records in the same order. Even though these lists are sorted by ID, external operations might change the number of records that are returned and make parallel list processing dangerous.

See Also

- *Bulk Processing Records in a Trigger* on page 149
- *Controlling Recursive Triggers* on page 150

Preventing Duplicate Records from Saving

Problem

You want to prevent users from saving duplicate records based on the value of one or more fields.

Solution

If you can determine whether a record is a duplicate based on the value of a single custom field, select the `Unique` and `Required` checkboxes on that field's definition:

- To edit a custom field on a standard object:

    1. Click **Setup ➤ Customize**.

"Preventing Duplicate Records from Saving" contributed by Steve Fisher, Senior Vice President of the Platform Division for salesforce.com

2. Select the link for the desired object, and click **Fields**.

3. Click **Edit** next to the name of the appropriate field.

- To edit a custom field on a custom object:

  1. Click **Setup ➤ Develop ➤ Objects**.

  2. Click the name of the object on which the field appears.

  3. Click **Edit** next to the name of the field in the Custom Fields and Relationships related list.

The `Unique` and `Required` checkboxes are only available on custom fields. If you want to check for uniqueness based on the value of a single standard field and your edition can't use Apex, you can also use the following workaround:

1. Create a custom field with the same type and label as the standard field. Select the `Unique` and `Required` checkboxes on the custom field's definition page.

2. Replace the standard field with your new custom field on all page layouts.

3. Use field-level security to make the standard field read-only for all user profiles. This prevents any user from mistakenly modifying the standard field through the API, unless the user has the "Modify All Data" profile permission.

4. Define a workflow rule that automatically updates the value of the standard field with the value of the custom field whenever the custom field changes. This ensures that any application functionality that relies on the value of the standard field continues to work properly. (For example, the **Send An Email** button on the Activity History related list relies on the standard `Email` field for a lead or contact.)

Note: Because this is a less-elegant solution than using Apex, creating a trigger on lead is the preferred solution for Unlimited Edition and Developer Edition.

If you need to require uniqueness based on the value of two or more fields, or a single standard field, write an Apex `before insert` and `before update` trigger. For example, the following trigger prevents leads from being saved if they have a matching `Email` field:

- The trigger first uses a map to store the updated leads with each lead's email address as the key.

- The trigger then uses the set of keys in the map to query the database for any existing lead records with the same email addresses. For every matching lead, the duplicate record is marked with an error condition.

```
trigger leadDuplicatePreventer on Lead
                          (before insert, before update) {

  Map<String, Lead> leadMap = new Map<String, Lead>();
  for (Lead lead : System.Trigger.new) {
```

```
            // Make sure we don't treat an email address that
            // isn't changing during an update as a duplicate.
            if ((lead.Email != null) &&
                    (System.Trigger.isInsert ||
                    (lead.Email !=
                        System.Trigger.oldMap.get(lead.Id).Email))) {

                // Make sure another new lead isn't also a duplicate
                if (leadMap.containsKey(lead.Email)) {
                    lead.Email.addError('Another new lead has the '
                                        + 'same email address.');
                } else {
                    leadMap.put(lead.Email, lead);
                }
            }
        }

        // Using a single database query, find all the leads in
        // the database that have the same email address as any
        // of the leads being inserted or updated.
        for (Lead lead : [SELECT Email FROM Lead
                        WHERE Email IN :leadMap.KeySet()]) {
            Lead newLead = leadMap.get(lead.Email);
            newLead.Email.addError('A lead with this email '
                                + 'address already exists.');
        }
    }
}
```

The following class can be used to test the trigger for both single- and bulk-record inserts and updates.

```
public class leadDupePreventerTests{
 static testMethod void testLeadDupPreventer() {

        // First make sure there are no leads already in the system
        // that have the email addresses used for testing
        Set<String> testEmailAddress = new Set<String>();
        testEmailAddress.add('test1@duptest.com');
        testEmailAddress.add('test2@duptest.com');
        testEmailAddress.add('test3@duptest.com');
        testEmailAddress.add('test4@duptest.com');
        testEmailAddress.add('test5@duptest.com');
        System.assert([SELECT count() FROM Lead
                    WHERE Email IN :testEmailAddress] == 0);

        // Seed the database with some leads, and make sure they can
        // be bulk inserted successfully.
        Lead lead1 = new Lead(LastName='Test1', Company='Test1 Inc.',
                        Email='test1@duptest.com');
        Lead lead2 = new Lead(LastName='Test2', Company='Test2 Inc.',
                        Email='test4@duptest.com');
        Lead lead3 = new Lead(LastName='Test3', Company='Test3 Inc.',
                        Email='test5@duptest.com');
        Lead[] leads = new Lead[] {lead1, lead2, lead3};
        insert leads;
```

```
// Now make sure that some of these leads can be changed and
// then bulk updated successfully. Note that lead1 is not
// being changed, but is still being passed to the update
// call. This should be OK.
lead2.Email = 'test2@duptest.com';
lead3.Email = 'test3@duptest.com';
update leads;

// Make sure that single row lead duplication prevention works
// on insert.
Lead dup1 = new Lead(LastName='Test1Dup',
                     Company='Test1Dup Inc.',
                     Email='test1@duptest.com');
try {
   insert dup1;
   System.assert(false);
} catch (DmlException e) {
   System.assert(e.getNumDml() == 1);
   System.assert(e.getDmlIndex(0) == 0);
   System.assert(e.getDmlFields(0).size() == 1);
   System.assert(e.getDmlFields(0)[0] == 'Email');
   System.assert(e.getDmlMessage(0).indexOf(
      'A lead with this email address already exists.') > -1);
}

// Make sure that single row lead duplication prevention works
// on update.
dup1 = new Lead(Id = lead1.Id, LastName='Test1Dup',
                Company='Test1Dup Inc.',
                Email='test2@duptest.com');
try {
   update dup1;
   System.assert(false);
} catch (DmlException e) {
   System.assert(e.getNumDml() == 1);
   System.assert(e.getDmlIndex(0) == 0);
   System.assert(e.getDmlFields(0).size() == 1);
   System.assert(e.getDmlFields(0)[0] == 'Email');
   System.assert(e.getDmlMessage(0).indexOf(
      'A lead with this email address already exists.') > -1);
}

// Make sure that bulk lead duplication prevention works on
// insert. Note that the first item being inserted is fine,
// but the second and third items are duplicates. Note also
// that since at least one record insert fails, the entire
// transaction will be rolled back.
dup1 = new Lead(LastName='Test1Dup', Company='Test1Dup Inc.',
                Email='test4@duptest.com');
Lead dup2 = new Lead(LastName='Test2Dup',
                     Company='Test2Dup Inc.',
                     Email='test2@duptest.com');
Lead dup3 = new Lead(LastName='Test3Dup',
                     Company='Test3Dup Inc.',
                     Email='test3@duptest.com');
```

```
Lead[] dups = new Lead[] {dup1, dup2, dup3};
try {
    insert dups;
    System.assert(false);
} catch (DmlException e) {
    System.assert(e.getNumDml() == 2);
    System.assert(e.getDmlIndex(0) == 1);
    System.assert(e.getDmlFields(0).size() == 1);
    System.assert(e.getDmlFields(0)[0] == 'Email');
    System.assert(e.getDmlMessage(0).indexOf(
        'A lead with this email address already exists.') > -1);
    System.assert(e.getDmlIndex(1) == 2);
    System.assert(e.getDmlFields(1).size() == 1);
    System.assert(e.getDmlFields(1)[0] == 'Email');
    System.assert(e.getDmlMessage(1).indexOf(
        'A lead with this email address already exists.') > -1);
}

// Make sure that bulk lead duplication prevention works on
// update. Note that the first item being updated is fine,
// because the email address is new, and the second item is
// also fine, but in this case it's because the email
// address doesn't change. The third case is flagged as an
// error because it is a duplicate of the email address of the
// first lead's value in the database, even though that value
// is changing in this same update call. It would be an
// interesting exercise to rewrite the trigger to allow this
// case. Note also that since at least one record update
// fails, the entire transaction will be rolled back.
dup1 = new Lead(Id=lead1.Id, Email='test4@duptest.com');
dup2 = new Lead(Id=lead2.Id, Email='test2@duptest.com');
dup3 = new Lead(Id=lead3.Id, Email='test1@duptest.com');
dups = new Lead[] {dup1, dup2, dup3};
try {
    update dups;
    System.assert(false);
} catch (DmlException e) {
    System.debug(e.getNumDml());
    System.debug(e.getDmlMessage(0));
    System.assert(e.getNumDml() == 1);
    System.assert(e.getDmlIndex(0) == 2);
    System.assert(e.getDmlFields(0).size() == 1);
    System.assert(e.getDmlFields(0)[0] == 'Email');
    System.assert(e.getDmlMessage(0).indexOf(
        'A lead with this email address already exists.') > -1);
}

// Make sure that duplicates in the submission are caught when
// inserting leads. Note that this test also catches an
// attempt to insert a lead where there is an existing
// duplicate.
dup1 = new Lead(LastName='Test1Dup', Company='Test1Dup Inc.',
                Email='test4@duptest.com');
dup2 = new Lead(LastName='Test2Dup', Company='Test2Dup Inc.',
                Email='test4@duptest.com');
dup3 = new Lead(LastName='Test3Dup', Company='Test3Dup Inc.',
```

```
                    Email='test3@duptest.com');
    dups = new Lead[] {dup1, dup2, dup3};
    try {
        insert dups;
        System.assert(false);
    } catch (DmlException e) {
        System.assert(e.getNumDml() == 2);
        System.assert(e.getDmlIndex(0) == 1);
        System.assert(e.getDmlFields(0).size() == 1);
        System.assert(e.getDmlFields(0)[0] == 'Email');
        System.assert(e.getDmlMessage(0).indexOf(
            'Another new lead has the same email address.') > -1);
        System.assert(e.getDmlIndex(1) == 2);
        System.assert(e.getDmlFields(1).size() == 1);
        System.assert(e.getDmlFields(1)[0] == 'Email');
        System.assert(e.getDmlMessage(1).indexOf(
            'A lead with this email address already exists.') > -1);
    }

    // Make sure that duplicates in the submission are caught when
    // updating leads. Note that this test also catches an attempt
    // to update a lead where there is an existing duplicate.
    dup1 = new Lead(Id=lead1.Id, Email='test4@duptest.com');
    dup2 = new Lead(Id=lead2.Id, Email='test4@duptest.com');
    dup3 = new Lead(Id=lead3.Id, Email='test2@duptest.com');
    dups = new Lead[] {dup1, dup2, dup3};
    try {
        update dups;
        System.assert(false);
    } catch (DmlException e) {
        System.assert(e.getNumDml() == 2);
        System.assert(e.getDmlIndex(0) == 1);
        System.assert(e.getDmlFields(0).size() == 1);
        System.assert(e.getDmlFields(0)[0] == 'Email');
        System.assert(e.getDmlMessage(0).indexOf(
            'Another new lead has the same email address.') > -1);
        System.assert(e.getDmlIndex(1) == 2);
        System.assert(e.getDmlFields(1).size() == 1);
        System.assert(e.getDmlFields(1)[0] == 'Email');
        System.assert(e.getDmlMessage(1).indexOf(
            'A lead with this email address already exists.') > -1);
    }
  }
}
```

Discussion

The first and most important lesson to learn from this recipe is that you should generally take advantage of native Force Platform functionality if it can solve your problem, rather than writing code. By using the point-and-click tools that are provided, you leverage the power of the platform. Why reinvent the wheel if you can take advantage of a native feature that performs the same functionality? As a result, we indicate in this recipe that you should first determine whether you can simply use the Unique and Required checkboxes on a single custom field definition to prevent duplicates.

If you do need to check for duplicates based on the value of a single standard field, or more than one field, Apex is the best way to accomplish this. Because Apex runs natively on the Force Platform servers, it's far more efficient than a deduplication algorithm that runs in an s-control or Web control. Additionally, Apex can execute every time a record is inserted or updated in the database, regardless of whether the database operation occurs as a result of a user clicking **Save** in the user interface, or as a result of a bulk `upsert` call to the API. S-controls and Web controls can only be triggered when a record is saved through the user interface.

The included trigger is production-ready because it meets the following criteria:

- The trigger only makes a single database query, regardless of the number of leads being inserted or updated.
- The trigger catches duplicates that are in the list of leads being inserted or updated.
- The trigger handles updates properly. That is, leads that are being updated with email addresses that haven't changed are not flagged as duplicates.
- The trigger has full unit test coverage, including tests for both single- and bulk-record inserts and updates.

See Also

Controlling Recursive Triggers on page 150

Creating a Child Record When a Parent Record is Created

Problem

You want to automatically create a new child record when you create a parent record. The child record should be populated with default values from the position.

Solution

Use an Apex trigger to automatically create the child record when a new parent record is created.

For this example, let's automatically create a new interviewer record (child) for the specified hiring manager whenever a new position (parent) is created.

```
trigger AutoCreateInterviewer on Position__c (after insert) {
    List<Interviewer__c> interviewers = new List<Interviewer__c>();

    //For each position processed by the trigger, add a new
    //interviewer record for the specified hiring manager.
    //Note that Trigger.New is a list of all the new positions
    //that are being created.
    for (Position__c newPosition: Trigger.New) {
```

```
            if (newPosition.Hiring_Manager__c != null) {
                interviewers.add(new Interviewer__c(
                            Name = '1',
                            Position__c = newPosition.Id,
                            Employee__c = newPosition.Hiring_Manager__c,
                            Role__c = 'Managerial'));
            }
        }
        insert interviewers;
}
```

See Also

- *Bulk Processing Records in a Trigger* on page 149
- *Controlling Recursive Triggers* on page 150
- *Comparing Queries Against Trigger.old and Trigger.new* on page 153

Using `System.runAs` in Test Methods

Problem

Generally, all Apex scripts run in system mode. The permissions and record sharing of the current user are not taken into account; however, you need to verify if a specific user has access to a specific object.

Solution

The system method `runAs` enables you to write test methods that change user contexts to either an existing user or a new user. All of that user's record sharing is then enforced.

In the following example, a new user is created, based on the standard user profile. In addition, a second user is instantiated, based on the system administrator profile, to demonstrate both ways of generating users for tests. Two accounts are created, and then `runAs` verifies that the standard user cannot view the administrator account.

```
@isTest
private class MyTestClass {

    static testMethod void test1(){

        // Retrieve two profiles, for the standard user and the system

        // administrator, then populate a map with them.

        Map<String,ID> profiles = new Map<String,ID>();
        List<Profile> ps = [select id, name from Profile where name =
```

```
        'Standard User' or name = 'System Administrator'];

for(Profile p : ps){
   profiles.put(p.name, p.id);
}

// Create the users to be used in this test.
// First make a new user.

User standard = new User(alias = 'standt',
email='standarduser@testorg.com',
emailencodingkey='UTF-8',
lastname='Testing', languagelocalekey='en_US',
localesidkey='en_US',
profileid = profiles.get('Standard User'),
timezonesidkey='America/Los_Angeles',
username='standarduser@testorg.com');

insert standard;

// Then instantiate a user from an existing profile

User admin = [SELECT Id FROM user WHERE profileid =
              :profiles.get('System Administrator')];

// Create some test data for testing these two users

List<Account> accnts = new List<Account>();
Account a1 =
   new Account(name='Admin Account', ownerid = admin.id);
Account a2 =
   new Account(name='Standard Account', ownerid = standard.id);

accnts.add(a1);
accnts.add(a2);
insert accnts;

// Confirm that the standard user cannot see the admin account

system.runas(standard){
   accnts.clear();
   accnts = [select id, name from account where id = :a1.id];
   system.debug(accnts.isEmpty() + ' really'+accnts);
   System.assertEquals(accnts.isEmpty(), true);

}
// Confirm that the admin user can see the standard account

system.runas(admin){
   accnts.clear();
   accnts = [select id, name from account where id = :a2.id];
   System.assertEquals(accnts.isEmpty(), false);
}
```

```
    }
}
```

Discussion

Note that this class is defined as `isTest`. Classes defined with the `isTest` annotation do not count against your organization limit of 1 MB for all Apex scripts.

You can only use `runAs` in a test method.

Only the following items use the permissions granted by the user specified with `runAs`:

- dynamic Apex
- methods using `with sharing` or `without sharing`
- shared records

The original permissions are reset after `runAs` completes.

See Also

"Testing and Code Coverage" in the *Apex Language Reference* available at
www.salesforce.com/us/developer/docs/apexcode/index_CSH.htm#apex_testing.htm

Chapter 5

Integrating with other Applications

You can integrate the operation of other applications with Salesforce in a number of ways. This chapter contains recipes for integration using email messaging, mobile applications, and delegated authentication.

Working with Email in Salesforce

By utilizing Apex classes, functions, and interfaces, Salesforce provides you with numerous ways to automate inbound and outbound message processing.

In this chapter, you'll learn how you can use Apex to retrieve contact information from a sender, determine whether an attachment is valid, and create a new contact based on received information. You will also learn how to send an automated reply, and use Visualforce to create powerful email templates.

Integrating with the Mobile Application

You can access and manipulate Salesforce data from your mobile device using the Mobile application.

Integrating with Delegated Authentication

You can create a delegated authentication application to manage single sign-on.

Retrieving Sender Information

Problem

You want to store the name, email address, and other contact information about a user that sends you an email.

Note: For the code sample in this Solution to work, you must have the Recruiting app metadata in your organization. See *The Sample Recruiting App* on page 3.

Solution

Create an Apex class that implements the `InboundEmailHandler` interface. For example:

```
global class ProcessApplicant implements Messaging.InboundEmailHandler
```

For every email received by Salesforce, an `InboundEmail` object is created that contains the contents and attachments of the email. To work with the object, the class needs to define the `handIeInboundEmail` method. For example:

```
global class ProcessApplicant implements Messaging.InboundEmailHandler
{
  global Messaging.InboundEmailResult
handleInboundEmail(Messaging.inboundEmail email,
  Messaging.InboundEnvelope env)
  {
  // Create an inboundEmailResult object for returning the
  // result of the Apex Email Service
  Messaging.InboundEmailResult result = new
  Messaging.InboundEmailResult();

  // Set the result to true, no need to send an email back
  // to the user with an error message
  result.success = true;

  //Return the result for the Apex Email Service
  return result;
  }
}
```

Note: The complete method is listed at the end of *Sending an Automatic Email* on page 171. Use the complete sample for testing.

To continue the implementation, we need to set up a position that a candidate can apply for, format an appropriate email, then incorporate Apex logic into the `handleInboundEmail` method to parse received emails.

1. Create a new Position that a Candidate can apply for:

   a. From the Positions tab, click **New**.

   b. Select Generic Position Record Type from the drop-down list and click **Continue**.

   c. Enter `Doc Writer` as a **Position Name**.

   d. Enter a `Job Description` and any `Responsibilities` you deem appropriate.

   e. Click **Save**.

2. Determine the format of the email which you would like to process. In this example, the email will look like this:

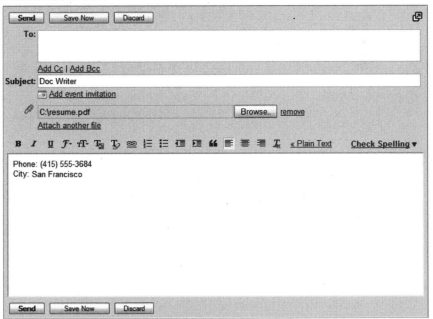

3. Within the `handleInboundEmail` method, create both a new Candidate representing the email sender, and a new Job Application that refers to the Candidate.

```
Candidate__c[] newCandidate = new Candidate__c[0];
Job_Application__c[] newJobApplication = new
Job_Application__c[0];
```

   These objects represent the user sending an email.

4. Within the `handleInboundEmail` method, you can manipulate the contents of the email through the passed `Messaging.inboundEmail` object. Add the following code within the `handleInboundEmail` method:

```
// Stores the email address of the sender
String email = env.fromAddress;
```

```
// Retrieves the first and last name of the sender
String fName =
email.fromname.substring(0,email.fromname.indexOf(' '));
String lName =
  email.fromname.substring(email.fromname.indexOf(' '));

// Looks for a job based on email subject
Position__c pos;
pos = [select ID from Position__c where name =
  :email.subject limit 1];
ID jobId = pos.ID;

// Retrieves content from the email. Splits each line
// by the terminating newline character
String[] emailBody = email.plainTextBody.split('\n', 0);
String phoneNumber = emailBody[0].substring(7);
String city = emailBody[1].substring(6);
```

Discussion

The content of an email can be formatted in any number of ways. Ensure that your code can handle different messages by parsing through the entire body of the email.

See Also

- "Managing Apex Classes" in the *Salesforce online help*
- "Using the InboundEmail Object" in the Salesforce online help
- "Inbound Email" in the *Apex Language Reference* at
  www.salesforce.com/us/developer/docs/apexcode/index_CSH.htm#apex_classes_email_inbound.htm
- "String Methods" in the *Apex Language Reference* at
  www.salesforce.com/us/developer/docs/apexcode/index_CSH.htm#apex_methods_system_string.htm

Retrieving Attachments from an Email

Problem

You want to save an attachment received in an email to a record.

Solution

First, verify that the email has either a binary or text attachment. Then, create an attachment from the file, and associate the attachment with a record.

Note: For the code sample in this Solution to work, you must have the Recruiting app metadata in your organization. See *The Sample Recruiting App* on page 3.

The attachment in this example is a PDF that we will associate with a Job Application as a resume. The following code snippet should be added to the `handIeInboundEmail` method started in *Retrieving Sender Information* on page 166:

```
if (email.binaryAttachments != null &&
  email.binaryAttachments.size() > 0)
{
 for (integer i = 0 ; i < email.binaryAttachments.size() ; i++)
 {
  Attachment a = new Attachment(ParentId = newJobApplication[0].Id,
  Name = email.binaryAttachments[i].filename,
  Body = email.binaryAttachments[i].body);
  insert a;
 }
}
```

 Note: The complete method is listed at the end of *Sending an Automatic Email* on page 171. Use the complete sample for testing.

Discussion

Attachments in email can be of a text or binary (for example, `.pdf` or `.doc`) type. You can define a different action to perform depending on the type of file you have received.

 Caution: Attachment validation is an essential part of processing emails. Malicious code can masquerade as a different file type.

See Also

- "InboundEmail.BinaryAttachment Object" in the *Apex Language Reference* at www.salesforce.com/us/developer/docs/apexcode/Content/apex_classes_email_inbound_binary.htm
- "Using the InboundEmail Object" in the Salesforce online help
- "InboundEmail.TextAttachment Object" in the *Apex Language Reference* at www.salesforce.com/us/developer/docs/apexcode/Content/apex_classes_email_inbound_text.htm

Creating a New Contact from an Email

Problem

You receive an email from a user for the first time, and want to create a new contact based on the sender's information.

Solution

Using Apex code, create a new recipient object and populate it.

For this example, we will assume that the sender of the email is a Candidate, and so we want to create a new object for the data through Apex.

 Note: For the code sample in this Solution to work, you must have the Recruiting app metadata in your organization. See *The Sample Recruiting App* on page 3.

The following code snippets should be added to the `handleInboundEmail` method started in *Retrieving Sender Information* on page 166.

```
Candidate__c[] newCandidate = new Candidate__c[0];

newCandidate.add(new Candidate__c(email__c = email,
first_name__c = fName,
last_name__c = lName,
phone__c = phoneNumber,
city__c = city));
```

Then, insert this object into the database:

```
insert newCandidate;
```

 Note: The complete method is listed at the end of *Sending an Automatic Email* on page 171. Use the complete sample for testing.

See Also

- *Retrieving Sender Information* on page 166
- "Using the InboundEmail Object" in the Salesforce online help
- "Inbound Email" in the *Apex Language Reference* at
  www.salesforce.com/us/developer/docs/apexcode/index_CSH.htm#apex_classes_email_inbound.htm

Sending an Automatic Email

Problem

You want to send an automatic reply to an individual that confirms their email was received.

Solution

The `Messaging.sendEmail` static method needs to be extended to process outbound email messaging. Before calling the function, compose an email by defining various fields, such as the subject and body of the email.

Use the following Apex code within the `handleInboundEmail` method, started in *Retrieving Sender Information* on page 166, to send an automatic response when a candidate's application is received.

 Note: For the code sample in this Solution to work, you must have the Recruiting app metadata in your organization. See *The Sample Recruiting App* on page 3.

The following code snippet should be added to the `handleInboundEmail` method started in *Retrieving Sender Information* on page 166:

```
public static void send (String emailTo)
{
 String[] toAddresses = new String[] {emailTo};

 Messaging.SingleEmailMessage mail = new Messaging.SingleEmailMessage();


 mail.setToAddresses(toAddresses);
 mail.setSenderDisplayName('HR Recruiter');
 mail.setSubject('Your job application has been received!');
 mail.setSaveAsActivity(true);
 mail.setPlainTextBody('Thank you for submitting your resume. We will
 contact you shortly to set an interview.');

 Messaging.sendEmail(new Messaging.SingleEmailMessage[] { mail });
}
```

The following Apex code is a complete version of the `ProcessApplicant` class when assembling the previous recipes:

```
global class ProcessApplicant implements Messaging.InboundEmailHandler
{
 global Messaging.InboundEmailResult
  handleInboundEmail(Messaging.inboundEmail email,
  Messaging.InboundEnvelope env)
 {
  // Create an inboundEmailResult object for returning the result
```

```
// of the Apex Email Service
Messaging.InboundEmailResult result = new
Messaging.InboundEmailResult();

Candidate__c[] newCandidate = new Candidate__c[0];
Job_Application__c[] newJobApplication = new Job_Application__c[0];


// Stores the email address of the sender
String emailAddress = env.fromAddress;

// Retrieves the first and last name of the sender
String fName =
 email.fromname.substring(0,email.fromname.indexOf(' '));
String lName =
 email.fromname.substring(email.fromname.indexOf(' '));

// Looks for a job name based on email subject
Position__c pos;
pos = [select ID from Position__c where name =
 :email.subject limit 1];
ID jobId = pos.ID;

// Retrieves content from the email. Splits each line
// by the terminating newline character
String[] emailBody = email.plainTextBody.split('\n', 0);
String phoneNumber = emailBody[0].substring(6);
String city = emailBody[1].substring(5);

try
{
 newCandidate.add(new Candidate__c(email__c = emailAddress,
 first_name__c = fName,
 last_name__c = lName,
 phone__c = phoneNumber,
 city__c = city));

 insert newCandidate;
}

catch (System.DmlException e)
{
 System.debug('ERROR: Not able to create candidate: ' + e);
}

// Associates a candidate with an application
newJobApplication.add(new Job_Application__c(Position__c = jobId,
candidate__c = newCandidate[0].id));

insert newJobApplication;

if (email.binaryAttachments != null &&
 email.binaryAttachments.size() > 0)
{
 for (integer i = 0 ; i < email.binaryAttachments.size() ; i++)
 {
```

```
   Attachment a = new Attachment(ParentId = newJobApplication[0].Id,

    Name = email.binaryAttachments[i].filename,
    Body = email.binaryAttachments[i].body);
    insert a;
  }
 }

 // Set the result to true, no need to send an email back to the user

 // with an error message
 result.success = true;

 // Return the result for the Apex Email Service
 return result;
}

public static void send (String emailTo)
{

 String[] toAddresses = new String[] {emailTo};

 Messaging.SingleEmailMessage mail =
 new Messaging.SingleEmailMessage();

 mail.setToAddresses(toAddresses);
 mail.setSenderDisplayName('HR Recruiter');
 mail.setSubject('Your job application has been received');
 mail.setSaveAsActivity(true);
 mail.setPlainTextBody('Thank you for submitting your resume!
  We will contact you shortly to set an interview date.');

 Messaging.sendEmail(new Messaging.SingleEmailMessage[] { mail });
 }
}
```

See Also

"Outbound Email" in the *Apex Language Reference* at
http://www.salesforce.com/us/developer/docs/apexcode/index_CSH.htm#apex_classes_email_outbound.htm

Activating Email Services

Problem

You want to create an email service that runs an Apex class.

Solution

You must activate an email service to automatically process the contents of an Apex class.

For the `ProcessApplicant` class you completed in *Sending an Automatic Email* on page 171, an email service will allow the `handleInboundEmail()` and `send()` functions to properly execute.

To associate `ProcessApplicant` with an email service:

1. Click **Setup ➤ Develop ➤ Email Services**.
2. Click **New Email Service**.
3. Enter `jobApplication` for the **Email Service Name**.
4. Enter `ProcessApplicant` for the **Apex Class**.
5. Click **Save and New Email Address**.
6. Since the **Email Address** and **Context User** fields have been automatically populated, click **Save**.

Salesforce then generates an email address unique to the email service. All email sent to this inbound email address runs the `ProcessApplicant` class.

Discussion

By themselves, Apex classes implementing `Messaging.InboundEmailHandler` won't achieve much unless they are activated. Utilizing them as an email service is the final step to process received messages.

See Also

- "What are Email Services?" in the *Salesforce Online Help*
- "Using the InboundEmail Object" in the Salesforce online help
- "Inbound Email" in the *Apex Language Reference* at http://www.salesforce.com/us/developer/docs/apexcode/index_CSH.htm#apex_classes_email_inbound.htm

Using Visualforce Email Templates

Problem

You want to send an email using a Visualforce email template.

Solution

First, create a Visualforce email template through the email template wizard, then send it to a contact, user, or lead in your organization.

Note: To create a Visualforce email template, you must have the "Customize Application" permission enabled.

Create a Visualforce email template:

1. Click **Setup ➤ Email ➤ My Templates**. If you have permission to edit public templates, click **Setup ➤ Communication Templates ➤ Email Templates**.
2. Click **New Template**.
3. Choose `Visualforce` and click **Next**.
4. Choose a folder in which to store the template.
5. Select the `Available For Use` checkbox if you would like this template offered to users when sending an email.
6. Enter an `Email Template Name`.
7. If necessary, change the `Unique Name`. This is a unique name used to refer to the component when using the Force Platform API. In managed packages, this unique name prevents naming conflicts on package installations. It can contain only alphanumeric characters and must begin with a letter. With the `Template Unique Name` field, a developer can change certain components' names in a managed package and the changes are reflected in a subscriber's organization.
8. Select an `Encoding` setting to determine the character set for the template.
9. Enter a `Description` of the template. Both template name and description are for your internal use only.
10. Enter the subject line for your template in `Email Subject`.
11. In the `Recipient Type` drop-down list, select the type of recipient that will receive the email template.
12. Optionally, in the `Related To Type` drop-down list, select the object from which the template will retrieve merge field data.
13. Click **Next**.
14. Enter markup text for your Visualforce email template.
15. Click **Save** to save your changes and view the details of the template, or click **Quick Save** to save your changes and continue editing your template. Your Visualforce markup must be valid before you can save your template.

 Note: The maximum size of a Visualforce email template cannot exceed 1 MB.

The following Visualforce markup sends a list of cases associated with an account to a contact, as well as creates and attaches a PDF containing the same information:

```
<messaging:emailTemplate recipientType="Contact"
 relatedToType="Account"
```

```
subject="Case report for Account: {!relatedTo.name}"
replyTo="support@acme.com">

<messaging:htmlEmailBody>
 <html>
  <body>

  <style type="text/css">
   p {font-family: arial; size: 8pt;}
   th {font-size: 11px; font-face: arial;
    background: #CCCCCC; border-width: 1;  text-align: center }
   td {font-size: 11px; font-face: verdana }
   table {border: solid #CCCCCC; border-width: 1}
   tr {border: solid #CCCCCC; border-width: 1}
  </style>

  <p>Dear {!recipient.name},</p>
  <p>Below is a list of cases related to  {!relatedTo.name}.</p>
  <table border="0" >
   <tr>
    <th>Case Number</th><th>Subject</th>
    <th>Creator Email</th><th>Status</th>
   </tr>
   <apex:repeat var="cx" value="{!relatedTo.Cases}">
    <tr>
    <td><a href =
"https://na1-blitz01.soma.salesforce.com/{!cx.id}">{!cx.CaseNumber}
    </a></td>
    <td>{!cx.Subject}</td>
    <td>{!cx.Contact.email}</td>
    <td>{!cx.Status}</td>
   </tr>
   </apex:repeat>
  </table>
  <p/>
  <center>
   <apex:outputLink value="http://www.salesforce.com">
    For more detailed information login to Salesforce.com
   </apex:outputLink>
   </center>
  </body>
 </html>
</messaging:htmlEmailBody>

<messaging:attachment renderas="pdf" filename="cases.pdf">
 <html>
  <body>
  <apex:datatable border="2" cellspacing="5" var="cx"
   value="{!relatedTo.Cases}">
   <apex:facet name="header">Cases currently associated with
   {!relatedTo.name}</apex:facet>
   <apex:column value="{!cx.CaseNumber}" headerValue="Case Number"/>

   <apex:column value="{!cx.Subject}" headerValue="Subject"/>
   <apex:column value="{!cx.Contact.email}"
```

```
        headerValue="Creator's Email" />
      <apex:column value="{!cx.Status}" headerValue="Status" />
    </apex:datatable>
    </body>
    </html>
  </messaging:attachment>
</messaging:emailTemplate>
```

Discussion

Every Visualforce email template must contain either an `htmlEmailBody` tag or a `plainTextEmailBody` tag. Visualforce email templates cannot be used to send mass email.

See Also

*   "Defining Visualforce Pages" in the *Salesforce online help*
*   "Creating Visualforce Email Templates" in the *Salesforce online help*

Using Apex to Update Salesforce Data in the Mobile Application

Problem

You want to modify related lists of Salesforce records in the mobile application, even when the records are not available locally on the mobile phone. Optionally, you'll use a Bluetooth peripheral device to update the data in the records.

Solution

For this recipe, let's assume that your organization sells servers. Your field service representatives want to update related list information on records from their mobile devices while at customer sites. For example, if they replace a broken component in a server, they want to be able to enter the new component's serial number and update the server record. The server will then be associated with the new component instead of the replaced one.

To accomplish this, we'll create three custom objects and some custom fields. We'll use an Apex trigger to update the server record when the field service representatives replace a component.

Before starting this recipe, make sure you meet the following requirements:

*   **Mobile Licenses:** Verify that your Developer Edition organization has mobile licenses. To find out, simply edit your user record. If the **Mobile User** checkbox is visible, select it, then edit your profile and enable the "Manage Mobile Configurations" permission. If the **Mobile User** checkbox is already selected, you don't need to do anything else.

If the **Mobile User** checkbox isn't available on your user record, you signed up for your account before mobile licenses were provided by default. Visit Developer Force and click **Getting Started** to sign up for a new Developer Edition organization.

- **Mobile Devices:** Verify that your mobile device will run Force Platform Mobile. See Force Platform Mobile Supported Devices in the Salesforce online help.

  If your mobile device is not supported, you can download and install the BlackBerry simulator package so you can run the mobile application on a simulator.

To use Apex to update data in Force Platform Mobile:

First, create a custom object named Server that has a lookup relationship to Account. This object allows your organization to keep track of the servers housed at each customer's site.

1. Click **Setup ➤ Create ➤ Objects ➤ New Custom Object**.
2. Enter the following information:

   - `Label:` Server
   - `Plural Label:` Servers

3. Accept the remaining defaults and click **Save**.
4. In the Custom Fields & Relationships related list, click **New** and define a field with the following attributes:

   - `Data Type:` Lookup Relationship
   - `Related To:` Account
   - `Field Label:` Account
   - `Field Name:` Account
   - `Field-Level Security:` Visible for all profiles
   - `Add Related List:` On all page layouts

5. In the Custom Fields & Relationships related list, click **New** and define a second field with the following attributes:

   - `Data Type:` Text Area
   - `Field Label:` Description
   - `Field Name:` Description
   - `Field-Level Security:` Visible for all profiles
   - `Add Related List:` On all page layouts

Next, create a custom object named Component that has a lookup relationship to Server. This object represents the various components that can be installed inside a server.

1. Click **Setup ➤ Create ➤ Objects ➤ New Custom Object**.

2. Enter the following information:

- `Label:` Component
- `Plural Label:` Components

3. Accept the remaining defaults and click **Save**.
4. In the Custom Fields & Relationships related list, click **New** and define a field with the following attributes:

- `Data Type:` Master-Detail Relationship
- `Related To:` Server
- `Field Label:` Server
- `Field Name:` Server
- `Field-Level Security:` Visible for all profiles
- `Add Related List:` On all page layouts

5. In the Custom Fields & Relationships related list, click **New** and define a second field with the following attributes:

- `Data Type:` Checkbox
- `Field Label:` Operational
- `Field Name:` Operational
- `Field-Level Security:` Visible for all profiles
- `Add Related List:` On all page layouts

6. In the Custom Fields & Relationships related list, click **New** and define a third field with the following attributes:

- `Data Type:` Picklist
- `Field Label:` Type
- `Values:` Motherboard, RAM, CPU, Network Card, Power Supply
- `Field Name:` Type
- `Field-Level Security:` Visible for all profiles
- `Add Related List:` On all page layouts

7. By default, one of the standard fields for the Component object is `Component Name`; however, the field service representatives reference the components by serial number. We'll change the standard field name to `Component Serial Number`. In the Standard Fields related list, click **Edit** next to **Component Name**.
8. In the `Record Name` field, type `Component Serial Number`.
9. Click **Save**.

Next, create a custom object named Replacement. This object allows the field service representatives to enter information about the new component.

1. Click **Setup ➤ Create ➤ Objects ➤ New Custom Object**.

2. Enter the following information:

   - `Label:` Replacement
   - `Plural Label:` Replacements

3. Accept the remaining defaults and click **Save**.
4. In the Custom Fields & Relationships related list, click **New** and define a field with the following attributes:

   - `Data Type:` Date
   - `Field Label:` Date
   - `Field Name:` Date
   - `Field-Level Security:` Visible for all profiles
   - `Add Related List:` On all page layouts

5. In the Custom Fields & Relationships related list, click **New** and define a second field with the following attributes:

   - `Data Type:` Lookup Relationship
   - `Related To:` Component
   - `Field Label:` New Component
   - `Field Name:` New Component
   - `Field-Level Security:` Hidden from all profiles
   - `Add Related List:` Hidden from all page layouts

6. In the Custom Fields & Relationships related list, click **New** and define a third field with the following attributes:

   - `Data Type:` Lookup Relationship
   - `Related To:` Component
   - `Field Label:` Replaced Component
   - `Field Name:` Replaced Component
   - `Field-Level Security:` Hidden from all profiles
   - `Add Related List:` Hidden from all page layouts

     In the next two steps, we'll create text versions of the `New Component` and `Replaced Component` lookup fields. This is because Force Platform Mobile handles lookup fields differently than the Salesforce website. Users can type in lookup fields on the website, but not in the mobile application. We want the field representatives to be able to quickly enter the serial number of the new component, so we'll create text fields to replace the lookup fields.

     To further complicate matters, mobile configurations deliver only a subset of a user's data to the mobile application. There is a possibility that the record the user is trying to look up is not stored locally on the mobile device. By allowing a user to enter text, the mobile application can send the information to Salesforce when the record is saved, and then Salesforce validates the user's text entry against the component records with the Apex trigger.

Additionally, if we want to pair the mobile device with a Bluetooth barcode scanner so that the field representatives can simply scan the serial numbers of the new and replaced components, it is imperative to set up the fields as text fields. For information about using a barcode reader, see the *Discussion* at the end of this recipe.

7. In the Custom Fields & Relationships related list, click **New** and define a fourth field with the following attributes:

   - `Data Type:` Text
   - `Field Label:` New Component Serial Number
   - `Field Name:` New Component Serial Number
   - `Field-Level Security:` Visible for all profiles
   - `Add Related List:` On all page layouts

8. In the Custom Fields & Relationships related list, click **New** and define a fifth field with the following attributes:

   - `Data Type:` Text
   - `Field Label:` Replaced Component Serial Number
   - `Field Name:` Replaced Component Serial Number
   - `Field-Level Security:` Visible for all profiles
   - `Add Related List:` On all page layouts

Next, create an Apex trigger on the Replacement object so that a server's components are automatically updated when a field representative creates a replacement record.

1. Click **Setup ➤ Create ➤ Objects ➤ Replacement**.
2. In the Triggers related list, click **New**.
3. In the `Body` text box, enter the following Apex trigger code:

```
trigger replacementPart on Replacement__c (before insert) {
    for(Replacement__c r : Trigger.new) {
        //first, find the old component
        //(the one we are replacing)
        Component__c oldCompInfo = [select id, type__c, Server__c
            from component__c where Name=
            :r.Replaced_Component_Serial_Number__c];
        //find the new component by name
        Component__c newCompInfo = [select id, type__c from
            component__c where
            Name=:r.New_Component_Serial_Number__c];
        if(oldCompInfo == null)
            r.Replaced_Component_Serial_Number__c.addError(
```

```
                        'The serial number you entered does not match '+
                        'any existing components.');
            if(newCompInfo == null)
                r.New_Component_Serial_Number__c.addError(
                    'The serial number you entered does not match '+
                    'any existing components.');
            //set the Replacement part's fields
            r.Replaced_Component__c = oldCompInfo.Id;
            r.New_Component__c = newCompInfo.Id;
            if(newCompInfo.type__c != oldCompInfo.type__c)
                r.New_Component__c.addError(
                'The new component type must be ' +
                'the same as the replaced component type.');
            //update the old component's Server__c to null
            Component__c oldComp = new Component__c(
                Id= oldCompInfo.Id, Server__c=null);
            //update the new component's Server__c
            //to the old component's Server__c
            component__c newComp = new Component__c(
                Id=r.New_Component__c, Server__c=
                    oldCompInfo.Server__c);
            //update both components
            List<Component__c> comps = new List<Component__c>();
            comps.add(oldComp);
            comps.add(newComp);
            update(comps);
            r.Date__c = System.Today();
        }
    }
```

4. Click **Save**.

Next, create a mobile configuration and mobilize the new objects.

1. Click **Setup ➤ Mobile Configurations ➤ New Mobile Configuration**.
2. In the `Name` field, type `Field Service`.
3. Select the `Active` checkbox.
4. Select the `Mobilize Recent Items` checkbox.
5. Select your name in the Available Members list box and click **Add**.
6. Click **Save**.
7. In the Data Sets related list, click **Edit**.
8. Click **Add...**.
9. Select **Server** and click **OK**.
10. Click the **Data Sets** node in the tree, click **Add...**. Select **Component**, and click **OK**.
11. Click the **Data Sets** node in the tree, and click **Add...**. Select **Replacement**, and click **OK**.

If this was a real mobile configuration for field representatives, you would probably also mobilize other objects, like Account and Case. For the recipe, we just need to mobilize the custom objects we created.

12. Click **Done**.

Finally, test the Apex trigger in the mobile application:

1. On the Salesforce website, create a server record and three related component records so you have some data to work with in the mobile application.

- `Server:` IBM BladeCenter S
- `Component Serial Number:` 100000; `Type:` CPU
- `Component Serial Number:` 100001; `Type:` Motherboard
- `Component Serial Number:` 100002; `Type:` Power Supply

2. Create one more component record that is not associated with any server record. Enter 100003 as the `Component Serial Number`, and set the `Type` to CPU.

3. Install the mobile application on your device. For installation instructions, see Installing Force Platform Mobile in the Salesforce online help. If you're using a BlackBerry simulator, the mobile application is already installed on the simulator device; you just need to activate your Salesforce Developer Edition account after launching Force Platform Mobile for the first time.

4. In the mobile application, select the Replacement tab.

5. Open the menu and select **New**.

6. In the `Replaced Component Serial Number` field, type `100000`.

7. In the `New Component Serial Number` field, type `100003`.

 Tip: Pairing the mobile device with a Bluetooth barcode scanner allows the field service representative to enter the serial numbers in the replacement record fields by scanning the barcodes.

8. Open the menu and select **Save**.

The mobile application sends the record to Salesforce and the new component is associated with the server record.

Discussion

To make this solution even more effective, implement the Apex trigger and give the field representatives barcode scanners so that they can quickly scan the serial numbers when replacing components. Many barcode scanners can operate wirelessly using a Bluetooth connection. Just pair the barcode scanner with a Bluetooth-enabled mobile device, and you'll be able to use the scanner for entering data in the mobile application.

See Also

- For information about extending your Visualforce pages to mobile users, see *Retrieving a User's Location from a GPS-enabled BlackBerry Smartphone* on page 184.
- For information about deploying the mobile solution to Salesforce users, see the *Force Platform Mobile Implementation Guide* at `http://na1.salesforce.com/help/doc/en/salesforce_mobile_implementation.pdf`.

Retrieving a User's Location from a GPS-enabled BlackBerry Smartphone

Problem

You want to capture the location where your mobile users enter Salesforce data by retrieving the GPS coordinates from the BlackBerry smartphone when users save a record.

Solution

Write a Visualforce page that sales representatives can use when logging sales visits. The Visualforce page contains JavaScript that sends the device's longitude and latitude to Salesforce when the record is saved. After writing the Visualforce page, we'll create a tab for the page and add the tab to the mobile application.

Before starting this recipe, make sure you complete the following prerequisites:

- **Mobile Licenses:** Verify that your Developer Edition organization has mobile licenses. To find out, simply edit your user record. If the **Mobile User** checkbox is visible, select it, then edit your profile and enable the "Manage Mobile Configurations" permission. If the **Mobile User** checkbox is already selected, you don't need to do anything else.

  If the **Mobile User** checkbox isn't available on your user record, you signed up for your account before mobile licenses were provided by default. Visit Developer Force and click **Getting Started** to sign up for a new Developer Edition organization.

- **Mobile Devices:** Verify that your BlackBerry smartphone can use Force Platform Mobile. See Force Platform Mobile Supported Devices in the Salesforce online help.

- **GPS Receiver:** Your BlackBerry smartphone must have an internal GPS receiver or an external Bluetooth GPS receiver; make sure that the receiver is enabled. To find out if your BlackBerry smartphone's GPS receiver is on, select **Options** ➤ **Advanced** ➤ **GPS** or **Options** ➤ **Advanced** ➤ **Location Based Services**.

  If your device does not meet these requirements, download and install the BlackBerry simulator package.

First, create a custom object named Sales Visit. This object allows sales representatives to enter information in Salesforce after making a sales visit.

1. Click **Setup ➤ Create ➤ Objects ➤ New Custom Object**.
2. Enter the following information:

   - `Label:` Sales Visit
   - `Plural Label:` Sales Visits
   - `Description:` Include a brief description so other developers know what this object does.

3. Accept the remaining defaults and click **Save**.
4. In the Custom Fields & Relationships related list, click **New** and define a field with the following attributes:

   - `Data Type:` Text Area
   - `Field Label:` Description
   - `Field Name:` Description
   - `Field-Level Security:` Visible for all profiles
   - `Add Related List:` Select for all page layouts

5. In the Custom Fields & Relationships related list, click **New** and define a second field with the following attributes:

   - `Data Type:` Number
   - `Field Label:` Longitude
   - `Length:` 3
   - `Decimal Places:` 10
   - `Field Name:` Longitude
   - `Field-Level Security:` Visible for all profiles
   - `Add Related List:` Select for all page layouts

6. In the Custom Fields & Relationships related list, click **New** and define a third field with the following attributes:

   - `Data Type:` Number
   - `Field Label:` Latitude
   - `Length:` 3
   - `Decimal Places:` 10
   - `Field Name:` Latitude
   - `Field-Level Security:` Visible for all profiles
   - `Add Related List:` Select for all page layouts

Create an Apex class that mimics the Sales Visit object but changes the save behavior:

1. Click **Setup ➤ Develop ➤ Apex Classes**, then click **New**.
2. Enter the following code:

```
public class visitController {

    public Sales_Visit__c visit {get;set;}

    public visitController() {
        visit = new Sales_Visit__c();
    }

    public PageReference save() {
        insert visit;
        visit = new Sales_Visit__c();
        return null;
    }
}
```

Normally after saving a record, the record's detail page displays, along with the tabs and sidebar. The Apex class suppresses all these screen elements—which would overload the mobile device's small screen—by displaying a blank Sales Visit record instead.

3. Click **Save**.

Create a Visualforce page that sends the user's GPS coordinates when the sales visit record is saved.

1. Click **Setup ➤ Develop ➤ Pages ➤ New**.
2. In the `Label` field, enter `Sales Visit Form`.
3. In the `Name` field, enter `Sales_Visit_Form`.
4. Replace the generic markup with the following Visualforce component:

```
<apex:page controller="visitController" showHeader="false"
  setup="true" standardStylesheets="false" id="ServiceForm">
  <apex:form id="form">
  <apex:pageBlock id="block">
    Sales Visit Name: <br />
      <apex:inputField value="{!visit.name}" /><br />
    Sales Visit Description: <br />
      <apex:inputField value="{!visit.Description__c}" />
                                                     <br />
    Longitude: <br />
      <apex:inputField value="{!visit.Longitude__c}"
        id="longitude" /><br />
    Latitude: <br />
      <apex:inputField value="{!visit.Latitude__c}"
        id="latitude" /><br />
    <apex:commandButton action="{!save}" value="Save!" />
  </apex:pageBlock>
  </apex:form>
  <script>
```

```
if( window.blackberry &&
  blackberry.location.GPSSupported) {
      blackberry.location.setAidMode(2);
      document.getElementById('{!
      $Component.form.block.longitude}').value =
          blackberry.location.longitude;
      document.getElementById('{!
      $Component.form.block.latitude}').value =
          blackberry.location.latitude;
  }
  else
  {
      document.write("You cannot view this page because " +

                     "your device does not support GPS.");

  }
</script>
</apex:page>
```

5. Click **Save**.

Create a tab for the Visualforce page.

1. Click **Setup ➤ Create ➤ Tabs ➤ New**.
2. Select Sales_Visit_Form from the Visualforce Page drop-down.
3. In the `Tab Label` field, enter `Sales Visit`.
4. Select a tab style.
5. Select the **Mobile Ready** checkbox.
6. Click **Next**.
7. Click **Next** again.
8. Click **Save**.

Create a mobile configuration and mobilize the new Visualforce page.

1. Click **Setup ➤ Mobile Configurations ➤ New Mobile Configuration**.
2. In the `Name` field, type `Sales Representative`.
3. Select the `Active` checkbox.
4. Select the `Mobilize Recent Items` checkbox.
5. Select your name in the Available Members list box, and then click **Add**.
6. Click **Save**.
7. In the Data Sets related list, click **Edit**.
8. Click **Add....**
9. Select **Account** and click **OK**.
10. Click the **Data Sets** node in the tree, and click **Add....** Select **Opportunity** and click **OK**.
11. Click the **Data Sets** node in the tree and click **Add....** Select **Lead** and click **OK**.
12. Click **Done**.

13. In the Mobile Tabs related list, click **Customize Tabs**.
14. Select the Account, Opportunity, Lead, and Sales Visit tabs and click **Add**.

    If the Sales Visit tab isn't in the Available Tabs list, you might not have selected the **Mobile Ready** checkbox when creating the Visualforce tab.

15. Click **Save**.

Test the Visualforce page in the mobile application.

1. Install the mobile application on your device. For installation instructions, see "Installing Force Platform Mobile" in the Salesforce online help. If you're using a BlackBerry simulator, the mobile application is already installed on the simulator device; you just need to activate your Salesforce Developer Edition account after launching Force Platform Mobile for the first time.

   If you already completed *Using Apex to Update Salesforce Data in the Mobile Application* on page 177, you don't need to reinstall the application. Simply open the mobile application on your BlackBerry smartphone, open the main menu, and select **System Info**. Select **Refresh All Data** to update the data on your device.

2. In the mobile application, select the Sales Visit tab.
3. Open the menu, and select **New**.
4. In the `Description` field, enter a description of the sales visit.
5. Open the menu and select **Save**.

   The record is saved and sent to Salesforce along with the user's GPS location.

   The application permissions on the BlackBerry smartphone control whether or not the browser is allowed to send the GPS coordinates. If the browser is not permitted to send the information, the Visualforce page doesn't display. To ensure that all mobile Salesforce users are able to properly view the page, the BlackBerry administrator should globally enable the application permissions on the BlackBerry Enterprise Server. To enable the permission on your BlackBerry smartphone:

   a. Select **Options** ➤ **Advanced Options** ➤ **Applications**.
   b. Highlight **Browser**, open the main menu, and select **Edit Default Permissions**.
   c. Change the value of `Location (GPS)` to Allow.

Discussion

Currently, the JavaScript class used in this recipe is only available for BlackBerry smartphones.

See Also

Using Apex to Update Salesforce Data in the Mobile Application on page 177

Enabling Single Sign-On with the Force Platform

Problem

You want to validate usernames and passwords for Salesforce against your corporate user database or another client application rather than having separate user passwords managed by Salesforce.

Solution

Salesforce offers two ways to use single sign-on:

- **Delegated Authentication:** You must request that this feature be enabled by salesforce.com. This recipe explains delegated authentication in more detail.
- **Federated Authentication using SAML:** For more information, see "Configuring SAML Settings for Single Sign-On" in the Salesforce online help.

When delegated authentication is enabled, salesforce.com does not validate a user's password. Instead, salesforce.com makes a Web services call to your organization to establish authentication credentials for the user.

 Note: Contact salesforce.com to enable delegated authentication for your organization if it is not already enabled.

To enable delegated authentication for your organization, build your delegated authentication Web service, and then configure your Salesforce organization to enable the Web service.

First, build your delegated authentication Web service:

1. In Salesforce, click **Setup ➤ Develop ➤ API ➤ Download Delegated Authentication WSDL** to download the Web Services Description Language (WSDL) file, `AuthenticationService.wsdl`.

   The WSDL describes the delegated authentication service and can be used to automatically generate a server-side stub to which you can add your specific implementation. For example, in the WSDL2Java tool from Apache Axis, you can use the `--server-side` switch. In the wsdl.exe tool from .NET, you can use the `/server` switch.

   A simple C# implementation of delegated authentication is shown below. The sample uses Microsoft .NET v1.1 and works with IIS6 on a Windows 2003 server. See `wiki.apexdevnet.com/index.php/How_to_Implement_Single_Sign-On_with_Force.com` for a more complex sample that demonstrates a solution using an authentication token.

```csharp
using System;
using System.DirectoryServices;

namespace samples.sforce.com
{
  /// <summary>
  /// This is a very basic implemention of an
  /// authentication service for illustration purposes.
  /// This sample should only be used
  /// with a HTTPS Delegated Gateway URL.
  /// It simply connects to your Active Directory
  /// server using the credentials that are passed in.
  /// If there is a bad username/password combination,
  /// it throws an exception and returns false;
  /// otherwise the credentials are ok
  /// and it returns true.
  /// Note that DirectoryEntry might not connect to
  /// Active Directory until we do something
  /// that actually requires it.
  /// That's why we read a property from the
  /// created DirectoryEntry object.
  /// </summary>
  public class SimpleAdAuth : System.Web.Services.WebService
  {
    [System.Web.Services.WebMethodAttribute()]
    [System.Web.Services.Protocols.SoapDocumentMethodAttribute(
      "",
      RequestNamespace = "urn:authentication.soap.sforce.com",
      ResponseElementName = "AuthenticateResult",
      ResponseNamespace = "urn:authentication.soap.sforce.com",
      Use = System.Web.Services.Description.SoapBindingUse.Literal,

      ParameterStyle =
System.Web.Services.Protocols.SoapParameterStyle.Wrapped)]
    [return:
System.Xml.Serialization.XmlElementAttribute("Authenticated")]

    public bool Authenticate (
      string username, string password, string sourceIp,
      [System.Xml.Serialization.XmlAnyElementAttribute()]
      System.Xml.XmlElement[] Any)
    {
      if(username.IndexOf("@")==-1)
        return false;

      // Attempt to bind to an Active Directory entry.
      // This will authenticate the username and password.
      // TODO: you'll need to change this to match
      // your Active Directory name
      const string root = "LDAP://DC=sample,DC=org";
      try
      {
        DirectoryEntry de
```

```
        = new DirectoryEntry(root, username, password);
    // retrieve a property
    string tempName = de.Name;
    return true;
    }
  catch(Exception)
  {
    return false;
    }
    }
  }
}
```

As part of the delegated authentication process, a salesforce.com server makes a SOAP 1.1 request to authenticate the user who is passing in the credentials. An example of this type of request is shown below.

```xml
<?xml version="1.0" encoding="UTF-8" ?>
<soapenv:Envelope
xmlns:soapenv="http://schemas.xmlsoap.org/soap/envelope/">
  <soapenv:Body>
    <Authenticate xmlns="urn:authentication.soap.sforce.com">
      <username>sampleuser@sample.org</username>
      <password>myPassword99</password>
      <sourceIp>1.2.3.4</sourceIp>
    </Authenticate>
  </soapenv:Body>
</soapenv:Envelope>
```

Your delegated authentication service needs to accept this request, process it, and return a `true` or `false` response. A sample response is shown below.

```xml
<?xml version="1.0" encoding="UTF-8"?>
<soapenv:Envelope
xmlns:soapenv="http://schemas.xmlsoap.org/soap/envelope/">
<soapenv:Body>
 <AuthenticateResponse
xmlns="urn:authentication.soap.sforce.com">
  <Authenticated>true</Authenticated>
 </AuthenticateResponse>
</soapenv:Body>
</soapenv:Envelope>
```

2. Add a link to your corporate intranet or other internally-accessible site that takes the authenticated user's credentials and passes them using an HTTPS POST to the Salesforce login page. For security reasons, you should make your service available by SSL only. This ensures that a password, if it is included, is not sent unencrypted. You must use an SSL certificate from a trusted provider, such as Verisign or Thawte.

Because Salesforce does not use the `password` field other than to pass it back to you, you do not need to send a password in this field. Instead, you could pass another authentication token, such as a Kerberos Ticket, so that your actual corporate passwords are not passed to or from Salesforce.

You can configure the Salesforce-delegated authentication authority to allow only tokens, or to accept either tokens or passwords. If the authority only accepts tokens, a Salesforce user cannot log in to Salesforce directly, because they cannot create a valid token; however, many companies choose to allow both tokens and passwords. In this environment, a user can still log in to Salesforce through the login page.

When the salesforce.com server passes these credentials back to you in the `Authenticate` message, verify them, and the user will gain access to the application.

Next, in Salesforce, specify your organization's delegated authentication gateway URL by clicking **Setup ➤ Security Controls ➤ Single Sign-On Settings ➤ Edit**. Enter the URL in the **Delegated Gateway URL** text box. For security reasons, Salesforce restricts the outbound ports you may specify to one of the following:

- 80: This port only accepts HTTP connections.
- 443: This port only accepts HTTPS connections.
- 7000-10000 (inclusive): These ports accept HTTP or HTTPS connections.

 Note: For security reasons, you should make your service available by SSL only.

Finally, modify your user profiles to enable the `Is Single Sign-On Enabled` user permission. In Salesforce, click **Setup ➤ Manage Users ➤ Profiles** to add or edit profiles.

Discussion

The actual implementation of delegated authentication is transparent to users, but involves a number of steps behind the scenes. When you configure Salesforce for delegated authentication, you are allowing a delegated authority to control authentication. When a user first logs onto their network environment, they are initially authenticated by this authority. When the user attempts to log on to subsequent protected applications, instead of passing a username and password to the application, the user requests a token from a token generator. (On Windows, this token request can use the NTLM protocol.) The received token is passed to the application, which verifies that the token properly identifies the user, and then allows the user access to the application.

Salesforce can use this method, since the password field is simply used to exchange information with the client, rather than specifying a particular data type. This flexibility means that Salesforce can accept a token, which is then used with the delegated authentication authority to verify the user. If the verification succeeds, the user is logged on to Salesforce. If the verification fails, the user receives an error. The process flow for Salesforce delegated authentication is shown in the figure below.

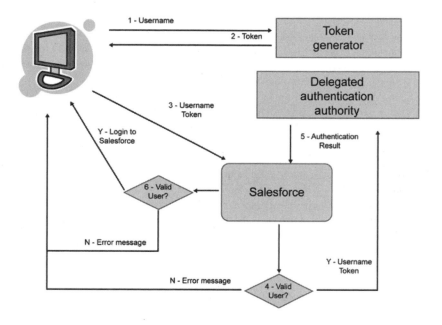

Figure 21: Delegated Authentication Process Flow

See Also

- *How to Implement Single Sign-On with the Force Platform* at
  wiki.apexdevnet.com/index.php/How_to_Implement_Single_Sign-On_with_Force.com
- "Configuring SAML Settings for Single Sign-On" in the Salesforce online help
- *The Single Sign-On Implementation Guide* in the Salesforce online help

Chapter 6

Integrating Applications with the API and Apex

As you become more experienced developing on the platform, you'll find that there are some types of applications and integrations that can't be handled by modifying a single app. For situations like these, you can leverage the powerful, SOAP-based API to write client applications that are created and executed outside of Salesforce.

In this chapter, you'll learn about choosing a development language, selecting a WSDL document, and managing API authentication, sessions, and timeouts. We'll also take a look at what it takes to build a full-fledged client application that demonstrates several API best practices.

Setting Up Your Salesforce Web Services API Applications

You should perform the following setup steps before working with the API in the recipes in the rest of this chapter.

1. *Select a Development Language* on page 196
2. *Create an Integration User* on page 196
3. *Select a WSDL* on page 197
4. *Generate a WSDL Document* on page 198
5. *If You Use the Partner WSDL* on page 199
6. *Log In to and Out of the API* on page 201
7. *Manage Sessions* on page 204
8. *Change the Session Timeout Value* on page 205

Select a Development Language

Choose the language or languages in which you'll write your application.

If you're interested in building a Web control or client application, write your code in any language that supports Web services, including Java, Perl, Python, PHP, Ruby on Rails, C#.NET, Visual Basic.NET, and Cocoa for Mac OS X. You can find toolkits and code samples for several Web-services-enabled languages on the Developer Force website at wiki.apexdevnet.com/index.php/API.

Create an Integration User

Client applications that access Salesforce through the API must first log in as a Salesforce user for authentication. Create a special user in your organization, solely for integration purposes. That way, even if an actual user leaves your organization, you'll always have a user with the correct permissions available. Assign this user a special profile with the following permissions selected:

- **API Only**. This permission specifies that the user can only log in through the API. This prevents the user from being used for any purpose other than integration scenarios.
- **Modify All Data**. This permission specifies that the user can view any data stored in the database and edit any field with the editable flag (some fields, like `CreatedDate`, do not have the editable flag set and cannot be edited by any user, regardless of the "Modify All Data" permission). This permission is also required for any user who wants to upsert non-unique external IDs through the API.

Select a WSDL

A WSDL document is an XML file that describes the format of messages you send and receive from a Web service. It's the protocol that your development environment's SOAP client uses to communicate with external services like Salesforce.

Salesforce provides two primary WSDL documents for operating on objects and fields in an organization, plus three additional WSDL documents for specific features of workflow rules and the API. Choose the WSDL document you should download and consume based on the type of application you're going to develop:

Enterprise WSDL

The Enterprise WSDL is a strongly-typed WSDL document for customers who want to build an integration with their Salesforce organization only, or for partners who are using tools like Tibco or webMethods to build integrations that require strong typecasting.

Strong typing means that an object in Salesforce has an equivalent object in Java, .NET, or whatever environment is accessing the API. This model generally makes it easier to write code because you don't need to deal with any underlying XML structures. It's also safer because data and schema dependencies are resolved at compile time, not at runtime.

The downside of the Enterprise WSDL, however, is that it only works with the schema of a single Salesforce organization because it's bound to all of the unique objects and fields that exist in that organization's data model. Consequently, if you use the Enterprise WSDL, you must download and re-consume it whenever your organization makes a change to its custom objects or fields. Additionally, you can't use it to create solutions that can work for multiple organizations.

Partner WSDL

The Partner WSDL is a loosely-typed WSDL document for customers, partners, and ISVs who want to build an integration or a Force Platform AppExchange app that can work across multiple Salesforce organizations.

With this WSDL document, the developer is responsible for marshaling data in the correct object representation, which typically involves editing the XML. However, you're also freed from being dependent on any particular data model or Salesforce organization. Consequently, if you use the Partner WSDL, you only need to download and consume it once, regardless of any changes to custom objects or fields.

Outbound Message WSDL

The Outbound Message WSDL document is for developers who want to send outbound messages from a workflow rule or approval process to an external service.

Apex WSDL

The Apex WSDL document is for developers who want to run or compile Apex scripts in another environment or build a new Force Platform IDE.

Metadata WSDL

The Metadata WSDL document is for users who want to use the API metadata calls. See "Understanding the Metadata API" in the *Force Platform Metadata API Developer's Guide.*

Delegated Authentication WSDL

The delegated authentication WSDL document is for users who want to created a delegated authentication application to support single-sign on. You can also download a client certificate for validating requests generated by Salesforce.

Generate a WSDL Document

If you want to generate a WSDL document other than an Outbound Message WSDL document, log in to your Salesforce organization and click **Setup ➤ Develop ➤ API**. Right-click the WSDL document you want to generate, and select **Save Link As** in Firefox, or **Save Target As** in Internet Explorer.

If you want to view a WSDL document without downloading it, simply click the download link for the WSDL document you want to view.

 Tip: To keep track of the WSDL documents you download, name them with a date/time stamp.

If you want to generate an Outbound Message WSDL document, click **Setup ➤ Create ➤ Workflow & Approvals ➤ Outbound Messagaes**. Select the name of the outbound message and then click **Click for WSDL**. This file is bound to the outbound message and contains the instructions about how to reach the endpoint service and what data is sent to it.

If You Use the Partner WSDL

If you want to use the Partner WSDL, but you don't know how to work with the loosely-typed SOAP messages, use the following information.

The Partner WSDL is based on a generic SObject, which represents a Salesforce record such as a particular account or contact. Every SObject has the following properties:

Name	Type	Description
Type	string	The API name of the object on which this SObject is based. For example, Account, Position__c, and so on.
ID	ID	The unique ID for this SObject. For the `create()` call, this value is null. For all other API calls, this value must be specified.
Any	XMLElement[] (in .NET) MessageElement[] (in Java)	An array of fields for the SObject. Each element of the array consists of an XML tag, where the name of the field is the name of the element, and the value of the field is the body of the tag. For example: `<name>value</name>`
FieldsToNull	string[]	An array of one or more field names whose value you want to explicitly set to `null`. This array is used only with the `update()` or `upsert()` calls. Note that you can only specify fields that you can update and that are nillable. For example, specifying an ID field or required field results in a runtime error.

The Partner WSDL provides methods that allow you to work with these properties so that you can perform the same tasks with the Partner WSDL as you can with the Enterprise WSDL. For example, the following Java code creates a job application record using the Enterprise WSDL:

```
public Job_Application__c createJobApp(String candidateId,
                                       String positionId) {
   Job_Application__c jobApp = new Job_Application__c();
```

"If You Use the Partner WSDL" contributed by Simon Fell, Principal Member of the Technical Staff at salesforce.com

```
        jobApp.setCandidate__c(new ID(candidateId));
        jobApp.setPosition__c(new ID(positionId));
        jobApp.setStatus__c("New");
        SaveResult [] sr = binding.create(new SObject[] {jobApp});
        if(!sr[0].isSuccess())
            throw new SaveException(sr[0]);
        jobApp.setId(sr[0].getId());
        return jobApp;
}
```

The same `createJobApp()` method can also be written in Java with the Partner WSDL:

```
public SObject createJobApp(String candidateId,
                            String positionId) {
    SObject jobApp = new SObject();
    // Submit four fields as part of the Any array on the 184
    // Chapter 11:Writing Web Controls and Client Applications
    // Job_Application__c record
    MessageElement[] fields = new MessageElement[3];
    // Candidate id
    field[0] = util.createNewXmlElement("Candidate__c", candidateId);

    // Position id
    field[1] = util.createNewXmlElement("Position__c", positionId);
    // Status
    field[2] = util.createNewXmlElement("Status__c", "New");
    jobApp.set_any(fields);
    jobApp.setType("Job_Application__c");
    SaveResult [] sr = binding.update(new SObject[] {jobApp});
    if(!sr[0].isSuccess())
        throw new SaveException(sr[0]);
    jobApp.setId(sr[0].getId());
    return jobApp;
}
```

The following VB.NET code creates a position record using the Enterprise WSDL:

```
Dim p as New Position__c
p.Id = "a00D0000005iYiq"
p.Name = "Analyst"
p.Status__c = "Open"
binding.create(New sObject() {p})
```

This code can be written using the Partner WSDL as follows:

```
Dim p as New SObject
  p.Type = "Position__c"
  p.Id = "a00D0000005iYiq"
  Dim doc as New XmlDocument
  Dim e1, e2 as XmlElement
  e1 = doc.CreateNewElement("Name")
  e2 = doc.CreateNewElement("Status")
  e1.InnerText = "Analyst"
```

```
e2.InnerText = "Open"
p.Any = new XmlElement() {e1,e2}
binding.update(New sObject() {p})
```

 Note: In these examples, notice that Java and .NET use different elements to represent field name/value pairs. For example, given the following name/value pair:

```
<City__c>Chicago</City__c>
```

- Java uses a `MessageElement` where:

    ◊ City__c is the `Name`

    ◊ Chicago is the `Value`

- .NET uses an `XMLElement` where:

    ◊ City__c is the `LocalName`

    ◊ Chicago is the `InnerText`

Use the Partner WSDL in conjunction with the `describeGlobal()` and `describeSObject()` metadata API calls. For example, a particular object's type is defined in the `name` field in the returned `DescribeSObjectResult`. Likewise, the name of an object's field is defined in the name field of the Field type in the returned `DescribeSObjectResult`.

Log In to and Out of the API

If a client application originates from outside the Salesforce user interface, it must first log in to the API. Best practice is to log out of the API when the client application completes its work. Use the following information to understand how to log in and log out from a client application. .

Similar to the way the login page works in the Salesforce user interface, the `login()` call takes a username and password and executes a login sequence on `https://www.salesforce.com/`. If the login is successful, the `login()` call returns a session ID and URL. The session ID represents the user's authentication token and the URL points to the host that contains data for the user's organization.

 Note: For performance and reliability, the platform runs on multiple instances (for example, na1.salesforce.com, na2.salesforce.com, and so on), but data for any single organization is always consolidated on a single instance. As long as you use the URL

"Log In to and Out of the API" contributed by Simon Fell, Principal Member of the Technical Staff at salesforce.com

that is returned from the `login()` call, you should never need to know the actual instance that hosts an organization's data.

Figure 22: Authenticating with the login() Call

Once you've obtained a session ID and server URL, you'll generally include the session ID in every API call, and you'll direct your client to make the API request to the host that you obtained.

 Tip: It's not necessary to use `login()` when writing an s-control that executes within the Salesforce user interface because the user accessing the s-control has already logged in and acquired a session ID.

To log in, acquire a Salesforce session ID and the appropriate host for your organization by using the `login()` call.

For example, the following Java code from the wrapper class described in *Using a Wrapper Class for Common API Functions* on page 210:

- Logs in to Salesforce
- Sets the login time
- Resets the URL for the SOAP binding stub to the returned server URL
- Creates a new session header for the binding class variable
- Updates the wrapper class' `sessionID` and `serverURL` variables

```
/**
 * This method is used to log in to salesforce and set the
 * private class variables for the wrapper, including the
 * session ID.
 */
public void login() throws UnexpectedErrorFault, InvalidIdFault,
                           LoginFault, RemoteException,
                           ServiceException {

    resetBindingStub();
    LoginResult loginResult = binding.login(username, password);
    this.nextLoginTime = System.currentTimeMillis() +
                         (this.sessionlength * 60000);

    this.binding._setProperty(SoapBindingStub.
```

```
                                ENDPOINT_ADDRESS_PROPERTY,
                                loginResult.getServerUrl());
        this.sessionId = loginResult.getSessionId();
        this.serverUrl = loginResult.getServerUrl();

        // Create a new session header object and set the
        // session id to that returned by the login
        SessionHeader sh = new SessionHeader();
        sh.setSessionId(loginResult.getSessionId());
        this.binding.setHeader(new
            SforceServiceLocator().getServiceName().getNamespaceURI(),

            "SessionHeader", sh);
    }
```

This VB .NET code performs the same logic as for the VB.NET version of the wrapper class (see *Using a Wrapper Class for Common API Functions* on page 210):

```
    Public Sub Login()
        Dim lr As sforce.LoginResult
        Me._binding.Url = Me._host
        lr = Me._binding.login(username, password)
        Me._nextLoginTime = Now().AddMinutes(Me.sessionlength)
        'Reset the SOAP endpoint to the returned server URL
        Me._binding.Url = lr.serverUrl
        Me._binding.SessionHeaderValue = New sforce.SessionHeader
        Me._binding.SessionHeaderValue.sessionId = lr.sessionId
        Me._sessionId = lr.sessionId
        Me._serverURL = lr.serverUrl
    End Sub
```

To log out of the session you created, issue the `logout()` call.

Java:

```
    /**
     * This method is used to log out of salesforce
     */
public void logout() {
    try {
        binding.logout();
    }
    catch (Exception e) {
        System.out.println("Unexpected error:\n\n" + e.getMessage());
    }
}
```

VB.NET:

```
    Public Sub Logout()
```

```
        Me._binding.logout()
    End Sub
```

Manage Sessions

An integration may last longer than the session timeout value specified for an organization, but logging in to Salesforce every time you need to make an API call is inefficient. To manage sessions, use the information in this section.

The session timeout value is the amount of time a single session ID remains valid before expiring. While a session is always valid for a user while he or she is working in the Web interface, sessions instantiated via the API expire after the duration of the session timeout, regardless of how many transactions are still taking place.

You can manage sessions by writing a method that checks to see whether your session ID is about to expire by comparing your last login time with the current session length. When this method returns true, log in again.

For example, the following Java code from the wrapper class discussed in *Using a Wrapper Class for Common API Functions* on page 210 implements a `loginRequired()` method:

```
/**
 * This method returns true if a login to Salesforce is
 * necessary, otherwise false. It should be used to check the
 * session length before performing any API calls.
 */
private boolean loginRequired() {
    if (sessionId == null || sessionId.length() == 0)
        return true;
    return !isConnected();
}

/**
 * This method checks whether the session is active or not
 * @return boolean
 */
public boolean isConnected() {
    return System.currentTimeMillis() < nextLoginTime;
}
```

This VB.NET function implements the same logic:

```
Private Function loginRequired() As Boolean
    loginRequired = Not (isConnected())
```

"Manage Sessions" contributed by Simon Fell, Principal Member of the Technical Staff at salesforce.com

```
End Function

Public Function isConnected() As Boolean
    If _sessionId <> "" And _sessionId <> Nothing Then
        If Now() > Me._nextLoginTime Then
            isConnected = False
        End If
        isConnected = True
    Else
        isConnected = False
    End If
End Function
```

Tip: Be sure that the value you use for session length is no more than the configured session timeout value. Because the session timeout value for an organization is not accessible through the API, it's a good idea to build applications that assume a thirty-minute session timeout so that administrators don't inadvertently break your integrations.

This example is very simple. Another, more robust option is to catch the session expiration remove exception (Exception Code - `INVALID_SESSION_ID`) and only then log in again. This ensures that you only log in when absolutely necessary and that you'll get a new session ID if your current session ever becomes invalid. This method is usually coupled with implementing retry logic.

Change the Session Timeout Value

If you want to change the session timeout value from the two hour default, so that your integrations can work longer without having to get a new session ID, change the value:

1. Log in to the application as an administrator.
2. Click **Setup ➤ Security Controls ➤ Session Settings**.
3. Change the `Timeout value` to one of the few preset values. They range from as little as 15 minutes to as long as 8 hours.

Note:

- Make sure you update any integration code so that it uses the new timeout value! Otherwise your integrations might break.
- Changing the session timeout value affects all users equally in an organization.

Implementing the Query/Query More Pattern

Problem

You need to issue queries that return more than 2000 records, but the `query()` call can only return up to 2000 at a time.

Solution

Use `queryMore()` to retrieve any additional records in batches of up to 2000 at a time. The `queryMore()` call takes a single `queryLocator` parameter that specifies the index of the last result record that was returned. This `queryLocator` is created and returned by the previous `query()` or `queryMore()` call.

When the `query()` or `queryMore()` calls return a result with the `isDone` flag set to true, there are no more records to process.

For example, the following Java code implements the `query()`/`queryMore()` pattern when querying leads:

```
QueryResult queryResult = this.stub.query("Select name From lead");
do {
    for(sObject lead : queryResult.getRecords()) {
        System.out.println(lead.get_any()[0].getValue());
    }
    if(queryResult.isDone())
        break;
    queryResult = this.stub.queryMore(queryResult.
                                        getQueryLocator());
} while(true);
```

This code implements `query()`/`queryMore()` in VB.NET:

```
Dim lead As sforce.sObject
Dim i As Integer
Dim qr As sforce.QueryResult = binding.query("select name from lead")
Do
    For i = 0 To qr.records.Length
        lead = qr.records(i)
        Console.WriteLine(lead.Any(0).InnerText)
    Next
        If qr.done Then Exit Do
        qr = binding.queryMore(qr.queryLocator)
Loop
```

"Implementing the Query/Query More Pattern" contributed by Simon Fell, Principal Member of the Technical Staff at salesforce.com, and Nick Tran, Developer Relations Senior Manager for salesforce.com

The `query()`/`queryMore()` batch size defaults to 500 records, but can be as small as 200 or as large as 2000. To change the batch size, use the `QueryOptions` header.

Note:

- If you use `query()`/`queryMore()` during a long-running integration scenario where you need to log in again to get new session IDs, the `queryLocator` cursor remains valid after you log in, as long as you get the next batch of records within fifteen minutes of idle time.
- Only ten `queryLocator` cursors can be active for an organization at any one time.

See Also

- *Manage Sessions* on page 204
- *Using a Wrapper Class for Common API Functions* on page 210
- *Batching Records for API Calls* on page 207

Batching Records for API Calls

Problem

You want to create, update, or delete records in the Salesforce database, but you have more than 200 records you want to process, which exceeds the maximum allowed per call.

Solution

Write a method that batches the records into multiple API calls.

For example, the following Java code from the wrapper class described in *Using a Wrapper Class for Common API Functions* on page 210 implements a `create()` method that takes an array of SObjects and a batch size as parameters. Any method that calls `create()` can pass in any number of records and dynamically vary the batch size to improve performance:

```
/**
 * This method creates an array of sObjects with a specified
 * batchSize.
 * @param records
 * @param batchSize
 * @return SaveResult[]
 */
public SaveResult[] create(SObject[] records, int batchSize)
```

Code for "Batching Records for API Calls" contributed by Simon Fell, Principal Member of the Technical Staff at salesforce.com

```
                throws InvalidSObjectFault, UnexpectedErrorFault,
                    InvalidIdFault, RemoteException,
                    ServiceException {
        if (batchSize > 200 || batchSize < 1)
            throw new IllegalArgumentException(
                        "batchSize must be between 1 and 200");
        return batch(records, batchSize, new CreateBatcher());
    }


    private SaveResult[] batch(SObject[] records, int batchSize,
                            Batcher batchOperation)
            throws UnexpectedErrorFault, InvalidIdFault,
                LoginFault, RemoteException, ServiceException {
        if (records.length <= batchSize) {
            checkLogin();
            return batchOperation.perform(records);
        }
        SaveResult[] saveResults = new SaveResult[records.length];
        SObject[] thisBatch = null;
        int pos = 0;
        while (pos < records.length) {
            int thisBatchSize = Math.min(batchSize,
                                        records.length - pos);
            if (thisBatch == null ||
                    thisBatch.length != thisBatchSize)
                thisBatch = new SObject[thisBatchSize];

            System.arraycopy(records, pos, thisBatch, 0,
                        thisBatchSize);
            SaveResult [] batchResults = batch(thisBatch,
                                        thisBatchSize,
                                        batchOperation);
            System.arraycopy(batchResults, 0, saveResults,
                        pos, thisBatchSize);
            pos += thisBatchSize;
        }
        return saveResults;
    }


    private abstract class Batcher {
        abstract SaveResult[] perform(SObject [] records)
                throws UnexpectedErrorFault, InvalidIdFault,
                    LoginFault, RemoteException,
                    ServiceException;
    }


    private class CreateBatcher extends Batcher {
        SaveResult [] perform(SObject [] records)
            throws UnexpectedErrorFault, InvalidIdFault,
                LoginFault, RemoteException, ServiceException {
            checkLogin();
            return binding.create(records);
        }
```

```
    }

    private class UpdateBatcher extends Batcher {
        SaveResult [] perform(SObject [] records)
            throws UnexpectedErrorFault, InvalidIdFault, LoginFault,
                RemoteException, ServiceException {
            checkLogin();
            return binding.update(records);
        }
    }
```

This VB.NET function implements the same logic:

```
    Public Function create(ByVal records() As sObject,
                        Optional ByVal batchSize As Integer = 200)

                    As sforce.SaveResult()
        Return batch(records, batchSize, New CreateBatcher)
    End Function


    Private Function batch(ByVal records() As sObject,
                    ByVal batchSize As Integer,
                    ByVal oper As Batcher)
                As sforce.SaveResult()
        If (records.Length <= batchSize) Then
            batch = oper.perform(Binding, records)
            Exit Function
        End If

        Dim saveResults(records.Length - 1) As sforce.SaveResult
        Dim thisBatch As sforce.sObject()
        Dim pos As Integer = 0
        Dim thisBatchSize As Integer

        While (pos < records.Length)
            thisBatchSize = Math.Min(batchSize,
                                records.Length - pos)
            ReDim thisBatch(thisBatchSize)
            System.Array.Copy(records, pos, thisBatch,
                        0, thisBatchSize)
            Dim sr As sforce.SaveResult() =
                            oper.perform(Binding, thisBatch)
            System.Array.Copy(sr, 0, saveResults, pos, thisBatchSize)

            pos += sr.Length
        End While
        batch = saveResults
    End Function

    Private Class Batcher
        Public Function perform(ByVal binding As sforce.SforceService,

                        ByVal records As sforce.sObject())
                    As sforce.SaveResult()
```

```
                perform = Nothing
        End Function
    End Class

    Private Class CreateBatcher
        Inherits Batcher
        Public Overloads Function perform(
                    ByVal binding As sforce.SforceService,
                    ByVal records As sforce.sObject())
                As sforce.SaveResult()
            perform = binding.create(records)
        End Function
    End Class

    Private Class UpdateBatcher
        Inherits Batcher
        Public Overloads Function perform(
                    ByVal binding As sforce.SforceService,
                    ByVal records As sforce.sObject())
                As sforce.SaveResult()
            perform = binding.update(records)
        End Function
    End Class
```

See Also

- *Manage Sessions* on page 204
- *Using a Wrapper Class for Common API Functions* on page 210
- *Log In to and Out of the API* on page 201

Using a Wrapper Class for Common API Functions

Problem

You find yourself writing similar sections of code wherever you need to make calls to the API in a client application.

Solution

Use an API wrapper class to abstract common functions whenever you write client applications and integrations. A wrapper class makes your integration more straightforward to develop and maintain, keeps the logic necessary to make API calls in one place, and affords easy reuse across all components that require API access.

"Using a Wrapper Class for Common API Functions" contributed by Simon Fell, Principal Member of the Technical Staff at salesforce.com

Wrapper classes typically include methods for the following types of actions:

- Logging in
- Managing sessions
- Querying with the `query()`/`queryMore()` pattern
- Batching records for create, update, delete, and so on

For example, the following Java code is a complete implementation of the wrapper class used in *Building a Web Portal with Salesforce Data* on page 223:

```
package com.sforce.client;

import java.net.MalformedURLException;
import java.net.URL;
import java.rmi.RemoteException;

import javax.xml.rpc.ServiceException;

import org.apache.axis.transport.http.HTTPConstants;

import com.sforce.soap.partner.AssignmentRuleHeader;
import com.sforce.soap.partner.LoginResult;
import com.sforce.soap.partner.QueryOptions;
import com.sforce.soap.partner.QueryResult;
import com.sforce.soap.partner.SaveResult;
import com.sforce.soap.partner.SessionHeader;
import com.sforce.soap.partner.SforceServiceLocator;
import com.sforce.soap.partner.SoapBindingStub;
import com.sforce.soap.partner.fault.InvalidIdFault;
import com.sforce.soap.partner.fault.InvalidSObjectFault;
import com.sforce.soap.partner.fault.LoginFault;
import com.sforce.soap.partner.fault.UnexpectedErrorFault;
import com.sforce.soap.partner.sobject.SObject;


public class Client {

    // Private wrapper class variables
    private String username;
    private String password;
    private URL host;
    private int querySize;
    private int sessionlength;
    private String sessionId;
    private String serverUrl;
    private long nextLoginTime;
    private SoapBindingStub binding;
    private boolean useCompression;

    private QueryOptions queryOptions;
    private AssignmentRuleHeader assignmentRules;


    /**
```

```
    * This method initializes the private class variables
    */
    public Client() throws MalformedURLException {
        this.querySize = 500;
        this.sessionlength = 29;
        this.useCompression = true;
        this.host = new URL(
                "https://www.salesforce.com/services/Soap/u/10.0");
    }

/**
    * These methods get and set the private class variables
    */
    public String getUsername() {
        return this.username;
    }

    public void setUsername(String value) {
        this.username = value;
    }

    public String getPassword() {
        return this.password;
    }

    public void setPassword(String value) {
        this.password = value;
    }

    public URL getHost() {
        return this.host;
    }

    public void setHost(URL value) {
        this.host = value;
    }

    public void setHost(String url) throws MalformedURLException {
        this.host = new URL(url);
    }

    public String getServerURL() {
        return this.serverUrl;
    }

    public int getQuerySize() {
        return this.querySize;
    }

    public void setQuerySize(int value) {
        this.querySize = value;
    }

    public int getSessionlength() {
        return this.sessionlength;
    }
```

```java
    public void setSessionlength(int value) {
        this.sessionlength = value;
    }

    public boolean getUseCompression() {
        return this.useCompression;
    }

    public void setUseCompression(boolean value) {
        this.useCompression = value;
        setCompressionOnBinding();
    }


    /**
     * This method is used to log in to salesforce and set the
     * private class variables for the wrapper, including the
     * session ID.
     */
    public void login() throws UnexpectedErrorFault, InvalidIdFault,
                               LoginFault, RemoteException,
                               ServiceException {

        resetBindingStub();
        LoginResult loginResult = binding.login(username, password);
        this.nextLoginTime = System.currentTimeMillis() +
                            (this.sessionlength * 60000);

        this.binding._setProperty(SoapBindingStub.
                                ENDPOINT_ADDRESS_PROPERTY,
                                loginResult.getServerUrl());
        this.sessionId = loginResult.getSessionId();
        this.serverUrl = loginResult.getServerUrl();

        // Create a new session header object and set the
        // session id to that returned by the login
        SessionHeader sh = new SessionHeader();
        sh.setSessionId(loginResult.getSessionId());
        this.binding.setHeader(new SforceServiceLocator().
            getServiceName().getNamespaceURI(),
            "SessionHeader", sh);
    }


    private void checkLogin() throws UnexpectedErrorFault,
                    InvalidIdFault, LoginFault, RemoteException,
                    ServiceException {
        if (this.loginRequired())
            login();
    }


    /**
     * This method is used to log in with an existing sessionId
     * @param String sid sessionId
```

```
 * @param String sURL serverUrl
 */
public void loginBySessionId(String sid, String sURL)
                             throws ServiceException {
    this.nextLoginTime = System.currentTimeMillis() +
                         (this.sessionlength * 60000);
    resetBindingStub();
    binding._setProperty(
            SoapBindingStub.ENDPOINT_ADDRESS_PROPERTY, sURL);
    this.sessionId = sid;
    this.serverUrl = sURL;
    SessionHeader sh = new SessionHeader();
    sh.setSessionId(sid);
    binding.setHeader(new SforceServiceLocator().
            getServiceName().getNamespaceURI(),
            "SessionHeader", sh);
}


/** This method resets the binding object back to its
  * initial state.
  */
private void resetBindingStub() throws ServiceException {
    this.binding = (SoapBindingStub) new
            SforceServiceLocator().getSoap(this.host);
    this.binding.setTimeout(60000);
    setCompressionOnBinding();
    this.assignmentRules = null;
    this.queryOptions = null;
}

private void setCompressionOnBinding() {
    binding._setProperty(HTTPConstants.MC_ACCEPT_GZIP,
                         useCompression);
    binding._setProperty(HTTPConstants.MC_GZIP_REQUEST,
                         useCompression);
}

/**
 * This method checks whether the session is active or not
 * @return boolean
 */
public boolean isConnected() {
    return System.currentTimeMillis() < nextLoginTime;
}

/**
 * This method returns true if a login to Salesforce is
 * necessary, otherwise false. It should be used to check the
 * session length before performing any API calls.
 */
private boolean loginRequired() {
    if (sessionId == null || sessionId.length() == 0)
        return true;
```

```
            return !isConnected();
    }

    private void setBatchSizeHeader(int batchSize) {
        if (queryOptions == null) {
            this.queryOptions = new QueryOptions();
            binding.setHeader(new SforceServiceLocator().
                    getServiceName().getNamespaceURI(),
                    "QueryOptions", queryOptions);
        }
        queryOptions.setBatchSize(batchSize);
    }


/**
 * This method queries the database and returns the results.
 * @param String strSOQLStmt
 * @return SObject[]
 */
    public QueryResult executeQuery(String strSOQLStmt,
            Integer queryBatchSize)
            throws UnexpectedErrorFault, InvalidIdFault, LoginFault,
                    RemoteException, ServiceException {

        checkLogin();
        setBatchSizeHeader(queryBatchSize ==
            null ? querySize : queryBatchSize);
        return binding.query(strSOQLStmt);
    }


    public QueryResult executeSOQL(String strSOQLStmt)
            throws UnexpectedErrorFault, InvalidIdFault, LoginFault,
                    RemoteException, ServiceException {
        return executeQuery(strSOQLStmt, null);
    }


    public QueryResult executeQueryMore(String queryLocator)
            throws UnexpectedErrorFault, InvalidIdFault, LoginFault,
                    RemoteException, ServiceException {
        checkLogin();
        return binding.queryMore(queryLocator);
    }

/**
 * This method sets the assignment rule header.
 * @param ruleId
 */
    public void setAssignmentRuleHeaderId(String ruleId) {
        setAssignmentRuleHeader(ruleId, false);
    }

/**
 * This method sets the assignment rule header with a
 * default ruleId.
```

```
        * @param ruleId
        */
       public void setAssignmentRuleHeaderToDefault
                                    (boolean runDefaultRule) {
           setAssignmentRuleHeader(null, runDefaultRule);
       }

       private void setAssignmentRuleHeader(String ruleId,
                                    boolean useDefault) {
           if (this.assignmentRules == null) {
              this.assignmentRules = new AssignmentRuleHeader();
              binding.setHeader(new SforceServiceLocator().
                     getServiceName().getNamespaceURI(),
                     "AssignmentRuleHeader", this.assignmentRules);
           }
           this.assignmentRules.setUseDefaultRule(useDefault);
           this.assignmentRules.setAssignmentRuleId(ruleId);
       }

       public SoapBindingStub getBinding()
              throws UnexpectedErrorFault, InvalidIdFault, LoginFault,
                     RemoteException, ServiceException {
           checkLogin();
           return this.binding;
       }

    /**
     * This method creates an array of sObjects with a specified
     * batchSize.
     * @param records
     * @param batchSize
     * @return SaveResult[]
     */
    public SaveResult[] create(SObject[] records, int batchSize)
           throws InvalidSObjectFault, UnexpectedErrorFault,
                  InvalidIdFault, RemoteException,
                  ServiceException {
        if (batchSize > 200 || batchSize < 1)
           throw new IllegalArgumentException(
                     "batchSize must be between 1 and 200");
        return batch(records, batchSize, new CreateBatcher());
    }

    public SaveResult[] create(SObject[] records)
           throws InvalidSObjectFault, UnexpectedErrorFault,
                  InvalidIdFault, RemoteException, ServiceException {

        return create(records, 200);
    }

    public SaveResult[] update(SObject[] records, int batchSize)
           throws UnexpectedErrorFault, InvalidIdFault, LoginFault,
                  RemoteException, ServiceException {
        if (batchSize > 200 || batchSize < 1)
```

```
                throw new IllegalArgumentException(
                            "batchSize must be between 1 and 200");

        return batch(records, batchSize, new UpdateBatcher());
    }

/**
 * This method updates an array of sObjects with a specified
 * batchSize.
 * @param records
 * @param batchSize
 * @return SaveResult[]
 */
public SaveResult[] update(SObject[] records)
        throws UnexpectedErrorFault, InvalidIdFault, LoginFault,
                RemoteException, ServiceException {
    return update(records, 200);
}

private SaveResult[] batch(SObject[] records, int batchSize,
                        Batcher batchOperation)
        throws UnexpectedErrorFault, InvalidIdFault,
                LoginFault, RemoteException, ServiceException {
    if (records.length <= batchSize) {
        checkLogin();
        return batchOperation.perform(records);
    }
    SaveResult[] saveResults = new SaveResult[records.length];
    SObject[] thisBatch = null;
    int pos = 0;
    while (pos < records.length) {
        int thisBatchSize = Math.min(batchSize,
                                    records.length - pos);
        if (thisBatch == null ||
                thisBatch.length != thisBatchSize)
            thisBatch = new SObject[thisBatchSize];

        System.arraycopy(records, pos, thisBatch, 0,
                        thisBatchSize);
        SaveResult [] batchResults = batch(thisBatch,
                                        thisBatchSize,
                                        batchOperation);
        System.arraycopy(batchResults, 0, saveResults,
                        pos, thisBatchSize);
        pos += thisBatchSize;
    }
    return saveResults;
}


private abstract class Batcher {
    abstract SaveResult[] perform(SObject [] records)
            throws UnexpectedErrorFault, InvalidIdFault,
                LoginFault, RemoteException,
                ServiceException;
}
```

```
    private class CreateBatcher extends Batcher {
        SaveResult [] perform(SObject [] records)
            throws UnexpectedErrorFault, InvalidIdFault,
                LoginFault, RemoteException, ServiceException {
            checkLogin();
            return binding.create(records);
        }
    }

    private class UpdateBatcher extends Batcher {
        SaveResult [] perform(SObject [] records)
            throws UnexpectedErrorFault, InvalidIdFault, LoginFault,
                RemoteException, ServiceException {
            checkLogin();
            return binding.update(records);
        }
    }
}
```

This code implements the VB.NET version of the wrapper class used in *Building a Web Portal with Salesforce Data* on page 223:

```
Imports Microsoft.VisualBasic
Imports System
Imports System.Collections
Imports sforce

Public Class Client

    Private _binding As SforceServiceCompressed
    Private _username As String
    Private _password As String
    Private _host As String
    Private _querySize As Integer
    Private _sessionlength As Integer
    Private _sessionId As String
    Private _serverURL As String
    Private _nextLoginTime As DateTime

    'Initialize private variables for the class
    Sub New()
        Me._binding = New SforceServiceCompressed
        Me._querySize = 500
        Me._sessionlength = 29
        Me._host = "https://www.salesforce.com/services/Soap/u/10.0"
    End Sub


    'Expose variables to calling function
    Public Property username() As String
        'Allows calling class to get values
        Get
            Return Me._username
```

```
        End Get
        'Allows calling class to set value
        Set(ByVal Value As String)
            Me._username = Value
        End Set
End Property

Public Property password() As String
        Get
            Return Me._password
        End Get
        Set(ByVal Value As String)
            Me._password = Value
        End Set
End Property

Public Property host() As String
        Get
            Return Me._host
        End Get
        Set(ByVal Value As String)
            Me._host = Value
        End Set
End Property

Public ReadOnly Property serverURL() As String
        Get
            Return Me._serverURL
        End Get
End Property

Public Property querySize() As Integer
        Get
            Return Me._querySize
        End Get
        Set(ByVal Value As Integer)
            Me._querySize = Value
        End Set
End Property

Public Property sessionlength() As Integer
        Get
            Return Me._sessionlength
        End Get
        Set(ByVal Value As Integer)
            Me._sessionlength = Value
        End Set
End Property

'In case of proxy server...
Public Property proxy() As System.Net.WebProxy
        Get
            Return Me._binding.Proxy
        End Get
        Set(ByVal Value As System.Net.WebProxy)
            Me._binding.Proxy = Value
```

```vb
            End Set
    End Property


    ' Compress SOAP messages
    Public Property useCompression() As Boolean
        Get
            Return Me._binding.AcceptCompressedResponse()
        End Get

        Set(ByVal Value As Boolean)
            Me._binding.AcceptCompressedResponse = Value
            Me._binding.SendCompressedRequest = Value
        End Set
    End Property


    Public Sub Login()
        Dim lr As sforce.LoginResult
        Me._binding.Url = Me._host
        lr = Me._binding.login(username, password)
        Me._nextLoginTime = Now().AddMinutes(Me.sessionlength)
        'Reset the SOAP endpoint to the returned server URL
        Me._binding.Url = lr.serverUrl
        Me._binding.SessionHeaderValue = New sforce.SessionHeader
        Me._binding.SessionHeaderValue.sessionId = lr.sessionId
        Me._sessionId = lr.sessionId
        Me._serverURL = lr.serverUrl
    End Sub


    Public Sub loginBySessionId(ByVal sid As String,
                                ByVal sURL As String)
        Me._nextLoginTime = Now().AddMinutes(Me.sessionlength)
        Me._binding.Url = sURL
        Me._binding.SessionHeaderValue = New sforce.SessionHeader
        Me._binding.SessionHeaderValue.sessionId = sid
        Me._sessionId = sid
        Me._serverURL = sURL
    End Sub


    Public Function isConnected() As Boolean
        If _sessionId <> "" And _sessionId <> Nothing Then
            If Now() > Me._nextLoginTime Then
                isConnected = False
            End If
            isConnected = True
        Else
            isConnected = False
        End If
    End Function


    Private Function loginRequired() As Boolean
        loginRequired = Not (isConnected())
    End Function
```

```
Public Function executeQuery(ByVal strSOQLStmt As String,
            Optional ByVal queryBatchSize As Integer = -1)
            As sforce.QueryResult
    If queryBatchSize = -1 Then
        queryBatchSize = _querySize
    End If
    If (Me.loginRequired()) Then
        Login()
    End If
    _binding.QueryOptionsValue = New sforce.QueryOptions
    _binding.QueryOptionsValue.batchSizeSpecified = True
    _binding.QueryOptionsValue.batchSize = queryBatchSize
    executeQuery = _binding.query(strSOQLStmt)
End Function


Public Function executeQueryMore(ByVal queryLocator As String)
            As sforce.QueryResult
    If loginRequired() Then Login()
    Return _binding.queryMore(queryLocator)
End Function


Public Sub setAssignmentRuleHeaderId(ByVal ruleId As String)
    _binding.AssignmentRuleHeaderValue =
                        New AssignmentRuleHeader
    _binding.AssignmentRuleHeaderValue.assignmentRuleId = ruleId
End Sub


Public Sub setAssignmentRuleHeaderToDefault(
                            ByVal runDefaultRule As Boolean)

    _binding.AssignmentRuleHeaderValue = New AssignmentRuleHeader

    _binding.AssignmentRuleHeaderValue.useDefaultRule =
                                        runDefaultRule

End Sub

Public ReadOnly Property Binding() As sforce.SforceService
    Get
        Return _binding
    End Get
End Property


Public Function create(ByVal records() As sObject,
                Optional ByVal batchSize As Integer = 200)

            As sforce.SaveResult()
    Return batch(records, batchSize, New CreateBatcher)
End Function
```

```vb
Public Function update(ByVal records() As sObject,
                Optional ByVal batchSize As Integer = 200)

            As sforce.SaveResult()
    Return batch(records, batchSize, New UpdateBatcher)
End Function


Private Function batch(ByVal records() As sObject,
                ByVal batchSize As Integer,
                ByVal oper As Batcher)
            As sforce.SaveResult()
    If (records.Length <= batchSize) Then
        batch = oper.perform(Binding, records)
        Exit Function
    End If

    Dim saveResults(records.Length - 1) As sforce.SaveResult
    Dim thisBatch As sforce.sObject()
    Dim pos As Integer = 0
    Dim thisBatchSize As Integer

    While (pos < records.Length)
        thisBatchSize = Math.Min(batchSize,
                        records.Length - pos)
        ReDim thisBatch(thisBatchSize)
        System.Array.Copy(records, pos, thisBatch,
                    0, thisBatchSize)
        Dim sr As sforce.SaveResult() =
                    oper.perform(Binding, thisBatch)
        System.Array.Copy(sr, 0, saveResults, pos, thisBatchSize)

        pos += sr.Length
    End While
    batch = saveResults
End Function

Private Class Batcher
    Public Function perform(ByVal binding
                        As sforce.SforceService,
                    ByVal records
                        As sforce.sObject())
                As sforce.SaveResult()
        perform = Nothing
    End Function
End Class

Private Class CreateBatcher
    Inherits Batcher
    Public Overloads Function perform(
                ByVal binding As sforce.SforceService,
                ByVal records As sforce.sObject())
        As sforce.SaveResult()
        perform = binding.create(records)
    End Function
```

```
      End Class

      Private Class UpdateBatcher
          Inherits Batcher
          Public Overloads Function perform(
                        ByVal binding As sforce.SforceService,
                        ByVal records As sforce.sObject())
              As sforce.SaveResult()
              perform = binding.update(records)
          End Function
      End Class
End Class
```

See Also

- *Building a Web Portal with Salesforce Data* on page 223
- *Log In to and Out of the API* on page 201
- *Manage Sessions* on page 204
- *Implementing the Query/Query More Pattern* on page 206
- *Batching Records for API Calls* on page 207

Building a Web Portal with Salesforce Data

Problem

You want to build a Web portal for the Recruiting app that allows visitors to apply online for open positions. The portal needs to include the following Web pages:

- A list view of all currently open positions, with data from the position records that are stored in Salesforce
- Detail views of all currently open positions, also with data from the position records that are stored in Salesforce
- An online application form that allows a visitor to apply for an open position. When the user clicks **Submit**, the data is sent back to Salesforce as a new job application and candidate record.

Most importantly, your Web portal visitors shouldn't have to log in to view the open positions in your organization.

Code for "Building a Web Portal with Salesforce Data" contributed by Sarah Whitlock, Senior Program Manager for Education Services former at salesforce.com, and Simon Fell, Principal Member of the Technical Staff at salesforce.com

Note: This Web portal is part of the Application Laboratory class offered by salesforce.com Training & Certification. For more information, see `www.salesforce.com/training`.

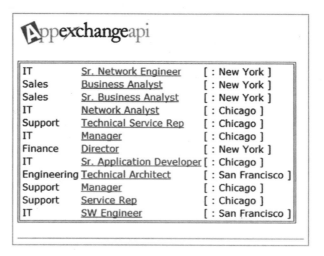

Figure 23: The Web Portal's Job Listings Page

Figure 24: The Web Portal's Position Detail Page

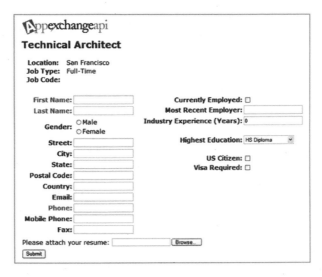

Figure 25: The Web Portal's Application Page

Solution

Write a client application that runs on an external server and uses the Force Platform API to access Salesforce data.

 Note: Because there's a lot of code involved with this solution, this recipe discusses how such a client can be designed, and some of the features that can be implemented. To download the complete Java, C#.NET, or VB.NET code that implements this client application, visit
`wiki.apexdevnet.com/index.php/Force_Platform_Cookbook`.

The following diagram shows the key components of such an application. While there can be some overlap, each component represents a different aspect of the MVC (Model-View-Controller) design paradigm:

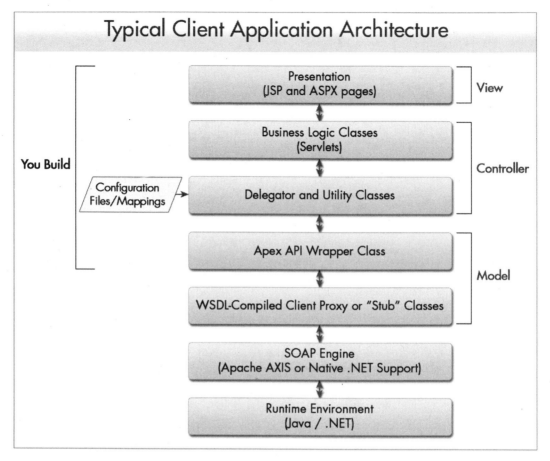

Figure 26: Typical Client Application Architecture

Model

The API wrapper class and the WSDL-compiled proxy classes provide non-application-specific access to the data in Salesforce. See *Using a Wrapper Class for Common API Functions* on page 210 for the wrapper class used to implement the Web portal application.

View

The JSP or ASPX pages contain the user interface of the application, including how the data is displayed for and captured from the user.

Controller

The delegator, utility, and business logic classes define the application-specific logic, including the logic that controls how captured data is returned to Salesforce as new or updated records.

Of particular note is the delegator class that the Web portal application uses to provide common, reusable code for creating and updating the key objects related to the application, such as Job Application and Candidate. Unlike the API wrapper class, which can be reused by many different client applications, the delegator is application-specific, providing an additional layer of abstraction between the API and the logic required to display the application's pages.

For example, the following Java-based delegator method provides the logic for creating a job application record. Based on the Partner WSDL, it prepares a single record and passes it to the wrapper class for creation via the API:

```
public SObject createJobApp(String candidateId,
                            String positionId) {

  SObject application = new SObject();

  try {
    MessageElement[] fields = new MessageElement[3];
    MessageElement field;

    //Candidate id
    field = util.createNewXmlElement("Candidate__c",
                                     candidateId);
    fields[0] = field;

    //Positionid
    field = util.createNewXmlElement("Position__c",
                                     positionId);
    fields[1] = field;

    //Status
    field = util.createNewXmlElement("Status__c",
                                     "New");
    fields[2] = field;

    application.set_any(fields);
    application.setType("Job_Application__c");
    application = createOneRecord(application);

  } catch (Exception e) {
    System.out.println(e.getMessage());
  }

  return application;
}
```

This same logic can be implemented in VB.NET as follows:

```
Public Function createJobApp(ByVal candidateId As String,
    ByVal positionId As String) As sforce.sObject
  Dim application As New sforce.sObject

  Dim fields(2) As System.Xml.XmlElement
  Dim field As System.Xml.XmlElement
```

```
' Candidate id
field = util.createNewXmlElement("Candidate__c",
                                   candidateId)
fields(0) = field

' Position id
field = util.createNewXmlElement("Position__c",
                                   positionId)
fields(1) = field

' Status
field = util.createNewXmlElement("Status__c",
                                   "New")
fields(2) = field

application.Any = fields
application.type = "Job_Application__c"

application = createOneRecord(application)

Return application
End Function
```

Discussion

The code that implements this Web portal client application also uses a configuration file and SOAP message compression, two best practices for client application development:

- Using a configuration file to control dynamic aspects of a client application is highly recommended because it reduces code maintenance time. It can include properties such as the API URL, username, password, and any SOQL or SOSL queries that drive business logic. For example, by storing the URL of the targeted Salesforce host in a configuration file, changing an integration target from sandbox to production only requires a simple configuration file edit.

  The Java-based solution uses a configuration file named `config.properties`, while the VB.NET and C#.NET solutions use configuration files named `web.config`.

- SOAP messages generated by both an API client and the API service can become very large, especially when they include large clobs of data, such as the resume attachment in the Web portal client application. To avoid lengthy transmission times across the Internet, you can configure your SOAP binding to use GZIP compression to reduce the size of SOAP messages by up to 90%. When the API server receives a compressed message, it decompresses the message, processes it, and then recompresses the response before returning it.

  The Java-based solution uses the following classes to compress and decompress SOAP messages:

  ◊ GZipWebRequest.java

◊ GZipWebResponse.java

◊ GZIP2WayRequestStream.java

◊ GZIP2WayRequestWrapper.java

◊ GZIP2WayResponseStream.java

◊ GZIP2WayResponseWrapper.java

The VB.NET and C#.NET solutions use these classes:

◊ GZipWebRequest.vb/GZipWebRequest.cs

◊ GZipWebResponse.vb/GZipWebResponse.cs

◊ SforceServiceCompressed.vb/SforceServiceCompressed.cs

For information about SOAP compression in Java, see
`wiki.apexdevnet.com/index.php/Compression_with_Axis_1.3`. For information
about SOAP compression in VB.NET and C#.NET, see
`wiki.apexdevnet.com/index.php/SOAP_Compression`.

See Also

- *Log In to and Out of the API* on page 201
- *Manage Sessions* on page 204
- *Implementing the Query/Query More Pattern* on page 206
- *Batching Records for API Calls* on page 207

Add and Remove Tags on a Single Record

Problem

You want to remove a public tag that is no longer applicable and add a new public tag for an
existing record.

Solution

To add or remove a tag on a single record, you should first query the record to determine which
tags are already present, before continuing with the `create()` and `delete()` operations.

1. To see the tags on a single contact, for example a contact named John Smith, execute
   the following in the AJAX Toolkit or your own client application:

```
var johnSmithTags = sforce.connection.query("SELECT Name, Id,
  ItemId
 FROM ContactTag WHERE Item.LastName = \'Smith\' AND
Item.FirstName = \'John\'");
```

`johnSmithTags` contains the following tag names:

- Northwest
- Staff

John Smith has been promoted from Staff to Senior Staff, a tag that does not yet exist.

2. To create the new Senior Staff tag, execute the following in the AJAX Toolkit or your own client application:

```
var SeniorStaffTag = new sforce.SObject('ContactTag');
SeniorStaffTag.ItemId = johnSmithResults.records[0].Id;
SeniorStaffTag.Name = "Senior Staff";
SeniorStaffTag.Type = "Public";
sforce.connection.create([SeniorStaffTag]);
```

3. Run the query in the first step again. `johnSmithTags` contains the following tag names:

- Northwest
- Senior Staff
- Staff

4. The Staff position is eliminated. To remove the Staff tag, delete its ID:

```
var staffID = sforce.connection.query("SELECT Id FROM ContactTag

 WHERE Name = 'Staff' AND ItemId = '" +
 johnSmithTags.records[0].ItemId + "'");
sforce.connection.deleteIds([staffID.records.Id]);
```

5. Run the query in the first step again. `johnSmithTags` contains the following tag names:

- Northwest
- Senior Staff

Discussion

Query to ensure that records have been tagged appropriately.

The API enforces the same limits as the Salesforce user interface on the number of tags that you can create.

Across all users, an organization is limited to:

- 1,000 unique public tags
- 50,000 instances of public tags applied to records

- 5,000,000 instances of personal and public tags applied to records

See Also

- "Tagging Limits" in the *Salesforce Online Help*
- "TagDefinition" in the *Force Platform Web Services API Developer's Guide* at
  http://www.salesforce.com/us/developer/docs/api/Content/sforce_api_objects_tagdefinition.htm
- "create()" in the *Force Platform Web Services API Developer's Guide* at
  http://www.salesforce.com/us/developer/docs/api/index_CSH.htm#sforce_api_calls_create.htm
- "delete()" in the *Force Platform Web Services API Developer's Guide* at
  http://www.salesforce.com/us/developer/docs/api/index_CSH.htm#sforce_api_calls_delete.htm
- *The AJAX Toolkit Developer's Guide* at http://www.salesforce.com/
  us/developer/docs/ajax/index.htm

Add and Remove Tags on Multiple Records

Problem

You want to remove public tags that are no longer applicable to multiple records of the same object type and replace them with a different tag.

Solution

To work with multiple records, loop through all records with a particular tag, collect their ItemIds, and edit them on an individual basis.

Suppose that all Northwest and Southwest tags need to be consolidated to a single West Coast tag. To remove the tags and replace them:

1. Store the accounts that contain the tags you want to delete. You can execute the following in the AJAX Toolkit or your own client application:

```
var westCoastAccounts = sforce.connection.query("SELECT ItemId,
Id
FROM AccountTag WHERE Name = 'Northwest' OR Name =
'Southwest'");
```

2. Create the new West Coast tag. Add the ItemIds by looping through the records:

```
var WestCoastTagArray = new Array();
for (var i = 0; i < westCoastAccounts.size; i++)
{
  WestCoastTagArray[i] = new sforce.SObject('AccountTag');
  WestCoastTagArray[i].Name = "West Coast";
  WestCoastTagArray[i].Type = "Public";
  WestCoastTagArray[i].ItemId =
```

```
westCoastAccounts.records[i].ItemId;
}
sforce.connection.create(WestCoastTagArray);
```

3. Delete all instances of the Northwest and Southwest tags:

```
var IdsToDelete = new Array();
for (var k = 0; k < westCoastAccounts.size; k++)
{
  IdsToDelete[k] = westCoastAccounts.records[k].Id;
}
sforce.connection.deleteIds(IdsToDelete);
```

Discussion

Make as few calls to the database as possible for the best performance. It is efficient to create a single array, populate it with a `for` loop, and call a single database operation, such as `create()` or `delete()`, on that array.

The API enforces the same limits as the Salesforce user interface on the number of tags that you can create.

Across all users, an organization is limited to:

- 1,000 unique public tags
- 50,000 instances of public tags applied to records
- 5,000,000 instances of personal and public tags applied to records

See Also

- "TagDefinition" in the *Force Platform Web Services API Developer's Guide* at
  www.salesforce.com/us/developer/docs/api/index_CSH.htm#sforce_api_objects_tagdefinition.htm
- "`create()`" in the *Force Platform Web Services API Developer's Guide* at
  www.salesforce.com/us/developer/docs/api/index_CSH.htm#sforce_api_calls_create.htm
- "`delete()`" in the *Force Platform Web Services API Developer's Guide* at
  www.salesforce.com/us/developer/docs/api/index_CSH.htm#sforce_api_calls_delete.htm

Updating Tag Definitions

Problem

You want to correct some public tags that have misspellings in them and remove some that are no longer useful in your application.

Solution

Run a query to determine the ID of the incorrect tag, then rename it. For example, suppose you see that a user has created a tag called WC. You want to retrieve the ID of this tag to see which records it is applied to. You canexecute the following in the AJAX Toolkit or your own client application:

To udpate the tag definition:

1. Query for all the tags with the name WC.

   ```
   var IDToUpdate = sforce.connection.query("SELECT Id FROM
   TagDefinition WHERE Name = 'WC'");
   ```

2. The name WC should be West Coast. Since this change affects multiple record types, create a new `TagDefinition` record with the correct value.

   ```
   var updateTD = new sforce.SObject('TagDefinition');
   updateTD.Id = IDToUpdate.records.Id;
   IDToUpdate.records.Name = "West Coast";
   ```

3. `updateTD` is used to replace the previous `TagDefinition` record. The final step is to call `update()` using the corrected record.

   ```
   sforce.connection.update([updateTD]);
   ```

   Since we essentially overwrote the ID, every record previously tagged with WC will now be tagged as West Coast.

Discussion

Operating on `TagDefinition` records does not take into consideration the types of any child tags. Ensure that the action you want to perform is appropriate for all types of tags. For instance, an `AccountTag` named WC and an `ContactTag` named WC will both be changed to West Coast. For information on changing tags on multiple records, see *Add and Remove Tags on Multiple Records* on page 231.

See Also

- "TagDefinition" in the *Force Platform Web Services API Developer's Guide* at
  www.salesforce.com/us/developer/docs/api/Content/sforce_api_objects_tagdefinition.htm
- "`update()`" in the *Force Platform Web Services API Developer's Guide* at
  www.salesforce.com/us/developer/docs/api/index_CSH.htm#sforce_api_calls_update.htm

Glossary

AJAX Toolkit

A JavaScript wrapper around the API that allows you to execute any API call and access any object you have permission to view from within JavaScript code.

AJAX Tools

A Force Platform AppExchange app that includes a collection of Web-based utilities for developers working with the AJAX Toolkit, s-controls, or Apex.

Anonymous block, Apex

An Apex script that does not get stored in the metadata, but that can be compiled and executed through the use of the `ExecuteAnonymousResult()` API call, or the equivalent in the AJAX toolkit.

Apex

A procedural scripting language that allows developers to execute flow and transaction control statements on the Force Platform server in conjunction with calls to the API. Using syntax that looks like Java and acts like database stored procedures, Apex allows developers to add business logic to most system events, including button clicks, related record updates, and custom s-control display.

Apex log

A debug console that displays the debug log for any Apex in your organization that executes as the result of a trigger while the console is open. The debug console also includes a text area at the bottom of the window that allows you to enter and execute anonymous statements.

App

A collection of components such as tabs, reports, dashboards, and custom s-controls that address a specific business need. Short for "application."

Application programming interface (API)

The interface that a computer system, library, or application provides in order to allow other computer programs to request services from it and exchange data between them.

Approval process

An automated process your organization can use to approve records on the platform. An approval process specifies the steps necessary for a record to be approved and who must approve it at each step. Approval processes also specify the actions to take when a record is approved, rejected, or first submitted for approval.

Auto number

A custom field type that automatically adds a unique sequential number to each record.

Cascading style sheets

Files that contain all of the information relevant to color, font, borders, and images that are displayed in a user interface.

Child relationship

A relationship that has been defined on an SObject that references a selected SObject as the "one" side of a one-to-many relationship. For example, if you expand the Child Relationships node under the Account object, contacts, opportunities, and tasks are included in this list.

Class, Apex

A template or blueprint from which Apex objects are created. Classes consist of other classes, user-defined methods, variables, exception types, and static initialization code. In most cases, Apex classes are modeled on their counterparts in Java and can be quickly understood by those who are familiar with them.

Client app

An app that runs outside the Salesforce user interface and uses only the API—typically running on a desktop or mobile device. These apps treat the platform as a data source, using the development model of whatever tool and platform for which they are designed. See also *Composite app* on page 236 and *Native app* on page 241.

Component library, Visualforce page

The list of tags and attributes that can be used in a Visualforce page.

Composite app

An app that combines native platform functionality with one or more external Web services, such as Yahoo! Maps. Composite apps allow for more flexibility and integration with other services, but may require running and managing external code. See also *Client app* on page 236 and *Native app* on page 241.

Controller, Visualforce page

An Apex class that provides a Visualforce page with the data and business logic it needs to run. Visualforce pages can use the standard controllers that come by default with every standard or custom object, or they can define custom controllers.

Controlling field

Any standard or custom picklist or checkbox field whose values control the available values in one or more corresponding dependent fields. See also *Dependent field* on page 237.

Custom field

Fields that can be added to customize an object for your organization's needs.

Custom link

A custom URL defined by an administrator to integrate your data with external websites and back-office systems.

Custom object

An entity that you build to store information that's unique to your app. See also *Object* on page 241 and *Standard object* on page 245.

Dashboard

A graphical representation of data from up to 20 summary or matrix reports arranged in a two- or three-column layout. Every user can select a favorite dashboard to display on his or her Home tab.

Database

An organized collection of information. The underlying architecture of the platform includes a database where your data is stored.

Database table

A list of information, presented with rows and columns, about the person, thing, or concept you want to track. See also *Object* on page 241.

Date literal

A keyword in a SOQL or SOSL query that represents a relative range of time such as *last month* or *next year*.

Dependent field

Any custom picklist or multi-select picklist field that displays available values based on the value selected in its corresponding controlling field. See also *Controlling field* on page 236.

Developer Edition

A free Salesforce edition that allows you to get hands-on experience with all aspects of the platform in an environment designed for development. Developer Edition accounts are available at developer.force.com.

Developer Force

The Developer Force website at developer.force.com provides a full range of resources for platform developers, including sample code, toolkits, an online developer community, and the test environments necessary for building apps.

DML statement

An Apex statement that inserts, updates, or deletes records from the Force Platform database.

Email template

A built-in feature that enables you to create form emails that communicate a standard message, such as a welcome letter to new employees or an acknowledgement that a customer service request has been received.

Enterprise Edition

A Salesforce edition designed to meet the needs of larger, more complex businesses. In addition to all of the functionality available in Professional Edition, Enterprise Edition organizations get advanced customization and administration tools that can support large-scale deployments.

Enterprise WSDL

A strongly-typed WSDL for customers who want to build an integration with their Salesforce organization only, or for partners who are using tools like Tibco or webMethods to build integrations that require strong typecasting. The downside of the Enterprise WSDL is that it only works with the schema of a single Salesforce organization because it's bound to all of the unique objects and fields that exist in that organization's data model. See also *Partner WSDL* on page 242.

Entity relationship diagram (ERD)

A data modeling tool that helps you organize your data into entities (or objects, as they are called in the Force Platform) and define the relationships between them.

Field

A part of an object that holds a specific piece of information, such as a text or currency value.

Field dependency

A filter that allows you to change the contents of a picklist based on the value of another field.

Field-level security

Settings that determine whether fields are hidden, visible, read only, or editable for users based on their profiles.

Flex Toolkit for the Force Platform

An Adobe® Flex™ library that allows you to access Salesforce data from within a Flex 2 application.

Force Platform

A platform for building cloud computing applications from salesforce.com. The Force Platform combines a powerful user interface, operating system, and database to allow you to customize and deploy cloud computing applications for your entire enterprise.

Force Platform API

A Web services-based application programming interface that provides access to your Salesforce organization's information.

Force Platform API WSDL

A WSDL for developers who want to run or compile Apex scripts in another environment, build a new Apex IDE, or create an integration or similar application.

Force Platform app menu

A menu that enables users to switch between customizable applications (or "apps") with a single click. The Force Platform app menu displays at the top of every page in the Salesforce user interface.

Force Platform AppExchange

A Web directory where hundreds of AppExchange apps are available to Salesforce customers to review, demo, comment upon, and/or install. Developers can submit their apps for listing on AppExchange if they wish to share them with the community.

Force Platform AppExchange package

A collection of application components that are posted as a unit on the Force Platform AppExchange. See also *Managed package* on page 240.

Force Platform point-and-click tools

The point-and-click tools that allow you to build app components declaratively, through the Salesforce administrative setup menu.

Force Platform Explorer

A lightweight, Windows-based tool that lets you browse the schema within your organization, edit data values, and build and test SOQL and SOSL queries.

Force Platform IDE

An Eclipse plug-in that allows developers to manage, author, and debug s-controls and Apex classes and triggers in the Eclipse development environment.

Force Platform Migration Tool

A toolkit that allows you to write an Apache Ant build script for migrating Apex between two Salesforce organizations.

Force Platform Metadata API WSDL

A WSDL for developers who want to manipulate organization setup information, usually to move metadata from one organization to another.

Foreign key

A field whose value is the same as the primary key of another table. You can think of a foreign key as a copy of a primary key from another table. A relationship is made between two tables by matching the values of the foreign key in one table with the values of the primary key in another. See also *Primary key* on page 243.

Formula field

A type of custom field that automatically calculates its value based on the values of merge fields, expressions, or other values.

Governor limits

Apex execution limits that prevent developers who write inefficient code from monopolizing the resources of other Salesforce users.

Group

A set of users that can contain individual users, other groups, or the users in a role. Groups can be used to help define sharing access to data.

Group Edition

A Salesforce edition designed for small businesses and workgroups with a limited number of users. Group Edition offers access to accounts, contacts, opportunities, leads, cases, dashboards, and reports.

Home tab

The starting page from which users can view a dashboard, choose sidebar shortcuts and options, view current tasks and activities, or select each of the major tabs.

HTML s-control

An s-control that contains the actual HTML that should be rendered on a page. When saved this way, the HTML is ultimately hosted on a platform server, but is executed in an end-user's browser. See also *S-Control* on page 244.

HTTP debugger

An application that can be used to identify and inspect SOAP requests that are sent from the AJAX Toolkit. They behave as proxy servers running on your local machine and allow you to inspect and author individual requests.

ID

A unique 15- or 18-character alphanumeric string that identifies a single record in Salesforce.

Inline s-control

An s-control that displays within a record detail page or dashboard, rather than on its own page.

Instance, Salesforce Server

A server that hosts an organization's Salesforce data (for example, na1.salesforce.com, na2.salesforce.com, and so on). The platform runs on multiple instances, but data for any single organization is always consolidated on a single instance. As long as you use the URL that is returned from the API login() call, you should never need to know the actual instance that hosts an organization's data.

Integration user

A Salesforce user defined solely for client apps or integrations.

Junction object

A custom object that enables a many-to-many relationship between two other objects.

Layout

See *Page layout* on page 242.

License Management Application (LMA)

A free Force Platform AppExchange app that allows you to track sales leads and accounts for every user who downloads a managed package of yours from AppExchange. See also *License Management Organization (LMO)* on page 240.

License Management Organization (LMO)

The organization in which you've installed the License Management Application (LMA). See also *Managed package* on page 240.

Lookup relationship

A relationship between two objects that allows you to associate records with each other. On one side of the relationship, a lookup field allows users to click a lookup icon and select another record from a list. On the associated record, you can then display a related list to show all of the records that have been linked to it.

Managed package

A collection of application components that are posted as a unit on Force Platform AppExchange, and that are associated with a namespace and a License Management Organization. A package must be managed for it to be published publicly on AppExchange, and for it to support upgrades. See also *Force Platform AppExchange package* on page 239.

Manual sharing

Record-level access rule that allows record owners to give read and edit permissions to other users who might not have access to the record any other way. See also *Record-level security* on page 243.

Merge field

A field you can place in an email template, custom link, s-control, or formula to incorporate values from a record. For example, Dear {!Contact.FirstName}, uses a contact merge field to obtain the value of a contact record's First Name field to address an email recipient by his or her first name.

Metadata-driven development

An app development model that allows apps to be defined as declarative "blueprints," with no code required. Apps built on the platform—their data models, objects, forms, workflows, and more—are defined by metadata.

Metadata WSDL

A WSDL for users who want to use the API metadata calls.

Multitenancy

An application model where all users and apps share a single, common infrastructure and code base.

MVC (Model-View-Controller)

A design paradigm that deconstructs applications into components that represent data (the model), ways of displaying that data in a user interface (the view), and ways of manipulating that data with business logic (the controller).

Namespace

A one- to 15-character alphanumeric identifier that distinguishes your package and its contents from packages of other developers on Force Platform AppExchange, similar to a domain name. Salesforce automatically prepends your namespace prefix, followed by two underscores ("__"), to all unique component names in your Salesforce organization.

Native app

A type of app that is built exclusively via metadata configuration and without coding. Native apps run entirely on the platform without need for external services or infrastructure. See also *Client app* on page 236 and *Composite app* on page 236

Object

In Force Platform terms, an object is similar to a database table—a list of information, presented with rows and columns, about the person, thing, or concept you want to track. Each object automatically has built-in features like a user interface, a security and sharing model, workflow processes, and much more.

Object-level security

Settings that allow an administrator to hide whole tabs and objects from a user, so that they don't even know that type of data exists. On the platform, you set object-level access rules with object permissions on user profiles. See also *Field-level security* on page 238 and *Record-level security* on page 243.

onClick JavaScript
JavaScript code that executes when a button or link is clicked.

One-to-many relationship
A relationship in which a single object is related to many other objects. For example, each Candidate may have one or more related Job Applications.

Organization-wide defaults
Settings that allow you to specify the baseline level of data access that a user has in your organization. For example, you can make it so that any user can see any record of a particular object that's enabled in their user profile, but that they'll need extra permissions to actually edit one.

Outbound message
A SOAP message from Salesforce to an external Web service. You can send outbound messages from a workflow rule or Apex.

Package
See *Force Platform AppExchange package* on page 239

Page layout
The organization of fields, custom links, related lists, and other components on a record detail or edit page. Use page layouts primarily for organizing pages for your users, rather than for security.

Partner WSDL
A loosely-typed WSDL for customers, partners, and ISVs who want to build an integration or a Force Platform AppExchange app that can work across multiple Salesforce organizations. With this WSDL, the developer is responsible for marshaling data in the correct object representation, which typically involves editing the XML. However, you're also freed from being dependent on any particular data model or Salesforce organization. See also *Enterprise WSDL* on page 238.

Personal Edition
A free Salesforce edition designed for an individual sales representative or other single user. Personal Edition provides access to key contact management features such as accounts, contacts, and synchronization with Outlook. It also provides sales representatives with critical sales tools such as opportunities.

Picklist
A selection list of options available for specific fields, for example, the `Country` field for a Candidate object. Users can choose a single value from a list of options rather than make an entry directly in the field.

Picklist values
The selections displayed in drop-down lists for particular fields. Some values come predefined, and other values can be changed or defined by an administrator.

Platform Edition
A Salesforce edition based on either Enterprise Edition or Unlimited Edition that does not include any of the standard Salesforce CRM apps, such as Sales or Service & Support.

Primary key

A relational database concept. Each table in a relational database has a field in which the data value uniquely identifies the record. This field is called the primary key. The relationship is made between two tables by matching the values of the foreign key in one table with the values of the primary key in another. See also *Foreign key* on page 239.

Production organization

A Salesforce organization that has live users accessing data.

Professional Edition

A Salesforce edition designed for businesses who need full-featured CRM functionality. Professional Edition includes straightforward and easy-to-use customization, integration, and administration tools to facilitate any small- to mid-sized deployment.

Profile

A component of the platform that defines a user's permission to perform different functions. The platform includes a set of standard profiles with every organization, and administrators can also define custom profiles to satisfy business needs.

Query locator

A parameter returned from the `query()` or `queryMore()` API call that specifies the index of the last result record that was returned.

Query string parameter

A name-value pair that's included in a URL, typically after a '?' character. For example:

```
http://na1.salesforce.com/001/e?name=value
```

Queue

A collection of records that don't have an owner. Users who have access to a queue can examine every record that's in it and claim ownership of the records they want.

Quirks mode

A browser implementation that supports legacy Web pages that rely on Web browsers' incomplete or incorrect implementations of HTML and CSS to display properly. Browsers revert to quirks mode if you forget to set the `DOCTYPE` properly at the top of a Web page, or if you don't use well-formed HTML. See also *Standards mode* on page 245.

Record

A single instance of an object. For example, Software Engineer is a single Position object record.

Record-level security

A method of controlling data in which we can allow particular users to view and edit an object, but then restrict the individual object records that they're allowed to see. See also *Organization-wide defaults* on page 242, *Role hierarchy* on page 244, *Sharing rules* on page 245, and *Manual sharing* on page 241.

Related list

A section of a record or other detail page that lists items related to that record.

Relationship

A connection between two objects in which matching values in a specified field in both objects are used to link related data. For example, if one object stores data about companies and another object stores data about people, a relationship allows you to find out which people work at the company.

Role hierarchy

A record-level security setting that defines different levels of users such that users at higher levels can view and edit information owned by or shared with users beneath them in the role hierarchy, regardless of the organization-wide sharing model settings. See also *Record-level security* on page 243.

Running user

The user whose security settings determine what data is displayed in a dashboard. Because only one running user is specified per dashboard, everyone who can access the dashboard sees the same data, regardless of their personal security settings.

S-Control

A component that allows you to embed custom HTML and JavaScript into Salesforce detail pages, custom links, Web tabs, or custom buttons. For example, you can define a custom s-control containing JavaScript and address merge fields to display a map of a contact's address. See also *HTML s-control* on page 239, *URL s-control* on page 246, and *Snippet* on page 245.

Salesforce.com Ideas

A forum where salesforce.com customers can suggest new product concepts, promote favorite enhancements, interact with product managers and other customers, and preview what salesforce.com is planning to deliver in future releases. Visit Salesforce.com Ideas at ideas.salesforce.com.

Sandbox organization

A nearly identical copy of a Salesforce production organization. You can create multiple sandboxes in separate environments for a variety of purposes, such as testing and training, without compromising the data and applications in your production environment.

Salesforce SOA (Service-Oriented Architecture)

A powerful capability of Apex that allows you to make calls to external Web services from within Apex code.

Search layout

The organization of fields included in search results, lookup dialogs, and the recent items lists on tab home pages.

Session ID

An authentication token that's returned when a user successfully logs in to Salesforce. The Session ID prevents a user from having to log in again every time he or she wants to perform another action in Salesforce.

Session timeout

The amount of time a single session ID remains valid before expiring. While a session is always valid for a user while he or she is working in the Web interface, sessions instantiated via the API expire after the duration of the session timeout, regardless of how many transactions are still taking place.

Sharing model

A security model that defines the default organization-wide access levels that users have to each other's information.

Sharing rules

Rules that allow an administrator to specify that all information created by users within a given group or role is automatically shared to the members of another group or role. Sharing rules also allow administrators to make automatic exceptions to org-wide defaults for particular groups of users.

Snippet

A type of s-control that's designed to be included in other s-controls. Similar to a helper method that is used by other methods in a piece of code, a snippet allows you to maintain a single copy of HTML or JavaScript that you can reuse in multiple s-controls. See also *S-Control* on page 244.

SOAP (Simple Object Access Protocol)

A protocol that defines a uniform way of passing XML-encoded data.

SOQL (Salesforce Object Query Language)

A query language that allows you to construct simple but powerful query strings and to specify the criteria that should be used to select the data from the database.

SoqlXplorer

A lightweight, OS-X-based tool that lets you graphically browse the schema within your organization, and build and test SOQL queries.

SOSL (Salesforce Object Search Language)

A query language that allows you to perform text-based searches using the API.

Standard object

A built-in object included with the Force Platform. You can also build custom objects to store information that's unique to your app. See also *Custom object* on page 237 and *Object* on page 241.

Standards mode

A browser implementation that respects all parts of the HTML and CSS language specifications. To use standards mode, you must set the DOCTYPE properly at the top of a Web page. See also *Quirks mode* on page 243.

Tab

An interface item that allows you to navigate around an app. A tab serves as the starting point for viewing, editing, and entering information for a particular object. When you click a tab at the top of the page, the corresponding tab home page for that object appears.

Test method

An Apex class method that verifies whether a particular piece of code is working properly. Test methods take no arguments, commit no data to the database, and can be executed by the runTests() system method either via the command line or in an Apex IDE, such as Eclipse with the Force Platform IDE.

Time-dependent workflow action

A workflow action that occurs before or after a certain amount of time has elapsed. Time-dependent workflow actions can fire tasks, field updates, outbound messages, and email alerts while the condition of a workflow rule remains true.

Time trigger

A setting that defines when time-dependent workflow actions should fire.

Trigger

A piece of Apex that executes before or after records of a particular type are inserted, updated, or deleted from the database. Every trigger runs with a set of context variables that provide access to the records that caused the trigger to fire, and all triggers run in bulk mode—that is, they process several records at once, rather than just one record at a time.

Trigger context variables

Default variables that provide access to information about the trigger and the records that caused it to fire.

Unit test

See *Test method* on page 245

Unlimited Edition

A Salesforce edition designed to extend customer success through the entire enterprise. Unlimited Edition includes all Enterprise Edition functionality, plus Apex, Force Platform Sandbox, Force Platform Mobile, premium support, and additional storage.

Unmanaged package

A Force Platform AppExchange package that cannot be upgraded or controlled by its developer. Unmanaged packages allow you to take any app components and move them "as is" to AppExchange without going through a lengthy publishing process. They're ideal for moving components between organizations for a one-time transfer.

URL (Uniform Resource Locator)

The global address of a website, document, or other resource on the Internet. For example, http://www.salesforce.com.

URL s-control

An S-Control that contains an external URL that hosts the HTML that should be rendered on a page. When saved this way, the HTML is hosted and run by an external website. URL s-controls are also called Web controls. See also *S-Control* on page 244.

Validation rule

A rule that prevents a record from being saved if it does not meet the standards that are specified.

Visualforce

A simple, tag-based markup language that allows developers to easily define custom pages and components for apps built on the platform. Each tag corresponds to a coarse or fine-grained component, such as a section of a page, a related list, or a field. The components can either be controlled by the same logic that's used in standard Salesforce pages, or developers can associate their own logic with a controller written in Apex.

Web control

See *URL s-control* on page 246.

Web service

A mechanism by which two applications can easily exchange data over the Internet, even if they run on different platforms, are written in different languages, or are geographically remote from each other.

WebService method

An Apex class method or variable that can be used by external systems, such as an s-control or mash-up with a third-party application. Web service methods must be defined in a global class.

Web tab

A custom tab that allows your users to use external websites from within the application.

Wizard

Any tool with a user interface that leads a user through a complex task in multiple steps.

Workflow action

An email alert, field update, outbound message, or task that fires when the conditions of a workflow rule are met.

Workflow email alert

A workflow action that sends an email when a workflow rule is triggered. Unlike workflow tasks, which can only be assigned to application users, workflow alerts can be sent to any user or contact, as long as they have a valid email address.

Workflow field update

A workflow action that changes the value of a particular field on a record when a workflow rule is triggered.

Workflow outbound message

A workflow action that sends data to an external Web service, such as another cloud computing application. Outbound messages are used primarily with composite apps.

Workflow queue

A list of workflow actions that are scheduled to fire based on workflow rules that have one or more time-dependent workflow actions.

Workflow rule

A "container" for a set of workflow instructions that includes the criteria for when the workflow should be activated, as well as the particular tasks, alerts, and field updates that should take place when the criteria for that rule are met.

Workflow task

A workflow action that assigns a task to an application user when a workflow rule is triggered.

Wrapper class

A class that abstracts common API functions such as logging in, managing sessions, and querying and batching records. A wrapper class makes your integration more straightforward to develop and maintain, keeps the logic necessary to make API calls in one place, and affords easy reuse across all components that require API access.

WSDL (Web Services Description Language)

An XML file that describes the format of messages you send and receive from a Web service. It's the language that your development environment's SOAP client uses to communicate with external services like Salesforce.

About the Authors

Stefanie Andersen is a Senior Technical Writer at salesforce.com, focused on the mobile platform. Stefanie earned a B.A. and an M.A. in English from Florida State University.

Steven Anderson is a Principal Technical Writer and Documentation Architect at salesforce.com. He has over 15 years of experience in technical communication as a writer, manager, and tools developer. His last three years have been at salesforce.com, focusing on Visualforce, Apex, and the Force Platform Web Services API. Steve earned a B.S. in Technical Communication from the New Mexico Institute of Mining and Technology.

Mysti Berry is a Lead Technical Writer at salesforce.com, focused on the Force Platform API and the Force Platform AJAX Toolkit. Mysti has 18 years experience in technical writing, the last three spent on the Force Platform. She earned a B.A. in linguistics from University of California Santa Cruz and an M.F.A. from University of San Francisco. She teaches technical writing courses at University of California Berkeley Extension.

Phil Choi is a Staff Technical Writer at salesforce.com, focusing on platform features including workflow and approvals, as well as Force Platform Sites. Phil earned a B.S. in Mechanical Engineering from The Pennsylvania State University and an M.F.A. in creative writing from Emerson College.

Leah Cutter is a Staff Technical Writer at salesforce.com, focused on Apex. Leah has a degree in Computer Science and another in English Literature from the University of Minnesota.

Mark Leonard is a Senior Technical Writer at salesforce.com, focused on the Force Platform Metadata API. Mark earned a B.E. in Electronic Engineering from University College Dublin and a M. Sc. by Research in Electronic Engineering from University of Dublin, Trinity College.

Chris McGuire is a Staff Technical Writer at salesforce.com, focused on the Force Platform. He is also a coauthor of *Force Platform Fundamentals: An Introduction to Custom Application Development in the Cloud.*

Garen Torikian is a Technical Writer at salesforce.com, focused on platform features including messaging and tags. Garen earned a degree in Computer Science and another in English Literature from the University of Southern California.

Index